Drawn & Engraved   by R. Woodman.

W. Wells Brown,

THE AMERICAN FUGITIVE IN EUROPE.

SKETCHES

OF

PLACES AND PEOPLE ABROAD.

BY

WM. WELLS BROWN.

WITH

A MEMOIR OF THE AUTHOR.

"Go, little book, from this my solitude!
I cast thee on the waters — go thy ways!
And if, as I believe, thy vein be good,
The world will find thee after many days."
SOUTHEY.

THE NEGRO UNIVERSITIES PRESS
NEW YORK

Originally published in 1855
by John P. Jewett and Company

Reprinted 1969 by
Negro Universities Press
A Division of Greenwood Publishing Corp.
New York

SBN 8371-1906-5

PREFACE

TO THE ENGLISH EDITION.

WHILE I feel conscious that most of the contents of these Letters will be interesting chiefly to American readers, yet I may indulge the hope that the fact of their being the first production of a Fugitive Slave as a history of travels may carry with them novelty enough to secure for them, to some extent, the attention of the reading public of Great Britain. Most of the letters were written for the private perusal of a few personal friends in America; some were contributed to *Frederick Douglass' Paper*, a journal published in the United States. In a printed circular sent some weeks since to some of my friends, asking subscriptions to this volume, I stated the reasons for its publication : these need not be repeated here. To those who so promptly and kindly responded to that appeal, I tender my most sincere thanks. It is with no little diffidence

that I lay these letters before the public ; for I am not
blind to the fact that they must contain many errors ;
and to those who shall find fault with them on that account, it may not be too much for me to ask them kindly
to remember that the author was a slave in one of the
Southern States of America until he had attained the
age of twenty years; and that the education he has
acquired was by his own exertions, he never having had
a day's schooling in his life.

W. WELLS BROWN.

22 Cecil Street, Strand,
        London.

NOTE

TO THE AMERICAN EDITION.

During my sojourn abroad I found it advantageous to my
purse to publish a book of travels, which I did under the title of
" Three Years in Europe, or Places I have seen and People I have
met." The work was reviewed by the ablest journals in Great
Britain, and from their favorable criticisms I have been induced
to offer it to the American public, with a dozen or more additional chapters.   W. W. B.

Boston, *November*, 1854.

CONTENTS.

CHAPTER VII.

CHAPTER VIII.

CHAPTER IX.

CHAPTER X.

CHAPTER XI.

CHAPTER XII.

CHAPTER XIII.

CHAPTER XIV.

CHAPTER XV.

CHAPTER XVI.

CONTENTS.

VIII CONTENTS.

Memoir of the Author.

"Shall tongues be mute when deeds are wrought
Which well might shame extremest Hell?
Shall freemen lack the indignant thought?
Shall Mercy's bosom cease to swell?
Shall Honor bleed? — shall Truth succumb?
Shall pen, and press, and *soul* be dumb?" — *Whittier.*

WILLIAM WELLS BROWN, the subject of this narrative, was born a slave in Lexington, Kentucky, not far from the residence of the late Hon. Henry Clay. His mother was the slave of Dr. John Young. His father was a slaveholder, and, besides being a near relation of his master, was connected with the Wickliffe family, one of the oldest, wealthiest, and most aristocratic of the Kentucky planters. Dr. Young was the owner of forty or fifty slaves, whose chief employment was in cultivating tobacco, hemp, corn, and flax. The doctor removed from Lexington, when William was five or six years old, to the State of Missouri, and commenced farming in a beautiful and fertile valley, within a mile of the Missouri river.

Here the slaves were put to work under a harsh and cruel overseer, named Cook. A finer situation for a farm could not have been selected in the state. With climate favorable to agriculture, and soil rich, the products came in abundance. At an early age William was separated from his mother, she being worked in the field, and he as a servant in his master's medical department. When about ten years of age, the young slave's feelings were much hurt at hearing the cries of his mother while being flogged by the negro-driver for being a few minutes behind the other hands in reaching the field. He heard her cry, " O, pray ! O, pray ! O, pray !" These are the words which slaves generally utter when imploring mercy at the hands of their oppressors. The son heard it, though he was some way off. He heard the crack of the whip, and the groans of his poor mother. The cold chill ran over him, and he wept aloud ; but he was a slave like his mother, and could render her no assistance. He was taught by the most bitter experience, that nothing could be more heart-rending than to see a dear and beloved mother or sister tortured by unfeeling men, and to hear her cries, and not to be able to render the least aid. When William was twelve years of age, his master left his farm and took up his residence near St. Louis. The doctor having more hands than he wanted for his own use, William was let out to a Mr. Freeland, an innkeeper. Here the young slave found himself in the hands of a most cruel and heartless master. Freeland was one of the real chivalry of the South ; besides being himself a slaveholder, he was a horse-racer, cock-fighter, gambler, and, to crown the whole, an inveterate drunkard. What else but bad treatment could be expected from such a character ? After enduring the tyrannical and inhuman usage of this man for five or six months, William resolved to stand it no longer, and therefore ran away, like other slaves who leave their masters, owing to severe treatment ;

and not knowing where to flee, the young fugitive went into the forest, a few miles from St. Louis. He had been in the woods but a short time, when he heard the barking and howling of dogs, and was soon satisfied that he was pursued by the negro-dogs ; and, aware of their ferocious nature, the fugitive climbed a tree, to save himself from being torn to pieces. The hounds were soon at the trunk of the tree, and remained there, howling and barking, until those in whose charge they were came up. The slave was ordered down, tied, and taken home. Immediately on his arrival there, he was, as he expected, tied up in the smoke-house, and whipped till Freeland was satisfied, and then smoked with tobacco-stems. This the slaveholder called " *Virginia play.*" After being well whipped and smoked. he was again set to work. William remained with this monster a few months longer, and was then let out to Elijah P. Lovejoy, who years after became the editor of an abolition newspaper, and was murdered at Alton, Illinois, by a mob of slaveholders from the adjoining State of Missouri. The system of letting out slaves is one among the worst of the evils of slavery. The man who hires a slave looks upon him in the same light as does the man who hires a horse for a limited period ; he feels no interest in him, only to get the worth of his money. Not so with the man who owns the slave ; he regards him as so much property, of which care should be taken. After being let out to a steamer as an under-steward, William was hired by James Walker, a slave-trader. Here the subject of our memoir was made superintendent of the gangs of slaves that were taken to the New Orleans market. In this capacity, William had opportunities, far greater than most slaves,

of acquiring knowledge of the different phases of the
"*peculiar institution.*" Walker was a negro specu-
lator, who was amassing a fortune by trading in the bones,
blood and nerves, of God's children. The thought of
such a traffic causes us to exclaim with the poet,

> "———— Is there not some chosen curse,
> Some hidden thunder in the stores of heaven,
> Red with uncommon wrath, to blast the man
> Who gains his fortune from the blood of souls?"

Between fifty and sixty slaves were chained together,
put on board a steamboat bound for New Orleans, and
started on the voyage. New and strange scenes began
to inspire the young slave with the hope of escaping to a
land of freedom. There was in the boat a large room on
the lower deck in which the slaves were kept, men and
women promiscuously, all chained two and two together,
not even leaving the poor slaves the privilege of choosing
their partners. A strict watch was kept over them, so
that they had no chance of escape. Cases had occurred
in which slaves had got off their chains and made their
escape at the landing-places, while the boat stopped to
take in wood. But, with all their care, they lost one
woman who had been taken from her husband and children, and, having no desire to live without them, in the
agony of her soul jumped overboard and drowned herself.
Her sorrows were greater than she could bear; slavery
and its cruel inflictions had broken her heart. She, like
William, sighed for freedom, but not the freedom which
even British soil confers and inspires, but freedom from
torturing pangs, and overwhelming grief.

At the end of the week they arrived at New Orleans,
the place of their destination. Here the slaves were

placed in a negro-pen, where those who wished to purchase could call and examine them. The negro-pen is a small yard surrounded by buildings, from fifteen to twenty feet wide, with the exception of a large gate with iron bars. The slaves are kept in the buildings during the night, and turned into the pen during the day. After the best of the gang were sold off, the balance was taken to the Exchange Coffee-house auction-rooms, and sold at public auction. After the sale of the last slave, William and Mr. Walker left New Orleans for St. Louis.

After they had been at St. Louis a few weeks, another cargo of human flesh was made up. There were amongst the lot several old men and women, some of whom had gray locks. On their way down to New Orleans William had to prepare the old slaves for market. He was ordered to shave off the old men's whiskers, and to pluck out the gray hairs where they were not too numerous; where they were, he colored them with a preparation of blacking with a blacking-brush. After having gone through the blacking process, they looked ten or fifteen years younger. William, though not well skilled in the use of scissors and razor, performed the office of the barber tolerably. After the sale of this gang of negroes they returned to St. Louis, and a second cargo was made up. In this lot was a woman who had a child at the breast, yet was compelled to travel through the interior of the country on foot with the other slaves. In a published memoir of his life, William says, "The child cried during the most of the day, which displeased Mr. Walker, and he told the mother that if her child did not stop crying he would stop its mouth. After a long and weary journey under a burning sun, we put up for the night at a country inn. The following morning, just as they were about to start, the child again commenced crying. Walker stepped up to her, and told her to give the child to him. The mother tremblingly obeyed. He took the child by one arm, as any one would a cat by the leg, and walked into the house where they had been staying, and said to the lady, 'Madam, I will make you a present of this little nigger ; it keeps making such a noise that I can't bear it.' ' Thank you, sir,' said the lady. The mother, as soon as she saw that the child was to be left, ran up to Mr. Walker, and, falling on her knees, begged of him, in an agony of despair, to let her have her child. She clung round his legs so closely that for some time he could not kick her off ; and she cried, ' O my child, my child ! Master, do let me have my dear, dear child ! O ! do, do ! I will stop its crying, and love you forever, if you will only let me have my child again.' But her prayers were not heeded ; they passed on, and the mother was separated from her child forever.

" After the woman's child had been given away, Mr. Walker rudely commanded her to retire into the ranks with the other slaves. Women who had children were not chained, but those who had none were. As soon as her child was taken she was chained to the gang."

Nothing was more grievous to the sensitive feelings of William than seeing the separation of families by the slave trader : husbands taken from their wives, and mothers from their children, without the least appearance of feeling on the part of those who separated them. While at New Orleans, on one occasion, William saw a slave murdered. The circumstances were as follows : In the evening, between seven and eight o'clock, a slave came running down the levee, followed by several men and boys. The whites were crying out, " Stop that nigger ! stop that nigger ! " while the poor panting slave, in almost breathless accents, was repeating, " I did not steal the meat — I did not steal the meat ! " The poor man at last took refuge in the river. The whites who were in pursuit of him ran on board of one of the boats to see if they could discover him. They finally espied him under the bow of the steamboat " Trenton." They got a pike-pole, and tried to drive him from his hiding-place. When they struck at him he would dive under the water. The water was so cold that it soon became evident that he must come out or be drowned.

While they were trying to drive him from under the boat or drown him, he, in broken and imploring accents, said, " I did not steal the meat! I did not steal the meat! My master lives up the river. I want to see my master. I did not steal the meat! Do let me go home to master! " After punching and striking him over the head for some time, he at last sunk in the water, to rise no more alive

On the end of the pike-pole with which they had been striking him was a hook, which caught in his clothing. and they hauled him up on the bow of the boat. Some said he was dead; others said he was " playing 'possum;" while others kicked him to make him get up ; but it was of no use — he was dead.

As soon as they became satisfied of this, they commenced leaving, one after another. One of the hands on the boat informed the captain that they had killed the man, and that the dead body was lying on the deck. The captain, whose name was Hart, came on deck, and said to those who were remaining, " You have killed this nigger ; now take him off my boat." The dead body was dragged on shore and left there. William went on board of the boat where the gang of slaves were, and during the whole night his mind was occupied with what he had seen. Early in the morning he went on shore to see if the dead body remained there. He found it in the same position that it was left the night before. He watched to see what they would do with it. It was left there until between eight and nine o'clock, when a cart, which took up the trash from the streets, came along, and the body was thrown in, and in a few minutes more was covered over with dirt, which they were removing from the streets.

At the expiration of the period of his hiring with Walker, William returned to his master, rejoiced to have escaped an employment as much against his own feelings as it was repugnant to human nature. But this joy was of short duration. The doctor wanted money, and resolved to sell William's sister and two brothers. The mother had been previously sold to a gentleman residing in the city of St. Louis. William's master now informed him that he intended to sell him, and, as he was his own nephew, he gave him the privilege of finding some one to purchase him, who would treat him better than if he was sold on the auction-block. William tried to make some arrangement by which he could purchase his own freedom, but the old doctor would hear nothing of the kind. If there is one thing more revolting in the trade of human flesh than another, it is the selling of one's own blood relations.

He accordingly set out for the city in search of a new master. When he arrived there, he proceeded to the jail with the hope of seeing his sister, but was again disappointed. On the following morning he made another attempt, and was allowed to see her once, for the last time. When he entered the room where she was seated in one corner, alone and disconsolate, there were four other women in the room, belonging to the same man, who were bought, the jailer said, for the master's own use.

William's sister was seated with her face towards the door when he entered, but her gaze was transfixed on nothingness, and she did not look up when he walked up to her ; but as soon as she observed him she sprang up, threw her arms around his neck, leaned her head upon his breast, and, without uttering a word, in silent, indescribable sorrow, burst into tears. She remained so for some minutes, but when she recovered herself sufficiently to speak she urged him to take his mother immediately, and try to get to the land of freedom. She said there was no hope for herself; she must live and die a slave. After giving her some advice, and taking a ring from his finger, he bade her farewell forever. Reader, did ever a fair sister of thine go down to the grave prematurely ? If so, perchance thou hast drank deeply from the cup of sorrow. But how infinitely better is it for a sister to " go into the silent land " with her honor untarnished, but with bright hopes, than for her to be sold to sensual slaveholders !

William had been in the city now two days, and, as he was to be absent for only a week, it was well that he should make the best use of his time, if he intended to escape. In conversing with his mother, he found her unwilling to make the attempt to reach the land of lib-

erty, but she advised him by all means to get there
himself, if he possibly could. She said, as all her children were in slavery, she did not wish to leave them;
but he loved his mother so intensely, that he could not
think of leaving without her. He consequently used all
his simple eloquence to induce her to fly with him, and, at
last, he prevailed. They consequently fixed upon the next
night as the time for their departure. The time at length
arrived, and they left the city just as the clock struck
nine. Having found a boat, they crossed the river in it.
Whose boat it was he did not know; neither did he care.
When it had served his purpose, he turned it adrift, and
when he saw it last it was going at a good speed down
the river. After walking in the main road as fast as
they could all night, when the morning came they made
for the woods, and remained there during the day; but
when night came again, they proceeded on their journey,
with nothing but the North Star to guide them. They
continued to travel by night, and to bury themselves in
the silent solitudes of the forest by day. Hunger and
fatigue could not stop them, for the prospect of freedom
at the end of the journey nerved them up. The very
thought of leaving slavery, with its democratic whips,
republican chains, and bloodhounds, caused the hearts of
the weary fugitives to leap with joy. After travelling ten
nights, and hiding in the woods during the day for fear of
being arrested and taken back, they thought they might
with safety go the rest of their way by daylight. In nearly
all the free states there are men who make a business of
catching runaway slaves and returning them to their
owners for the reward that may be offered; some of those
were on the alert for William and his mother, for they

had already seen the runaways advertised in the St. Louis newspapers.

All at once they heard the click of a horse's hoof, and looking back saw three men on horseback galloping towards them. They soon came up, and demanded them to stop. The three men dismounted, arrested them on a warrant, and showed them a handbill, offering two hundred dollars for their apprehension and delivery to Dr. Young and Isaac Mansfield, in St. Louis.

While they were reading the handbill, William's mother looked him in the face and burst into tears. "A cold chill ran over me," says he, "and such a sensation I never experienced before, and I trust I never shall again." They took out a rope and tied him, and they were taken back to the house of the individual who appeared to be the leader. They then had something given them to eat, and were separated. Each of them was watched over by two men during the night. The religious characteristic of the American slaveholder soon manifested itself, as, before the family retired to rest, they were all called together to attend prayers; and the very man who, but a few hours before, had arrested poor, panting, fugitive slaves, now read a chapter from the Bible, and offered a prayer to God; as if that benignant and omnipotent One consecrated the infernal act he had just committed.

The next morning they were chained and handcuffed, and started back to St. Louis. A journey of three days brought the fugitives again to the place they had left twelve days previously, with the hope that they would never return. They were put in prison to await the orders of their owners. When a slave attempts to escape and fails, he feels sure of either being severely punished, or sold to the negro-traders and taken to the far south, there to be worked up on a cotton, sugar or rice plantation. This William and his mother dreaded. While they were in suspense as to what would be their fate, news came to them that the mother had been sold to a slave-speculator. William was soon sold to a merchant residing in the city, and removed to his new owner's dwelling. In a few days the gang of slaves, of which William's mother was one, were taken on board a steamer, to be carried to the New Orleans market. The young slave obtained permission from his new owner to go and take a last farewell of his mother. He went to the boat, and found her there, chained to another woman, and the whole number of slaves, amounting to some fifty or sixty, chained in the same manner. As the son approached his mother she moved not, neither did she weep; her emotions were too deep for tears. William approached her, threw his arms around her neck, kissed her, fell upon his knees begging her forgiveness, for he thought he was to blame for her sad condition, and if he had not persuaded her to accompany him she might not have been in chains then.

She remained for some time apparently unimpressionable, tearless, sighless, but in the innermost depths of her heart moved mighty passions. William says, "She finally raised her head, looked me in the face,—and such a look none but an angel can give!—and said, 'My dear son, you are not to blame for my being here. You have done nothing more nor less than your duty. Do not, I pray you, weep for me; I cannot last long upon a cotton plantation. I feel that my heavenly Master will soon call me home, and then I shall be out of the hands of the slaveholders.' I could hear no more; my heart struggled to free itself from the human form. In a moment she saw Mr. Mansfield, her master, coming toward that part of the boat, and she whispered in my ear, ' My child, we must soon part to meet no more on this side of the grave. You have ever said that you would not die a slave; that you would be a freeman. Now try to get your liberty! You will soon have no one to look after but yourself!' and just as she whispered the last sentence into my ear, Mansfield came up to me, and, with an oath, said, ' Leave here this instant! you have been the means of my losing one hundred dollars to get this wench back,' at the same time kicking me with a heavy pair of boots. As I left her she gave one shriek, saying, ' God be with you!' It was the last time that I saw her, and the last word I heard her utter.

"I walked on shore. The bell was tolling. The boat was about to start. I stood with a heavy heart, waiting to see her leave the wharf. As I thought of my mother, I could but feel that I had lost

' The glory of my life,
My blessing and my pride !
I half forgot the name of slave
When she was by my side.'

"The love of liberty that had been burning in my bosom had well-nigh gone out. I felt as though I was ready to die. The boat moved gently from the wharf, and while she glided down the river I realized that my mother was indeed

' Gone — gone — sold and gone
To the rice-swamp, dank and lone.'

" After the boat was out of sight I returned home; but my thoughts were so absorbed in what I had witnessed that I knew not what I was about. Night came, but it brought no sleep to my eyes." When once the love of freedom is born in the slave's mind, it always increases and brightens; and William having heard so much about Canada, where a number of his acquaintances had found a refuge and a home, he heartily desired to join them. Building castles in the air in the day-time, incessantly thinking of freedom, he would dream of the land of liberty, but on waking in the morning would weep to find it but a dream.

> " He would dream of Victoria's domain,
> And in a moment he seemed to be there;
> But the fear of being taken again
> Soon hurried him back to despair."

Having been for some time employed as a servant in a hotel, and being of a very active turn, William's new owner resolved to let him out on board a steamboat. Consequently the young slave was hired out to the steamer St. Louis, and soon after sold to Captain Enoch Price, the owner of that boat. Here he was destined to remain but a short period, as Mrs. Price wanted a carriage-driver, and had set her heart upon William for that purpose.

Scarcely three months had elapsed from the time that William became the property of Captain Price, ere that gentleman's family took a pleasure-trip to New Orleans, and William accompanied them. From New Orleans the family proceeded to Louisville. The hope of escape again dawned upon the slave's mind, and the trials of the past were lost in hopes for the future. The love of liberty, which had been burning in his bosom for years, and which, at times, had been well-nigh extinguished, was now resuscitated. Hopes nurtured in childhood, and strengthened as manhood dawned, now spread their sails to the gales of his imagination. At night, when all around was peaceful, and in the mystic presence of the everlasting starlight, he would walk the steamer's decks, meditating on his happy prospects, and summoning up gloomy reminiscences of the dear hearts he was leaving behind him. When not thinking of the future his mind would dwell on the past. The love of a dear mother, a dear and affectionate sister, and three brothers yet living, caused him to shed many tears. If he could only be assured of their being dead, he would have been comparatively happy; but he saw, in imagination, his mother in the cotton-field, followed by a monster task-master, and no one to speak a consoling word to her. He beheld his sister in the hands of the slave-driver, compelled to submit to his cruelty, or, what was unutterably worse, his lust; but still he was far away from them, and could not do anything for them if he remained in slavery; consequently he resolved, and consecrated the resolve with a prayer, that he would start on the first opportunity.

That opportunity soon presented itself. When the boat got to the wharf where it had to stay for some time, at the first convenient moment William made towards the woods, where he remained until night-time. He dared not walk during the day, even in the State of Ohio, he had seen so much of the perfidy of white men, and resolved, if possible, not to get into their hands. After darkness covered the world, he emerged from his hiding-place; but he did not know east from west, or north from south; clouds hid the North Star from his view. In this desolate condition he remained for some hours, when the clouds rolled away, and his friend, with its shining face,— the North Star,— welcomed his sight. True as the needle to the pole, he obeyed its attractive beauty, and walked on till daylight dawned.

It was winter-time; the day on which he started was the first of January, and, as it might be expected, it was intensely cold; he had no overcoat, no food, no friend, save the North Star, and the God which made it. How ardently must the love of freedom burn in the poor slave's bosom, when he will pass through so many difficulties, and even look death in the face, in winning his birthright freedom ! But what crushed the poor slave's heart in his flight most was, not the want of food or clothing, but the thought that every white man was his deadly enemy. Even in the free States the prejudice against color is so strong, that there appears to exist a deadly antagonism between the white and colored races.

William in his flight carried a tinder-box with him, and when he got very cold he would gather together dry leaves and stubble and make a fire, or certainly he would have perished. He was determined to enter into no house, fearing that he might meet a betrayer.

It must have been a picture which would have inspired an artist, to see the fugitive roasting the ears of corn that he found or took from barns during the night, at solitary fires in the deep solitudes of woods.

The suffering of the fugitive was greatly increased by the cold, from the fact of his having just come from the warm climate of New Orleans. Slaves seldom have more than one name, and William was not an exception to this, and the fugitive began to think of an additional name. A heavy rain of three days, in which it froze as fast as it fell, and by which the poor fugitive was completely drenched, and still more chilled, added to the depression of his spirits already created by his weary journey. Nothing but the fire of hope burning within his breast could have sustained him under such overwhelming trials.

> "Behind he left the whip and chains;
> Before him were sweet Freedom's plains."

Through cold and hunger, William was now ill, and he could go no further. The poor fugitive resolved to seek protection, and accordingly hid himself in the woods near the road, until some one should pass. Soon a traveller came along, but the slave dared not speak. A few moments more and a second passed; the fugitive attempted to speak, but fear deprived him of voice. A third made his appearance. He wore a broad-brimmed hat and a long coat, and was evidently walking only for exercise. William scanned him well, and, though not much skilled in physiognomy, he concluded he was the man. William approached him, and asked him if he knew any one who would help him, as he was sick. The gentleman asked whether he was not a slave. The poor slave hesitated; but, on being told that he had nothing to fear, he answered "Yes." The gentleman told him he was in a pro-slavery neighborhood, but, if he would wait a little, he would go and get a covered wagon, and convey him to his house. After he had gone, the fugitive meditated whether he should stay or not, being apprehensive that the broad-brimmed gentleman had

gone for some one to assist him: he however concluded
to remain.

After waiting about an hour — an hour big with fate
to him — he saw the covered-wagon making its appearance, and no one in it but the person he before accosted.
Trembling with hope and fear, he entered the wagon,
and was carried to the person's house. When he got
there, he still halted between two opinions, whether he
should enter or take to his heels; but he soon decided,
after seeing the glowing face of the wife. He saw something in her that bid him welcome, something that told
him he would not be betrayed.

He soon found that he was under the shed of a Quaker,
and a Quaker of the George Fox stamp. He had heard
of Quakers and their kindness; but was not prepared to
meet with such hospitality as now greeted him. He saw
nothing but kind looks, and heard nothing but tender
words. He began to feel the pulsations of a new existence. White men always scorned him, but now a white
benevolent woman felt glad to wait on him; it was a revolution in his experience. The table was loaded with
good things, but he could not eat. If he were allowed
the privilege of sitting in the kitchen, he thought he
could do justice to the viands. The surprise being over,
his appetite soon returned.

" I have frequently been asked," says William, " how
I felt upon finding myself regarded as a man by a white
family; especially having just run away from one. I
cannot say that I have ever answered the question yet.
The fact that I was, in all probability, a freeman,
sounded in my ears like a charm. I am satisfied that
none but a slave could place such an appreciation upon

liberty as I did at that time. I wanted to see my mother and sister, that I might tell them that 'I was free!' I wanted to see my fellow-slaves in St. Louis, and let them know that the chains were no longer upon my limbs. I wanted to see Captain Price, and let him learn from my own lips that I was no more a chattel, but a MAN. I was anxious, too, thus to inform Mrs. Price that she must get another coachman, and I wanted to see Eliza more than I did Mr. Price or Mrs. Price. The fact that I was a freeman — could walk, talk, eat, and sleep as a man, and no one to stand over me with the blood-clotted cow-hide — all this made me feel that I was not myself."

The kind Quaker, who so hospitably entertained William, was called Wells Brown. He remained with him about a fortnight, during which time he was well fed and clothed. Before leaving, the Quaker asked him what was his name besides William. The fugitive told him he had no other. "Well," said he, "thee must have another name. Since thee has got out of slavery, thee has become a man, and men always have two names."

William told him that as he was the first man to extend the hand of friendship to him, he would give him the privilege of naming him.

"If I name thee," said he, "I shall call thee Wells Brown, like myself."

"But," said he, "I am not willing to lose my name of William. It was taken from me once against my will, and I am not willing to part with it on any terms."

"Then," said the benevolent man, "I will call thee William Wells Brown."

"So be it," said William Wells Brown, and he has been known by this name ever since.

After giving the newly-christened freeman " a name," the Quaker gave him something to aid him to get "a local habitation." So, after giving him some money, Brown again started for Canada. In four days he reached a public-house, and went in to warm himself. He soon found that he was not out of the reach of his enemies. While warming himself, he heard some men in an adjoining bar-room talking about some runaway slaves. He thought it was time to be off, and, suiting the action to the thought, he was soon in the woods out of sight. When night came, he returned to the road and walked on; and so, for two days and two nights, till he was faint and ready to perish of hunger.

In this condition he arrived in the town of Cleveland, Ohio, on the banks of Lake Erie, where he determined to remain until the spring of the year, and then to try and reach Canada. Here he was compelled to work merely for his food.

Having tasted the sweets of freedom himself, his great desire was to extend its blessing to his race, and in the language of the poet he would ask himself,

> " Is true freedom but to break
> Fetters for our own dear sake,
> And with leathern hearts forget
> That we owe mankind a debt?
>
> " No ! true freedom is to share
> All the chains our brothers wear,
> And with heart and hand to be
> Earnest to make others free."

While acting as a servant to one of the steamers on Lake Erie, Brown often took fugitives from Cleveland and other ports to Buffalo, or Detroit, from either of which places they could cross to Canada in an hour. During the season of 1842, this fugitive slave conveyed no less than *sixty-nine* runaway slaves across Lake Erie, and placed them safe on the soil of Canada.

In proportion as his mind expanded under the more favorable circumstances in which he was placed, Brown became anxious, not merely for the redemption of his race from personal slavery, but for the moral and religious elevation of those who were free. Finding that habits of intoxication were too prevalent among his colored brethren, he, in conjunction with others, commenced a temperance reformation in their body. Such was the success of their efforts that, in three years, in the city of Buffalo alone, a society of upwards of five hundred members was raised out of a colored population of less than seven hundred. Of that society Mr. Brown was thrice elected president.

In the spring of 1844 he became an agent of the Western New York Anti-Slavery Society, and afterwards spent some time in the service of the Massachusetts Society. In 1849 Mr. Brown embarked for Europe as a delegate to the Paris Peace Conference.

The reception of Mr. Brown at the Peace Congress, in Paris, was most flattering. He admirably maintained his reputation as a public speaker. His brief address upon that "war spirit of America, which holds in bondage nearly four millions of his brethren," produced a profound sensation. At its conclusion the speaker was warmly greeted by Victor Hugo, the Abbé Duguerry, Emile de Girardin, Richard Cobden, and every man of note in the assembly. At the soirée given by M. de Tocqueville, the Minister for Foreign Affairs, and the other fêtes given to the members of the Congress, Mr. Brown was received with marked attention.

Having finished his peace mission in France, he returned to England, where he was received with a hearty welcome by some of the most influential abolitionists of that country. Most of the fugitive slaves, and, in fact, nearly all of the colored men who have visited Great Britain from the United States, have come upon begging missions, either for some society or for themselves. Mr. Brown has been almost the only exception. With that independence of feeling which those who are acquainted with him know to be one of his chief characteristics, he determined to maintain himself and family by his own exertions,— by his literary labors, and the honorable profession of a public lecturer. From nearly all the cities and large provincial towns he received invitations to lecture or address public meetings. The mayors, or other citizens of note, presided over many of these meetings. At Newcastle-upon-Tyne a soirée was given him, and an address presented by the citizens. A large and influential meeting was held at Bolton, Lancashire, which was addressed by Mr. Brown, and at its close the ladies presented to him the following address:

" An Address presented to Mr. William Wells Brown, the Fugitive Slave from America, by the Ladies of Bolton, March 22nd, 1850 :

" Dear Friend and Brother : We cannot permit you to depart from among us without giving expression to the feelings which we entertain towards yourself personally, and to the sympathy which you have awakened in our breasts for the three millions of our sisters and brothers who still suffer and groan in the prison-house of American bondage. You came among us an entire stranger; we received you for the sake of your mission; and having heard the story of your personal wrongs, and gazed with horror on the atrocities of slavery as seen through the medium of your touching descriptions, we are resolved, henceforward, in reliance on divine assistance, to render what aid we can to the cause which you have so eloquently pleaded in our presence.

"We have no words to express our detestation of the crimes which, in the name of liberty, are committed in the country which gave you birth. Language fails to tell our deep abhorrence of the impiety of those who, in the still more sacred name of religion, rob immortal beings not only of an earthly citizenship, but do much to prevent them from obtaining a heavenly one; and, as mothers and daughters, we embrace this opportunity of giving utterance to our utmost indignation at the cruelties perpetrated upon our sex, by a people professedly acknowledging the equality of all mankind. Carry with you, on your return to the land of your nativity, this our solemn protest against the wicked institution which, like a dark and baleful cloud, hangs over it; and ask the unfeeling enslavers, as best you can, to open the prison-doors to them that are bound, and let the oppressed go free.

"Allow us to assure you that your brief sojourn in our town has been to ourselves, and to vast multitudes, of a character long to be remembered; and when you are far removed from us, and toiling, as we hope you may be long spared to do, in this righteous enterprise, it may be some solace to your mind to know that your

name is cherished with affectionate regard, and that the
blessing of the Most High is earnestly supplicated in
behalf of yourself, your family, and the cause to which
you have consecrated your distinguished talents."

A most respectable and enthusiastic public meeting
was held at Sheffield to welcome Mr. Brown, and the
next day he was invited to inspect several of the large
establishments there. While going through the manu-
factory of Messrs. Broadhead and Atkin, silver and elec-
tro platers, &c., in Love-street, and whilst he was being
shown through the works, a subscription was hastily set
on foot on his behalf, by the workmen and women of the
establishment, which was presented to Mr. Brown, in the
counting-house, by a deputation of the subscribers. The
spokesman (the designer to Messrs. Broadhead & Atkin),
addressing Mr. Brown on behalf of the work-people,
begged his acceptance of the present as a token of es-
teem, as well as an expression of their sympathy in the
cause he advocates, namely, that of the American slave.
Mr. Brown briefly thanked the parties for their spon-
taneous free-will offering, accompanied, as it was, by a
generous expression of sympathy for his afflicted brethren
and sisters in bondage.

Mr. Brown was in England five years, and during
his sojourn there travelled above twenty-five thousand
miles through Great Britain, addressed more than one
thousand public meetings, lectured in twenty-three mechanics' and literary institutions, and gave his services
to many of the benevolent and religious societies on the
occasion of their anniversary meetings. After a lecture
which he delivered before the Whittington Club, he

received from the managers of that institution the following testimonial:

    "WHITTINGTON CLUB AND METROPOLITAN ATHENÆUM,
              189 STRAND, *June* 21, 1850.

"MY DEAR SIR: I have much pleasure in conveying to you the best thanks of the Managing Committee of this institution for the excellent lecture you gave here last evening, and also in presenting you in their names with an honorary membership of the club. It is hoped that you will often avail yourself of its privileges by coming amongst us. You will then see, by the cordial welcome of the members, that they protest against the odious distinctions made between man and man, and the abominable traffic of which you have been the victim.

"For my own part, I shall be happy to be serviceable to you in any way, and at all times be glad to place the advantages of the institution at your disposal.

    "I am, my dear sir, yours, truly,
        "WILLIAM STRUDWICKE, *Secretary.*
"Mr. W. WELLS BROWN."

————

The following lines were read at a soirée given to Mr. Brown at Bristol, in 1850:

TO WILLIAM WELLS BROWN,

THE AMERICAN FUGITIVE SLAVE.

BY E. S. MATHEWS.

Brother, farewell to thee!
  His blessing on thee rest
Who hates all slavery
  And helps the poor oppressed.

Go forth with power to break
  The bitter, galling yoke;

Go forth 'mongst strong and weak,
    The aid of all invoke.

O, thou wilt have much woe,
    Tossed on a sea of strife,
Hunted by many a foe
    Eager to take thy life.

Perchance thou 'lt have to brook
    The taunts of bond and free,
The cold, disdainful look
    Of men — less men than thee.

We feel thy soul will rise
    Superior to it all ;
For thou hast heard the cries,
    And drained the cup of gall.

Thine eyes have wept the tears
    Which tyrants taught to flow,
While craven scorn and sneers
    Fell with the shameful blow.

And now that thou art come
    To Freedom's blessed land,
Thou broodest on thy home
    And Slavery's hateful brand.

Thou thinkest thou canst hear
    Three million voices call ;
They raise to thee their prayer, —
    Haste, help to break their thrall !

Say, wilt thou have, thy steps to guard,
    Some powerful spell or charm ?
Then listen to thy sister's word,
    Nor fear thou hurt or harm.

When shines the North Star, cold and bright,
    Cheer thou thy heart, lift up thy head !
Feel, as thou look'st upon its light,
    That blessings on its beams are shed !
For rich, and poor, and bond, and free,
Will also gaze and pray for thee.

CHAPTER I.

" Adieu, adieu ! — my native shore
  Fades o'er the waters blue ;
The night-winds sigh, the breakers roar,
  And shrieks the wild sea-mew.
Yon sun that sets upon the sea
  We follow in his flight ;
Farewell a while to him and thee !
  My native land, good-night ! "

CHILDE HAROLD.

On the 18th July, 1849, I took passage in the steam-ship *Canada*, Captain Judkins, bound for Liverpool. The day was a warm one; so much so, that many persons on board, as well as on shore, stood with their umbrellas up, so intense was the heat of the sun. The ringing of the ship's bell was a signal for us to shake hands with our friends, which we did, and then stepped on the deck of the noble craft. The *Canada* quitted her moorings at half-past twelve, and we were soon in motion. As we were passing out of Boston Bay, 1 took my stand on the quarter-deck, to take a last farewell (at least for a time) of my native land. A visit to the Old World, up to that time, had seemed but a dream. As

I looked back upon the receding land, recollections of the past rushed through my mind in quick succession. From the treatment that I had received from the Americans as a victim of slavery, and the knowledge that I was at that time liable to be seized and again reduced to whips and chains, I had supposed that I would leave the country without any regret; but in this I was mistaken, for when I saw the last thread of communication cut off between me and the land, and the dim shores dying away in the distance, I almost regretted that I was not on shore.

An anticipated trip to a foreign country appears pleasant when talking about it, especially when surrounded by friends whom we love; but when we have left them all behind, it does not seem so pleasant. Whatever may be the fault of the government under which we live, and no matter how oppressive her laws may appear, yet we leave our native land (if such it be) with feelings akin to sorrow. With the steamer's powerful engine at work, and with a fair wind, we were speedily on the bosom of the Atlantic, which was as calm and as smooth as our own Hudson in its calmest aspect. We had on board above one hundred passengers, forty of whom were the " Vienneise children " — a troop of dancers. The passengers represented several different nations, English, French, Spaniards, Africans, and Americans. One man, who had the longest mustache that mortal man was ever doomed to wear, especially attracted my attention. He appeared to belong to no country in particular, but was yet the busiest man on board. After viewing for some time the many strange faces round me, I descended to the cabin to look after my luggage, which had been put hurriedly on board. I hope that all who take a trip of so great a distance may be as fortunate as I was, in being supplied with books to read on the voyage. My friends had furnished me with literature, from "Macaulay's History of England" to "Jane Eyre," so that I did not want for books to occupy my time.

A pleasant passage of about thirty hours brought us to Halifax, at six o'clock in the evening. In company with my friend the President of the Oberlin Institute, I took a stroll through the town ; and from what little I saw of the people in the streets, I am sure that the taking of the temperance pledge would do them no injury. Our stay at Halifax was short. Having taken in a few sacks of coals, the mails, and a limited number of passengers, we were again out, and soon at sea.

As the steamer moved gently from the shore I felt like repeating those lines of a distinguished poet :

> " With thee, my bark, I 'll swiftly go
>   Athwart the foaming brine ;
> Nor care what land thou bear'st me to,
>   So not again to mine.
> Welcome, welcome, ye dark blue waves !
>   And when you fail my sight
> Welcome ye deserts and ye caves !
>   My native land, good-night ! "

Nothing occurred during the passage to mar the pleasure which we anticipated from a voyage by sea in such fine weather. And, after a splendid run of seven days more, I heard the welcome cry of "Land a-head." It was early in the morning, and I was not yet out of bed ; but I had no wish to remain longer in my berth. Although the passage had been unprecedently short, yet this news was hailed with joy by all on board.

For my own part, I was soon on deck. Away in the distance, and on our larboard quarter, were the gray hills of old Ireland. Yes; we were in sight of the land of Curran, Emmet and O'Connell. While I rejoiced with the other passengers at the sight of land, and the near approach to the end of our voyage, I felt low-spirited, because it reminded me of the great distance I was from home, and of dear ones left behind. But the experience of above twenty years' travelling had prepared me to undergo what most persons must, in visiting a strange country. This was the last day but one that we were to be on board ; and, as if moved by the sight of land, all seemed to be gathering their different things together—brushing up their old clothes and putting on their new ones, as if this would bring them any sooner to the end of their journey.

The last night on board was the most pleasant, apparently, that we had experienced ; probably, because it was the last. The moon was in her meridian splendor, pouring her broad light over the calm sea ; while near to us, on our starboard side, was a ship, with her snow-white sails spread aloft, and stealing through the water like a thing of life. What can present a more picturesque view than two vessels at sea on a moonlight night, and within a few rods of each other? With a gentle breeze, and the powerful engine at work, we seemed to be flying to the embrace of our British neighbors.

The next morning I was up before the sun, and found that we were within a few miles of Liverpool. The taking of a pilot on board at eleven o'clock warned us to prepare to quit our ocean palace, and seek other quarters. At a little past three o'clock, the ship cast anchor, and we were all tumbled, bag and baggage, into a small steamer, and in a few moments were at the door of the custom-house. The passage had only been nine days and twenty-two hours, the quickest on record at that time, yet it was long enough. I waited nearly three hours before my name was called, and when it was I unlocked my trunks and handed them over to one of the officers, whose dirty hands made no improvement on the work of the laundress. First one article was taken out, and then another, till an *Iron Collar* that had been worn by a female slave on the banks of the Mississippi was hauled out, and this democratic instrument of torture became the centre of attraction; so much so, that instead of going on with the examination, all hands stopped to look at the "Negro Collar."

Several of my countrymen who were standing by were not a little displeased at answers which I gave to questions on the subject of slavery; but they held their peace. The interest created by the appearance of the iron collar closed the examination of my luggage. As if afraid that they would find something more hideous, they put the custom-house mark on each piece, and passed them out, and I was soon comfortably installed at Brown's Temperance Hotel, Clayton-square.

No person of my complexion can visit this country without being struck with the marked difference between the English and the Americans. The prejudice which I have experienced on all and every occasion in the United States, and to some extent on board the *Canada*, vanished as soon as I set foot on the soil of Britain. In America I had been bought and sold as a slave in the Southern States. In the so-called Free States, I had been treated as one born to occupy an inferior position,— in steamers, compelled to take my fare on the deck; in hotels, to take my meals in the kitchen; in coaches, to ride on the outside; in railways, to ride in the "negro-car;" and in churches, to sit in the "negro-pew." But no sooner was I on British soil, than I was recognized as a man, and an equal. The very dogs in the streets appeared conscious of my manhood. Such is the difference, and such is the change that is brought about by a trip of nine days in an Atlantic steamer.

I was not more struck with the treatment of the people than with the appearance of the great seaport of the world. The gray stone piers and docks, the dark look of the magnificent warehouses, the substantial appearance of everything around, causes one to think himself in a new world instead of the old. Everything in Liverpool looks old, yet nothing is worn out. The beautiful villas on the opposite side of the river, in the vicinity of Birkenhead, together with the countless number of vessels in the river, and the great ships to be seen in the stream, give life and animation to the whole scene.

Everything in and about Liverpool seems to be built for the future as well as the present. We had time to examine but few of the public buildings, the first of which was the custom-house, an edifice that would be an ornament to any city in the world.

CHAPTER II.

" It seems as if every ship their sovereign knows,
        His awful summons they so soon obey ;
    So hear the scaly herds when Proteus blows,
        And so to pasture follow through the sea."

AFTER remaining in Liverpool two days, I took passage in the little steamer *Adelaide* for Dublin. The wind being high on the night of our voyage, the vessel had scarcely got to sea ere we were driven to our berths; and, though the distance from Liverpool to Dublin is short, yet, strange to say, I witnessed more effects of the sea and rolling of the steamer upon the passengers, than was to be seen during the whole of our voyage from America. We reached Kingstown, five miles below Dublin, after a passage of nearly fifteen hours, and were soon seated on a car, and on our way to the city. While coming into the bay, one gets a fine view of Dublin and the surrounding country. Few sheets of water make a more beautiful appearance than Dublin Bay. We found it as still and smooth as a mirror, with a soft mist on its surface,— a strange contrast to the boisterous sea that we had left a moment before.

The curious phrases of the Irish sounded harshly upon my ear, probably because they were strange to me. I lost no time, on reaching the city, in seeking out some to whom I had letters of introduction, one of whom gave me an invitation to make his house my home during my stay, — an invitation which I did not think fit to decline.

Dublin, the metropolis of Ireland, is a city of above two hundred thousand inhabitants, and is considered by the people of Ireland to be the second city in the British empire. The Liffey, which falls into Dublin Bay a little below the custom-house, divides the town into two nearly equal parts. The streets are — some of them — very fine, especially Sackville-street, in the centre of which stands a pillar erected to Nelson, England's most distinguished naval commander. The Bank of Ireland, to which I paid a visit, is a splendid building, and was formerly the Parliament House. This magnificent edifice fronts College Green, and near at hand stands a bronze statue of William III. The Bank and the Custom-House are two of the finest monuments of architecture in the city; the latter of which stands near the river Liffey, and its front makes an imposing appearance, extending three hundred and seventy-five feet. It is built of Portland stone, and is adorned with a beautiful portico in the centre, consisting of four Doric columns, supporting an enriched entablature, decorated with a group of figures in alto-relievo, representing Hibernia and Britannia presenting emblems of peace and liberty. A magnificent dome, supporting a cupola, on whose apex stands a colossal figure of Hope, rises nobly from the centre of the building to a height of one hundred and twenty-five feet. It is, withal, a fine specimen of what man can do.

From this noble edifice we bent our steps to another part of the city, and soon found ourselves in the vicinity of St. Patrick's, where we had a heart-sickening view of the poorest of the poor. All the recollections of poverty which I had ever beheld seemed to disappear in comparison with what was then before me. We passed a filthy and noisy market, where fruit and vegetable women were screaming and begging those passing by to purchase their commodities; while in and about the market-place were throngs of beggars fighting for rotten fruit, cabbage-stocks, and even the very trimmings of vegetables. On the side-walks were great numbers hovering about the doors of the more wealthy, and following strangers, importuning them for " pence to buy bread." Sickly and emaciated looking creatures, half naked, were at our heels at every turn.

In our return home, we passed through a respectable-looking street, in which stands a small three-story brick building, that was pointed out to us as the birthplace of Thomas Moore, the poet. The following verse from one of his poems was continually in my mind while viewing this house :

> " Where is the slave so lowly,
> Condemned to chains unholy,
> Who, could he burst
> His bonds at first,
> Would pine beneath them slowly ? "

The next day was the Sabbath, but it had more the appearance of a holiday than a day of rest. It had been announced the day before that the royal fleet was expected, and at an early hour on Sunday the entire town seemed to be on the move towards Kingstown, and, as the family with whom I was staying followed the multitude, I was not inclined to remain behind, and so went with them. On reaching the station, we found it utterly impossible to get standing room in any of the trains, much less a seat, and therefore determined to reach Kingstown under the plea of a morning's walk ; and in this we were not alone, for during the walk of five miles the road was filled with thousands of pedestrians, and a countless number of carriages, phaëtons, and vehicles of a more humble order.

We reached the lower town in time to get a good dinner, and rest ourselves before going to make further searches for her majesty's fleet. At a little past four o'clock, we observed the multitude going towards the pier, a number of whom were yelling, at the top of their voices, " It 's coming, it 's coming ! " but on going to the quay we found that a false alarm had been given. However, we had been on the look-out but a short time, when a column of smoke, rising, as it were, out of the sea, announced that the royal fleet was near at hand. The concourse in the vicinity of the pier was variously estimated at from eighty to one hundred thousand.

It was not long before the five steamers were entering the harbor, the one bearing her majesty leading the way.

As each vessel had a number of distinguished persons on
board, the people appeared to be at a loss to know which
was the queen; and as each party made its appearance
on the promenade deck, they were received with great
enthusiasm, the party having the best-looking lady being
received with the greatest applause. The Prince of
Wales, and Prince Alfred, while crossing the deck were
recognized, and greeted with three cheers; the former,
taking off his hat and bowing to the people, showed that
he had had some training as a public man, although not
ten years of age. But not so with Prince Alfred; for,
when his brother turned to him and asked him to take
off his hat, and make a bow to the people, he shook his
head, and said, "No." This was received with hearty
laughter by those on board, and was responded to by the
thousands on shore. But greater applause was yet in
store for the young prince; for the captain of the
steamer being near by, and seeing that the Prince of
Wales could not prevail on his brother to take off his hat,
stepped up to him and undertook to take it off for him,
when, seemingly to the delight of all, the prince put both
hands to his head, and held his hat fast. This was
regarded as a sign of courage and future renown, and
was received with the greatest enthusiasm, many crying
out, " Good, good ! he will make a brave king when his
day comes."

After the greetings and applause had been wasted on
many who had appeared on deck, all at once, as if by
some magic power, we beheld a lady, rather small in

stature, with auburn hair, attired in a plain dress, and wearing a sky-blue bonnet, standing on the larboard paddle-box, by the side of a tall, good-looking man, with a mustache. The thunders of applause that now rent the air, and cries of "The queen, the queen!" seemed to set at rest the question of which was her majesty. But a few moments were allowed to the people to look at the queen, before she again disappeared; and it was understood that she would not be seen again that evening. A rush was then made for the railway, to return to Dublin.

*   *   *   *   *   *

The seventh of August was a great day in Dublin. At an early hour the bells began their merry peals, and the people were soon seen in groups in the streets and public squares. The hour of ten was fixed for the procession to leave Kingstown, and it was expected to enter the city at eleven. The windows of the houses in the streets through which the royal train was to pass were at a premium, and seemed to find ready occupants.

Being invited the day previous to occupy part of a window in Sackville-street, I was stationed at my allotted place at an early hour, with an outstretched neck and open eyes. My own color differing from those about me, I attracted not a little attention from many; and often, when gazing down the street to see if the royal procession was in sight, would find myself eyed by all around. But neither while at the window or in the streets was I once insulted. This was so unlike the American prejudice, that it seemed strange to me. It

was near twelve o'clock before the procession entered
Sackville-street, and when it did all eyes seemed to beam
with delight.   The first carriage contained only her
majesty and the Prince Consort; the second the royal
children, and the third the lords in waiting.   Fifteen
carriages were used by those that made up the royal
party.   I had a full view of the queen and all who followed in the train.   Her majesty — whether from
actual love for her person, or the novelty of the occasion,
I know not which — was received everywhere with the
greatest enthusiasm.   One thing, however, is certain, and that is, Queen Victoria is beloved by her
subjects.

But the grand *fête* was reserved for the evening.
Great preparations had been made to have a grand illumination on the occasion, and hints were thrown out that
it would surpass anything ever witnessed in London.   In
this they were not far out of the way; for all who
witnessed the scene admitted that it could scarcely have
been surpassed.   My own idea of an illumination, as I
had seen it in the back-woods of my native land, dwindled
into nothing when compared with this magnificent
affair.

In company with a few friends, and a lady under my
charge, I undertook to pass through Sackville and one
or two other streets about eight o'clock in the evening,
but we found it utterly impossible to proceed.   Masses
thronged the streets, and the wildest enthusiasm seemed
to prevail.   In our attempt to cross the bridge, we were

wedged in and lost our companions; and on one occasion I was separated from the lady, and took shelter under a cart standing in the street. After being jammed and pulled about for nearly two hours, I returned to my lodgings, where I found part of my company, who had come in one after another. At eleven o'clock we had all assembled, and each told his adventures and "hair-breadth escapes;" and nearly every one had lost a pocket-handkerchief or something of the kind; my own was among the missing. However, I lost nothing; for a benevolent lady, who happened to be one of the company, presented me with one which was of far more value than the one I had lost.

Every one appeared to enjoy the holiday which the royal visit had caused. But the Irish are indeed a strange people. How varied their aspect, how contradictory their character! Ireland, the land of genius and degradation, of great resources and unparalleled poverty, noble deeds and the most revolting crimes, the land of distinguished poets, splendid orators, and the bravest of soldiers, the land of ignorance and beggary! Dublin is a splendid city, but its splendor is that of chiselled marble rather than real life. One cannot behold these architectural monuments without thinking of the great men that Ireland has produced. The names of Burke, Sheridan, Flood, Grattan, O'Connell and Shiel, have become as familiar to the Americans as household words. Burke is known as the statesman; Sheridan for his great speech on the trial of Warren

Hastings; Grattan for his eloquence; O'Connell as the agitator, and Shiel as the accomplished orator.

But, of Ireland's sons, none stands higher in America than Thomas Moore, the poet. The vigor of his sarcasm, the glow of his enthusiasm, the coruscations of his fancy, and the flashing of his wit, seem to be as well understood in the New World as the Old; and the support which his pen has given to civil and religious liberty throughout the world entitles the Minstrel of Erin to this elevated position.

CHAPTER III.

"There is no other land like thee,
No dearer shore;
Thou art the shelter of the free, —
The home, the port of Liberty."

AFTER a pleasant sojourn of three weeks in Ireland, I took passage in one of the mail-steamers for Liverpool, and, arriving there, was soon on the road to the metropolis. The passage from Dublin to Liverpool was an agreeable one. The rough sea that we passed through on going to Ireland had given way to a dead calm; and our noble little steamer, on quitting the Dublin wharf, seemed to understand that she was to have it all her own way. During the first part of the evening, the boat appeared to feel her importance, and, darting through the water with majestic strides, she left behind her a dark cloud of smoke suspended in the air like a banner; while, far astern in the wake of the vessel, could be seen the rippled waves sparkling in the rays of the moon, giving strength and beauty to the splendor of the evening.

On reaching Liverpool, and partaking of a good breakfast, for which we paid double price, we proceeded

to the railway station, and were soon going at a rate unknown to those accustomed to travel only on American
railways.   At a little past two o'clock in the afternoon
we saw in the distance the outskirts of London.   We
could get but an indistinct view, which had the appearance of one architectural mass, extending all round to
the horizon, and enveloped in a combination of fog and
smoke ; and towering above every other object to be seen
was the dome of St. Paul's Cathedral.

A few moments more, and we were safely seated in a
" Hansom's Patent," and on our way to Hughes's — one
of the politest men of the George Fox stamp we have
ever met.   Here we found forty or fifty persons, who,
like ourselves, were bound for the Peace Congress.   The
Sturges, the Wighams, the Richardsons, the Allens, the
Thomases, and a host of others not less distinguished as
friends of peace, were of the company — of many of whom
I had heard, but none of whom I had ever seen ; yet I
was not an entire stranger to many, especially to the
abolitionists.   In company with a friend, I sallied forth
after tea to take a view of the city.   The evening was
fine — the dense fog and smoke, having to some extent
passed away, left the stars shining brightly, while the
gas-light from the street-lamps and the brilliant shop-
windows gave it the appearance of day-light in a new
form.   "What street is this ? " we asked.   " Cheapside,"
was the reply.   The street was thronged, and everybody
seemed to be going at a rapid rate, as if there was something of importance at the end of the journey.   Flying

vehicles of every description passing each other with a
dangerous rapidity, men with lovely women at their
sides, children running about as if they had lost their
parents — all gave a brilliancy to the scene scarcely to
be excelled. If one wished to get jammed and pushed
about, he need go no further than Cheapside. But
everything of the kind is done with a degree of propriety
in London that would put the New Yorkers to blush.
If you are run over in London, they " beg your pardon ; "
if they run over you in New York, you are "laughed
at : " in London, if your hat is knocked off it is picked up
and handed to you ; if in New York, you must pick it
up yourself. There is a lack of good manners among
Americans that is scarcely known or understood in Europe. Our stay in the great metropolis gave us but
little opportunity of seeing much of the place ; for in
twenty-four hours after our arrival we joined the rest
of the delegates, and started on our visit to our Gallic
neighbors.

We assembled at the London Bridge Railway Station,
a few minutes past nine, to the number of six hundred.
The day was fine, and every eye seemed to glow with
enthusiasm. Besides the delegates, there were probably
not less than six hundred more, who had come to see the
company start. We took our seats, and appeared to be
waiting for nothing but the iron-horse to be fastened to
the train, when all at once we were informed that we
must go to the booking-office and change our tickets. At
this news every one appeared to be vexed. This caused

great trouble; for, on returning to the train, many persons got into the wrong carriages; and several parties were separated from their friends, while not a few were calling out, at the top of their voices, "Where is my wife? Where is my husband? Where is my luggage? Who's got my boy? Is this the right train?" "What is that lady going to do with all these children?" asked the guard. "Is she a delegate? are all the children delegates?" In the carriage where I had taken my seat was a good-looking lady, who gave signs of being very much annoyed. "It is just so when I am going anywhere: I never saw the like in my life!" said she. "I really wish I was at home again."

An hour had now elapsed, and we were still at the station. However, we were soon on our way, and going at express speed. In passing through Kent we enjoyed the scenery exceedingly, as the weather was altogether in our favor; and the drapery which nature hung on the trees, in the part through which we passed, was in all its gayety. On our arrival at Folkstone, we found three steamers in readiness to convey the party to Boulogne. As soon as the train stopped, a general rush was made for the steamers, and in a very short time the one in which I had embarked was passing out of the harbor. The boat appeared to be conscious that we were going on a holy mission, and seemed to be proud of her load. There is nothing in this wide world so like a thing of life as a steamer, from the breathing of her steam and smoke, the energy of her motion, and the beauty of her shape;

while the ease with which she is managed by the command of a single voice makes her appear as obedient as the horse is to the rein.

When we were about half way between the two great European powers, the officer began to gather the tickets. The first to whom he applied, and who handed out his "Excursion Ticket," was informed that we were all in the wrong boat. "Is this not one of the boats to take over the delegates?" asked a pretty little lady, with a whining voice. "No, madam," said the captain. "You must look to the committee for your pay," said one of the company to the captain. "I have nothing to do with committees," the captain replied. "Your fare, gentlemen, if you please."

Here the whole party were again thrown into confusion. "Do you hear that? We are in the wrong boat." "I knew it would be so," said the Rev. Dr. Ritchie, of Edinburgh. "It is indeed a pretty piece of work," said a plain-looking lady in a handsome bonnet. "When I go travelling again," said an elderly-looking gent, with an eye-glass to his face, "I will take the phaëton and old Dobbin." Every one seemed to lay the blame on the committee, and not, too, without some just grounds. However, Mr. Sturge, one of the committee, being in the boat with us, an arrangement was entered into by which we were not compelled to pay our fare the second time.

As we neared the French coast, the first object that attracted our attention was the Napoleon Pillar, on the top of which is a statue of the emperor in the imperial robes. We landed, partook of refreshment that had been prepared for us, and again repaired to the railway station. The arrangements for leaving Boulogne were no better than those at London. But after the delay of another hour we were again in motion.

It was a beautiful country through which we passed from Boulogne to Amiens. Straggling cottages which bespeak neatness and comfort abound on every side. The eye wanders over the diversified views with unabated pleasure, and rests in calm repose upon its superlative beauty. Indeed, the eye cannot but be gratified at viewing the entire country from the coast to the metropolis. Sparkling hamlets spring up, as the steam-horse speeds his way, at almost every point, showing the progress of civilization, and the refinement of the nineteenth century.

We arrived at Paris a few minutes past twelve o'clock at night, when, according to our tickets, we should have been there at nine. Elihu Burritt, who had been in Paris some days, and who had the arrangements there pretty much his own way, was at the station waiting the arrival of the train, and we had demonstrated to us the best evidence that he understood his business. In no other place on the whole route had the affairs been so well managed ; for we were seated in our respective carriages and our luggage placed on the top, and away we went to our hotels, without the least difficulty or inconvenience. The champion of an " Ocean Penny Postage " received, as he deserved, thanks from the whole company for his admirable management.

The silence of the night was only disturbed by the rolling of the wheels of the omnibus, as we passed through the dimly-lighted streets. Where, a few months before, was to be seen the flash from the cannon and the musket, and the hearing of the cries and groans behind the barricades, was now the stillness of death — nothing save here and there a *gens d'arme* was to be seen going his rounds in silence.

The omnibus set us down at the hotel Bedford, Rue de L'Card, where, although near one o'clock, we found a good supper waiting for us; and, as I was not devoid of an appetite, I did my share towards putting it out of the way.

The next morning I was up at an early hour, and out on the Boulevards to see what might be seen. As I was passing from the hotel to the Place de La Concord, all at once, and as if by some magic power, I found myself in front of the most splendid edifice imaginable, situated at the end of the Rue Nationale. Seeing a number of persons entering the church at that early hour, and recognizing among them my friend the President of the Oberlin (Ohio) Institute, and wishing not to stray too far from my hotel before breakfast, I followed the crowd and entered the building. The church itself consisted of a vast nave, interrupted by four pews on each side, fronted with lofty fluted Corinthian columns standing on pedestals, supporting colossal arches, bearing up cupolas pierced with skylights and adorned with compartments gorgeously gilt; their corners supported with saints and

apostles in *alto relievo*. The walls of the church were
lined with rich marble. The different paintings and
figures gave the interior an imposing appearance. On
inquiry, I found that I was in the Church of the
Madeleine. It was near this spot that some of the
most interesting scenes occurred during the Revolution
of 1848, which dethroned Louis Philippe. Behind the
Madeleine is a small but well-supplied market; and on
an esplanade east of the edifice a flower-market is held
on Tuesdays and Fridays.

At eleven o'clock the same day, the Peace Congress met in the Salle St. Cecile, Rue de la St.
Lazare. The Parisians have no " Exeter Hall;" in
fact, there is no private hall in the city of any size,
save this, where such a meeting could be held. This
hall had been fitted up for the occasion. The room
is long, and at one end has a raised platform ; and at the
opposite end is a gallery, with seats raised one above
another. On one side of the hall was a balcony with
sofas, which were evidently the " reserved seats."

The hall was filled at an early hour with the delegates, their friends, and a good sprinkling of the French.
Occasionally, small groups of gentlemen would make
their appearance on the platform, until it soon appeared
that there was little room left for others ; and yet the
officers of the Convention had not come in. The different countries were, many of them, represented here.
England, France, Belgium, Germany, Switzerland,
Greece, Spain, and the United States, had each their

delegates. The assembly began to give signs of impatience, when very soon the train of officials made their appearance amid great applause. Victor Hugo led the way, followed by M. Duguerry, curé of the Madeleine, Elihu Burritt, and a host of others of less note. Victor Hugo took the chair as President of the Congress, supported by vice-presidents from the several nations represented. Mr. Richard, the secretary, read a dry report of the names of societies, committees, etc., which was deemed the opening of the Convention.

The president then arose, and delivered one of the most impressive and eloquent appeals in favor of peace that could possibly be imagined. The effect produced upon the minds of all present was such as to make the author of "*Notre Dame de Paris*" a great favorite with the Congress. An English gentleman near me said to his friend, "I can't understand a word of what he says, but is it not good?" Victor Hugo concluded his speech amid the greatest enthusiasm on the part of the French, which was followed by hurras in the old English style. The Convention was successively addressed by the President of the Brussels Peace Society; President Mahan, of the Oberlin (Ohio) Institute, U. S.; Henry Vincent; and Richard Cobden. The latter was not only the *lion* of the English delegation, but the great man of the Convention. When Mr. Cobden speaks there is no want of hearers. The great power of this gentleman lies in his facts and his earnestness, for he cannot be called an eloquent speaker. Mr. Cobden addressed the Congress first in French, then in English; and, with the single exception of Mr. Ewart, M. P., was the only one of the English delegation that could speak to the French in their own language.

The first day's proceedings were brought to a close at five o'clock, when the numerous audience dispersed — the citizens to their homes, and the delegates to see the sights.

I was not a little amused at an incident that occurred at the close of the first session. On the passage from America, there were in the same steamer with me several Americans, and among these three or four appeared to be much annoyed at the fact that I was a passenger, and enjoying the company of white persons; and, although I was not openly insulted, I very often heard the remark, that "That nigger had better be on his master's farm," and "What could the American Peace Society be thinking about, to send a black man as a delegate to Paris?" Well, at the close of the first sitting of the convention, and just as I was leaving Victor Hugo, to whom I had been introduced by an M. P., I observed near me a gentleman with his hat in hand, whom I recognized as one of the passengers who had crossed the Atlantic with me in the *Canada*, and who appeared to be the most horrified at having a negro for a fellow-passenger. This gentleman, as I left M. Hugo, stepped up to me and said, "How do you do, Mr. Brown?" "You have the advantage of me," said I. "O, don't you know me? I was a fellow-passenger with you from

America; I wish you would give me an introduction to
Victor Hugo and Mr. Cobden." I need not inform you
that I declined introducing this pro-slavery American to
these distinguished men. I only allude to this, to show
what a change came over the dreams of my white American brother by crossing the ocean. The man who would
not have been seen walking with me in the streets of
New York, and who would not have shaken hands with
me with a pair of tongs while on the passage from the
United States, could come with hat in hand in Paris,
and say, "I was your fellow-passenger." From the
Salle de St. Cecile, I visited the Column Vendome, from
the top of which I obtained a fine view of Paris and its
environs. This is the Bunker Hill Monument of Paris.
On the top of this pillar is a statue of the Emperor
Napoleon, eleven feet high. The monument is built
with stone, and the outside covered with a metallic composition, made of cannons, guns, spikes, and other warlike implements taken from the Russians and Austrians
by Napoleon. Above twelve hundred cannons were
melted down to help to create this monument of folly, to
commemorate the success of the French arms in the German campaign. The column is in imitation of the Tra-
jan pillar at Rome, and is twelve feet in diameter at the
base. The door at the bottom of the pillar, and where
we entered, was decorated above with crowns of oak,
surmounted by eagles, each weighing five hundred
pounds. The bas-relief of the shaft pursues a spiral
direction to the top, and displays, in a chronological

order, the principal actions of the French army, from the departure of the troops from Boulogne to the battle of Austerlitz. The figures are near three feet high, and their number said to be two thousand. This sumptuous monument stands on a plinth of polished granite, surmounted by an iron railing; and, from its size and position, has an imposing appearance when seen from any part of the city.

Everything here appears strange and peculiar — the people not less so than their speech. The horses, carriages, furniture, dress and manners, are in keeping with their language. The appearance of the laborers in caps, resembling night-caps, seemed particularly strange to me. The women without bonnets, and their caps turned the right side behind, had nothing of the look of our American women. The prettiest woman I ever saw was without a bonnet, walking on the Boulevards. While in Ireland, and during the few days I was in England, I was struck with the marked difference between the appearance of the women and those of my own country. The American women are too tall, too sallow, and too long-featured, to be called pretty. This is most probably owing to the fact that in America the people come to maturity earlier than in most other countries.

My first night in Paris was spent with interest. No place can present greater street attractions than the Boulevards of Paris. The countless number of cafés, with tables before the doors, and these surrounded by men with long moustaches, with ladies at their sides, whose very smiles give indication of happiness, together with the sound of music from the gardens in the rear, tell the stranger that he is in a different country from his own.

CHAPTER IV.

"―――― A town of noble fame,
Where monuments are found in ancient guise,
Where kings and queens in pomp did long abide,
And where God pleased that good King Louis died."

AFTER the Convention had finished its sittings yesterday, I accompanied Mrs. C―― and sisters to Versailles,
where they are residing during the summer. It was
really pleasing to see among the hundreds of strange
faces in the Convention those distinguished friends of the
slave from Boston.

Mrs. C――'s residence is directly in front of the
great palace where so many kings have made their
homes, the prince of whom was Louis XIV. The palace
is now unoccupied. No ruler has dared to take up his
residence here since Louis XVI. and Marie Antoinette
were driven from it by the mob from Paris on the eighth
of October, 1789. The town looks like the wreck of what
it once was. At the commencement of the first revolution,
it contained one hundred thousand inhabitants; now it
has only about thirty thousand. It seems to be going
back to what it was in the time of Louis XIII., when, in
1624, he built a small brick chateau, and from it arose

the magnificent palace which now stands here, and which attracts strangers to it from all parts of the world.

I arose this morning at an early hour, and took a walk through the grounds of the palace, and remained three hours among the fountains and statuary of this more than splendid place. At ten o'clock we again returned to Paris, to the Peace Congress.

The session was opened by a speech from M. Coquerel, the Protestant clergyman in Paris. His speech was received with much applause, and seemed to create great sensation in the Congress, especially at the close of his remarks, when he was seized by the hand by the Abbé Duguerry, amid the most deafening and enthusiastic applause of the entire multitude. The meeting was then addressed in English by a short gentleman, of florid complexion. His words seemed to come without the least difficulty, and his gestures, though somewhat violent, were evidently studied; and the applause with which he was greeted by the English delegation showed that he was a man of no little distinction among them. His speech was one continuous flow of rapid, fervid eloquence, that seemed to fire every heart; and although I disliked his style, I was prepossessed in his favor. This was Henry Vincent, and his speech was in favor of disarmament.

Mr. Vincent was followed by M. Emile de Girardin, the editor of *La Presse*, in one of the most eloquent speeches that I ever heard; and his exclamation of "Soldiers of Peace" drew thunders of applause from

his own countrymen. M. Girardin is not only the leader
of the French press, but is a writer on politics of great
distinction, and a leader of no inconsiderable party in the
National Assembly; although still a young man, apparently not more than thirty-eight or forty years of
age.

After a speech from Mr. Ewart, M. P., in French,
and another from Mr. Cobden in the same language, the
Convention was brought to a close for the day. I spent
the morning yesterday in visiting some of the lions of the
French capital, among which was the Louvre. The
French government having kindly ordered that the
members of the Peace Congress should be admitted free,
and without ticket, to all the public works, I had nothing
to do but present my card of membership, and was immediately admitted.

The first room I entered was nearly a quarter of a
mile in length; is known as the "Long Gallery," and
contains some of the finest paintings in the world.
On entering this superb palace, my first impression was
that all Christendom had been robbed, that the Louvre
might make a splendid appearance. This is the Italian
department, and one would suppose by its appearance
that but few paintings had been left in Italy. The
entrance end of the Louvre was for a long time in an
unfinished state, but was afterwards completed by that
master workman, the Emperor Napoleon. It was long
thought that the building would crumble into decay, but
the genius of the great Corsican rescued it from ruin.

During our walk through the Louvre, we saw some twenty or thirty artists copying paintings; some had their copies finished and were going out, others half done, while many had just commenced. I remained some minutes near a pretty French girl, who was copying a painting of a dog rescuing a child from a stream of water into which it had fallen.

I walked down one side of the hall and up the other, and was about leaving, when I was informed that this was only one room, and that a half-dozen more were at my service; but a clock on a neighboring church reminded me that I must quit the Louvre for the Salle de St. Cecile.

  *   *   *   *   *   *

At the meeting of the third session of the Congress, the hall was filled at an early hour with rather a more fashionable-looking audience than on any former occasion, and all appeared anxious for its commencement, as it was understood to be the last day. After the reading of several letters from gentlemen, apologizing for their not being able to attend, the speech of Elihu Burritt was read by a son of M. Coquerel. I felt somewhat astonished that my countryman, who was said to be master of fifty languages, had to get some one to read his speech in French.

The Abbé Duguerry now came forward amid great cheering, and said that "the eminent journalist, Girardin, and the great English logician, Mr. Cobden, had made it unnecessary for any further advocacy in that

assembly of the peace cause ; that if the principles laid
down in the resolutions were carried out, the work would
be done.   He said that the question of general pacifica-
tion was built on truth,— truth which emanated from
God,— and it were as vain to undertake to prevent air
from expanding as to check the progress of truth.   It
must and would prevail."

A pale, thin-faced gentleman next ascended the platform (or tribune, as it was called) amid shouts of applause from the English, and began his speech in rather
a low tone, when compared with the sharp voice of Vincent, or the thunder of the Abbé Duguerry.   An audience is not apt to be pleased or even contented with an
inferior speaker, when surrounded by eloquent men, and
I looked every moment for manifestations of disapprobation, as I felt certain that the English delegation had
made a mistake in applauding this gentleman, who
seemed to make such an unpromising beginning.   But the
speaker soon began to get warm on the subject, and even
at times appeared as if he had spoken before.   In a very
short time, with the exception of his own voice, the stillness of death prevailed throughout the building, and the
speaker delivered one of the most logical speeches made
in the Congress, and, despite of his thin, sallow look,
interested me much more than any whom I had before
heard.   Towards the close of his remarks, he was several
times interrupted by manifestations of approbation; and
finally concluded amid great cheering.   I inquired the

gentleman's name, and was informed that it was Edward Miall, editor of the *Nonconformist*.

After speeches from several others, the great Peace Congress of 1849, which had brought men together from nearly all the governments of Europe, and many from America, was brought to a final close by a speech from the president, returning thanks for the honor that had been conferred upon him. He said : " My address shall be short, and yet I have to bid you adieu ! How resolve to do so ? Here, during three days, have questions of the deepest import been discussed, examined, probed to the bottom; and during these discussions counsels have been given to governments which they will do well to profit by. If these days' sittings are attended with no other result, they will be the means of sowing in the minds of those present germs of cordiality which must ripen into good fruit. England, France, Belgium, Europe and America, would all be drawn closer by these sittings. Yet the moment to part has arrived, but I can feel that we are strongly united in heart. But, before parting, I may congratulate you and myself on the result of our proceedings. We have been all joined together without distinction of country ; we have all been united in one common feeling during our three days' communion. The good work cannot go back ; it must advance, it must be accomplished. The course of the future may be judged of by the sound of the footsteps of the past. In the course of that day's discussion, a reminiscence had been handed up to one of the speakers, that

this was the anniversary of the dreadful massacre of St.
Bartholomew : the reverend gentleman who was speaking
turned away from the thought of that sanguinary scene
with pious horror, natural to his sacred calling.   But I,
who may boast of firmer nerve, I take up the remem-
brance. Yes, it was on this day, two hundred and
seventy-seven years ago, that Paris was roused from
slumber by the sound of that bell which bore the name
of *cloche d'argent*.   Massacre was on foot, seeking
with keen eye for its victim ; man was busy in slaying
man. That slaughter was called forth by mingled passions of the worst description. Hatred of all kinds was
there urging on the slayer,— hatred of a religious, a
political, a personal character. And yet on the anniversary of that same day of horror, and in that very city
whose blood was flowing like water, has God this day
given a rendezvous to men of peace, whose wild tumult is
transformed into order, and animosity into love. The
stain of blood is blotted out, and in its place beams forth
a ray of holy light. All distinctions are removed, and
Papist and Huguenot meet together in friendly communion. (Loud cheers.)   Who that thinks of these
amazing changes can doubt of the progress that has been
made ? But whoever denies the force of progress must
deny God, since progress is the boon of Providence, and
emanated from the great Being above. I feel gratified
for the change that has been effected, and, pointing
solemnly to the past, I say let this day be ever held
memorable ; let the twenty-fourth of August, 1572,

be remembered only for the purpose of being compared with the twenty-fourth of August, 1849; and when we think of the latter, and ponder over the high purpose to which it has been devoted,— the advocacy of the principles of peace,— let us not be so wanting in reliance on Providence as to doubt for one moment of the eventual success of our holy cause."

The most enthusiastic cheers followed this interesting speech. A vote of thanks to the government, and three times three cheers, with Mr. Cobden as "fugleman," ended the great Peace Congress of 1849.

Time for separating had arrived, yet all seemed unwilling to leave the place, where, for three days, men of all creeds and of no creed had met upon one common platform. In one sense the meeting was a glorious one, in another it was mere child's play; for the Congress had been restricted to the discussion of certain topics. They were permitted to dwell on the blessings of peace, but were not allowed to say anything about the very subjects above all others that should have been brought before the Congress. A French army had invaded Rome and put down the friends of political and religious freedom, yet not a word was said in reference to it. The fact is, the committee permitted the Congress to be *gagged* before it had met. They put padlocks upon their own mouths, and handed the keys to the government. And this was sorely felt by many of the speakers. Richard Cobden, who had thundered his anathemas against the corn-laws of his own country, and against wars in every clime, had to sit quiet in his fetters. Henry Vincent, who can make a louder speech in favor of peace than almost any other man, and whose denunciations of "all war," have gained him no little celebrity with peace men, had to confine himself to the blessings of peace. O, how I wished for a Massachusetts atmosphere, a New England convention platform, with Wendell Phillips as the speaker, before that assembled multitude from all parts of the world!

But the Congress is over, and cannot now be made different; yet it is to be hoped that neither the London Peace Committee, nor any other men having the charge of getting up such another great meeting, will commit such an error again.

CHAPTER V.

THE day after the close of the Congress, the delegates and their friends were invited to a soirée by M. de Tocqueville, Minister for Foreign Affairs, to take place on the next evening (Saturday) ; and, as my colored face and curly hair did not prevent my getting an invitation, I was present with the rest of my peace brethren.

Had I been in America, where color is considered a crime, I would not have been seen at such a gathering, unless as a servant. In company with several delegates, we left the Bedford Hotel for the mansion of the Minister of Foreign Affairs ; and, on arriving, we found a file of soldiers drawn up before the gate. This did not seem much like peace : however, it was merely done in honor of the company. We entered the building through massive doors, and resigned ourselves into the hands of good-looking waiters in white wigs ; and, after our names were duly announced, were passed from room to room, till I was presented to Madame de Tocqueville, who was standing near the centre of the large drawing-room, with a bouquet in her hand. I was about passing on, when the gentleman who introduced me intimated that I was an "American slave." At the announcement of this fact, the distinguished lady extended her hand and gave me a cordial welcome, at the same time saying, "I hope you feel yourself free in Paris." Having accepted an invitation to a seat by the lady's side, who seated herself on a sofa, I was soon what I most dislike, "the observed of all observers." I recognized, among many of my own countrymen who were gazing at me, the American Consul, Mr. Walsh. My position did not improve his looks. The company present on this occasion were variously estimated at from one thousand to fifteen hundred. Among these were the ambassadors from the different countries represented at the French metropolis, and many of the *élite* of Paris. One could not but be interested with the difference in dress, looks and manners, of this assemblage of strangers, whose language was as different as their general appearance. Delight seemed to beam in every countenance, as the living stream floated from one room to another. The house and gardens were illuminated in the most gorgeous manner. Red, yellow, blue, green, and many other colored lamps, suspended from the branches of the trees in the gardens, gave life and animation to the whole scene out of doors. The soirée passed off satisfactorily to all parties; and by twelve o'clock I was again at my hotel.

Through the politeness of the government the members of the Congress have not only had the pleasure of seeing all the public works free, and without special ticket, but the palaces of Versailles and St. Cloud, together with their splendid grounds, have been thrown open, and the water-works set to playing in both places. This mark of respect for the peace movement is commendable in the French; and were I not such a strenuous friend of free speech, this act would cause me to overlook the padlocks that the government put upon our lips in the Congress.

Two long trains left Paris at nine o'clock for Versailles; and at each of the stations the company were loudly cheered by the people who had assembled to see them pass. At Versailles we found thousands at the station, who gave us a most enthusiastic welcome. We were blessed with a goodly number of the fair sex, who always give life and vigor to such scenes. The train had scarcely stopped, ere the great throng were wending their ways in different directions, — some to the cafés to get what an early start prevented their getting before leaving Paris, and others to see the soldiers who were on review. But most bent their steps towards the great palace.

At eleven o'clock we were summoned to the *déjeuner* which had been prepared by the English delegates in honor of their American friends. About six hundred sat down at the tables. Breakfast being ended, Mr. Cobden was called to the chair, and several speeches were made. Many who had not an opportunity to speak at the Congress thought this a good chance; and the written addresses which had been studied during the passage from America, with the hope that they would immortalize their authors before the Congress, were produced at the breakfast-table. But speech-making was not the order of the day. Too many thundering addresses had been delivered in the Salle de St. Cecile to allow the company to sit and hear dryly written and worse delivered speeches in the Teniscourt.

There was no limited time given to the speakers, yet no one had been on his feet five minutes before the cry was heard from all parts of the house, "Time, time!" One American was hissed down; another took his seat with a red face; and a third opened his bundle of paper, looked around at the audience, made a bow, and took his seat amid great applause. Yet some speeches were made, and to good effect; the best of which was by Elihu Burritt, who was followed by the Rev. James Freeman Clarke. I regretted very much that the latter did not deliver his address before the Congress, for he is a man of no inconsiderable talent, and an acknowledged friend of the slave.

The cry of "The water-works are playing!" "The water is on!" broke up the meeting, without even a vote of thanks to the chairman; and the whole party were soon revelling among the fountains and statues of Louis XIV. Description would fail to give a just idea of the grandeur and beauty of this splendid place. I do not think that anything can surpass the fountain of Neptune, which stands near the Grand Trianon. One may easily get lost in wandering through the grounds of Versailles, but he will always be in sight of some life-like statue. These monuments, erected to gratify the fancy of a licentious king, make their appearance at every turn. Two lions, the one overturning a wild boar, the other a wolf, both the production of Fillen, pointed out to us the fountain of Diana. But I will not attempt to describe to you any of the very beautiful sculptured gods and goddesses here.

With a single friend I paid a visit to the two Trianons. The larger was, we were told, just as King Louis Philippe left it. One room was splendidly fitted up for the reception of Her Majesty Queen Victoria, who, it appeared, had promised a visit to the French court; but the French monarch ran away from his throne before the time arrived. The Grand Trianon is not larger than many noblemen's seats that may be seen in a day's ride through any part of the British empire. The building has only a ground floor, but its proportions are very elegant.

We next paid our respects to the Little Trianon. This appears to be the most republican of any of the French palaces. I inspected this little palace with much interest, not more for its beauty than because of its having been the favorite residence of that purest of princesses, and most affectionate of mothers, Marie Antoinette. The grounds and building may be said to be only a palace in miniature, and this makes it a still more lovely spot. The building consists of a square pavilion two stories high, and separated entirely from the accessory buildings, which are on the left, and among them a pretty chapel. But a wish to be with the multitude, who were roving among the fountains, cut short my visit to the Trianons.

The day was very fine, and the whole party seemed to enjoy it. It was said that there were more than one hundred thousand persons at Versailles during the day. The company appeared to lose themselves with the pleasure of walking among the trees, flower-beds, fountains, and statues. I met more than one wife seeking a lost husband, and *vice versa.* Many persons were separated from their friends, and did not meet them again till at the hotels in Paris. In the train returning to Paris, an old gentleman who was seated near me said, " I would rest contented if I thought I should ever see my wife again ! "

At four o'clock we were *en route* to St. Cloud, the much-loved and favorite residence of the Emperor Napoleon. It seemed that all Paris had come out to St. Cloud to see how the English and Americans would enjoy the playing of the water-works. Many kings and rulers of the French have made St. Cloud their residence, but none have impressed their image so indelibly upon it as Napoleon. It was here he was first elevated to power, and here Josephine spent her most happy hours.

The apartments where Napoleon was married to Marie Louise, the private rooms of Josephine and Marie Antoinette, were all in turn shown to us. While standing on the balcony looking at Paris one cannot wonder that the emperor should have selected this place as his residence, for a more lovely spot cannot be found than St. Cloud.

The palace is on the side of a hill, two leagues from Paris, and so situated that it looks down upon the French capital. Standing, as we did, viewing Paris from St. Cloud, and the setting sun reflecting upon the domes, spires, and towers of the city of fashion, made us feel that this was the place from which the monarch should watch his subjects. From the hour of arrival at St. Cloud till near eight o'clock, we were either inspecting the splendid palace, or roaming the grounds and gardens, whose beautiful walks and sweet flowers made it appear a very paradise on earth.

At eight o'clock the water-works were put in motion, and the variegated lamps, with their many devices, displaying flowers, stars and wheels, all with a brilliancy that can scarcely be described, seemed to throw everything in the shade we had seen at Versailles. At nine o'clock the train was announced, and after a good deal of jamming and pushing about, we were again on the way to Paris.

CHAPTER VI.

"Types of a race who shall the invader scorn,
  As rocks resist the billows round their shore ;
Types of a race who shall to time unborn
  Their country leave unconquered as of yore."

CAMPBELL.

I STARTED at an early hour for the palace of the Tuileries. A show of my card of membership of the Congress (which had carried me through so many of the public buildings) was enough to gain me immediate admission. The attack of the mob on the palace, on the 20th of June, 1792; the massacre of the Swiss guard, on the 10th of August of the same year; the attack by the people, in July, 1830, together with the recent flight of King Louis Philippe and family, made me anxious to visit the old pile.

We were taken from room to room, until the entire building had been inspected. In front of the Tuileries are a most magnificent garden and grounds. These were all laid out by Louis XIV., and are left nearly as they were during that monarch's reign. Above fifty acres, surrounded by an iron rail-fence, fronts the Place de la Concorde, and affords a place of promenade for the

Parisians. I walked the grounds, and saw hundreds of well-dressed persons under the shade of the great chestnuts, or sitting on chairs, which were kept to let at two sous a piece. Near by is the Place de Carrousel, noted for its historical remembrances. Many incidents connected with the several revolutions occurred here, and it is pointed out as the place where Napoleon reviewed that formidable army of his, before its departure for Russia.

From the Tuileries I took a stroll through the Place de la Concorde, which has connected with it so many acts of cruelty, that it made me shudder as I passed over its grounds. As if to take from one's mind the old associations of this place, the French have erected on it, or rather given a place to, the celebrated obelisk of Luxor, which now is the chief attraction on the grounds. The obelisk was brought from Egypt at an enormous expense, for which purpose a ship was built, and several hundred men employed above three years in its removal. It is formed of the finest red syenite, and covered on each side with three lines of hieroglyphic inscriptions, commemorative of Sesostris,— the middle lines being the most deeply cut and most carefully finished; and the characters altogether number more than sixteen hundred. The obelisk is of a single stone, is seventy-two feet in height, weighs five hundred thousand pounds, and stands on a block of granite that weighs two hundred and fifty thousand pounds. He who can read

Latin will see that the monument tells its own story, but to me its characters were all blank.

It would be tedious to follow the history of this old and venerated stone, which was taken from the quarry fifteen hundred and fifty years before the birth of Christ, placed in Thebes, its removal, the journey to the Nile, and down the Nile, thence to Cherbourg, and lastly its arrival in Paris on the 23d of December, 1833,— just one year before I escaped from slavery. The obelisk was raised on the spot where it now stands, on the 25th of October, 1836, in the presence of Louis Philippe, and amid the greetings of one hundred and sixty thousand persons.

Having missed my dinner, I crossed over to the Palais Royal, to a dining saloon, and can assure you that a better dinner may be had there for three francs than can be got in New York for twice that sum,— especially if the person who wants the dinner is a colored man. I found no prejudice against my complexion in the Palais Royal.

Many of the rooms in this once abode of royalty are most splendidly furnished, and decorated with valuable pictures. The likenesses of Madame de Stael, J. J. Rousseau, Cromwell and Francis I., are among them.

After several unsuccessful attempts to-day, in company with R. D. Webb, Esq., to seek out the house where once resided the notorious Robespierre, I was fortunate enough to find it, but not until I had lost the company of my friend. The house is No. 396, Rue St.

Honore, opposite the Church of the Assumption. It stands back, and is reached by entering a court. During the first revolution it was occupied by M. Duplay, with whom Robespierre lodged. The room used by the great man of the revolution was pointed out to me. It is small, and the ceiling low, with two windows looking out upon the court. The pin upon which the blue coat once hung is still in the wall. While standing there, I could almost imagine that I saw the great " Incorruptible," sitting at the small table, composing those speeches which gave him so much power and influence in the convention and the clubs.

Here the disciple of Rousseau sat and planned how he should outdo his enemies and hold on to his friends. From this room he went forth, followed by his dog Brunt, to take his solitary walk in a favorite and neighboring field, or to the fiery discussions of the National Convention. In the same street is the house in which Madame Roland — one of Robespierre's victims — resided.

A view of the residence of one of the master-spirits of the French Revolution inclined me to search out more: and, therefore, I proceeded to the old town, and after winding through several small streets — some of them so narrow as not to admit more than one cab at a time — I found myself in the Rue de L'Ecole de Medecine, and standing in front of house No. 20. This was the residence, during the early days of the revolution, of that blood-thirsty demon in human form, Marat.

As this was private property, my blue card of membership to the Congress was not available. But after slipping a franc into the old lady's hand, I was informed that I could be admitted. We entered a court and ascended a flight of stairs, the entrance to which is on the right; then, crossing to the left, we were shown into a moderate-sized room on the first floor, with two windows looking out upon a yard. Here it was where the "Friend of the People" (as he styled himself) sat and wrote those articles that appeared daily in his journal, urging the people to "hang the rich upon lamp-posts." The place where the bath stood, in which he was bathing at the time he was killed by Charlotte Corday, was pointed to us; and even something representing an old stain of blood was shown as the place where he was laid when taken out of the bath. The window, behind whose curtains the heroine hid, after she had plunged the dagger into the heart of the man whom she thought was the cause of the shedding of so much blood by the guillotine, was pointed out with a seeming degree of pride by the old woman.

With my Guide Book in hand, I again went forth to "hunt after new fancies."

After walking over the ground where the guillotine once stood, cutting off its hundred and fifty heads per day, and then visiting the place where some of the chief movers in that sanguinary revolution once lived, I felt little disposed to sleep, when the time for it had arrived. However, I was out the next morning at an early hour,

and on the Champs Elysees; and again took a walk over
the place where the guillotine stood when its fatal blade
was sending so many unprepared spirits into eternity.
When standing here, you have the palace of the Tuileries on one side, the arch on the other, on a third the
classic Madeleine, and on the fourth the National Assembly. It caused my blood to chill, the idea of being
on the identical spot where the heads of Louis XVI. and
his queen, after being cut off, were held up to satisfy
the blood-thirsty curiosity of the two hundred thousand
persons that were assembled on the Place de la Revolution. Here royal blood flowed as it never did before or
since. The heads of patricians and plebeians were
thrown into the same basket, without any regard to birth
or station. Here Robespierre and Danton had stood
again and again, and looked their victims in the face as
they ascended the scaffold; and here these same men
had to mount the very scaffold that they had erected for
others. I wandered up the Seine, till I found myself
looking at the statue of Henry IV., over the principal entrance of the Hotel de Ville. When we take into
account the connection of the Hotel de Ville with the
different revolutions, we must come to the conclusion
that it is one of the most remarkable buildings in Paris.
The room was pointed out where Robespierre held his
counsels, and from the windows of which he could look
out upon the Place de Greve, where the guillotine stood
before its removal to the Place de la Concorde. The
room is large, with gilded hangings, splendid old-fash-

ioned chandeliers, and a chimney-piece with fine, anti-
quated carvings, that give it a venerable appearance.
Here Robespierre not only presided at the counsels that
sent hundreds to the guillotine, but from this same spot
he, with his brother, St. Just and others, were dragged
before the Committee of Public Safety, and thence to
the guillotine, and justice and revenge satisfied.

The window from which Lafayette addressed the people in 1830, and presented to them Louis Philippe as
the king, was shown to us. Here the poet, statesman,
philosopher and orator, Lamartine, stood in February,
1848, and, by the power of his eloquence, succeeded in
keeping the people quiet. Here he forced the mob,
braved the bayonets presented to his breast, and, by his
good reasoning, induced them to retain the tri-colored
flag, instead of adopting the red flag, which he considered the emblem of blood.

Lamartine is a great heroic genius, dear to liberty and
to France; and successive generations, as they look back
upon the revolution of 1848, will recall to memory the
many dangers which nothing but his dauntless courage
warded off. The difficulties which his wisdom surmounted, and the good service that he rendered to
France, can never be adequately estimated, or too highly
appreciated. It was at the Hotel de Ville that the
republic of 1848 was proclaimed to the people.

I next paid my respects to the Column of July, that
stands on the spot formerly occupied by the Bastile. It
is one hundred and sixty-three feet in height, and on the

top is the Genius of Liberty, with a torch in his right hand, and in the left a broken chain. After a fatiguing walk up a winding stair, I obtained a splendid view of Paris from the top of the column.

I thought I should not lose the opportunity of seeing the Church de Notre Dame while so near to it, and, therefore, made it my next rallying-point. No edifice connected with religion has had more interesting incidents occurring in it than this old church. Here Pope Pius VII. placed the imperial crown on the head of the Corsican,— or, rather, Napoleon took the crown from his hands, and placed it on his own head. Satan dragging the wicked to ——, the rider on the red horse at the opening of the second seal, the blessedness of the saints, and several other striking sculptured figures, were among the many curiosities in this splendid place. A hasty view from the gallery concluded my visit to the Notre Dame.

Leaving the old church, I strayed off in a direction towards the Seine, and passed by an old-looking building of stately appearance, and recognized, among a throng passing in and out, a number of the members of the Peace Congress. I joined a party entering, and was soon in the presence of men with gowns on, and men with long staffs in their hands, and, on inquiry, found that I was in the Palais de Justice, beneath which is the Conciergerie, a noted prison. Louis XVI. and Marie Antoinette were tried and condemned to death here.

A bas-relief, by Cortat, representing Louis in conference with his Council, is here seen. But I had visited too many places of interest during the day to remain long in a building surrounded by officers of justice, and took a stroll upon the Boulevards.

The Boulevards may be termed the Regent-street of Paris, or a New Yorker would call it Broadway. While passing a café, my German friend Faigo, whose company I had enjoyed during the passage from America, recognized me, and I sat down and took a cup of delicious coffee for the first time on the side-walk, in sight of hundreds who were passing up and down the street every hour. From three till eleven o'clock, P. M., the Boulevards are lined with men and women sitting before the doors of the saloons, drinking their coffee or wines, or both at the same time, as fancy may dictate. All Paris appeared to be on the Boulevards, and looking as if the great end of this life was enjoyment.

Anxious to see as much as possible of Paris in the limited time I had to stay in it, I hired a cab on the following morning, and commenced with the Hotel des Invalides, a magnificent building, within a few minutes' walk of the National Assembly. On each side of the entrance-gate are figures representing nations conquered by Louis XIV., with colossal statues of Mars and Minerva. The dome on the edifice is the loftiest in Paris, the height from the ground being three hundred and twenty-three feet.

Immediately below the dome is the tomb of the man at whose word the world turned pale. A statue of the

Emperor Napoleon stands in the second piazza, and is of the finest bronze.

This building is the home of the pensioned soldiers of France. It was enough to make one sick at the idea of war, to look upon the mangled bodies of these old soldiers. Men with arms and no legs; others had legs but no arms; some with canes and crutches, and some wheeling themselves about in little hand-carts. About three thousand of the decayed soldiers were lodged in the Hotel des Invalides, at the time of my visit. Passing the National Assembly on my return, I spent a moment or two in it. The interior of this building resembles an amphitheatre. It is constructed to accommodate nine hundred members, each having a separate desk. The seat upon which the Duchess of Orleans and her son, the Comte de Paris, sat, when they visited the National Assembly after the flight of Louis Philippe, was shown with considerable alacrity. As I left the building, I heard that the president of the republic was on the point of leaving the Elysee for St. Cloud, and, with the hope of seeing the "prisoner of Ham," I directed my cabman to drive me to the Elysee.

In a few moments we were between two files of soldiers, and entering the gates of the palace. I called out to the driver, and told him to stop; but I was too late, for we were now in front of the massive doors of the palace, and a liveried servant opened the cab door, bowed, and asked if I had an engagement with the president. You may easily "guess" his surprise when I told him

no.   In my best French I asked the cabman why he had
come to the palace, and was answered, " You told me
to."   By this time a number had gathered round, all
making inquiries as to what I wanted.   I told the driver
to retrace his steps, and, amid the shrugs of their shoulders, the nods of their heads, and the laughter of the
soldiers, I left the Elysee without even a sight of the
president's moustache for my trouble.   This was only
one of the many mistakes I made while in Paris.

CHAPTER VII.

"The moon on the east oriel shone
    Through slender shafts of shapely stone,
        By foliaged tracery combined.
    Thou wouldst have thought some fairy's hand
    'Twixt poplars straight the osier wand
        In many a freakish knot had twined :
    Then framed a spell, when the work was done,
    And changed the willow wreaths to stone."
                                        SIR WALTER SCOTT.

HERE I am, within ten leagues of Paris, spending the
time pleasantly in viewing the palace and grounds of the
great chateau of Louis XIV. Fifty-seven years ago, a
mob, composed of men, women and boys, from Paris,
stood in front of this palace, and demanded that the king
should go with them to the capital. I have walked over
the same ground where the one hundred thousand stood
on that interesting occasion. I have been upon the same
balcony, and stood by the window from which Marie
Antoinette looked out upon the mob that were seeking
her life.

Anxious to see as much of the palace as I could, and
having an offer of the company of my young friend,
Henry G. Chapman, to go through the palace with me, I

set out early this morning, and was soon in the halls that
had often been trod by royal feet. We passed through
the private as well as the public apartments; through
the secret door by which Marie Antoinette had escaped
from the mob of 1792; and viewed the room in which her
faithful guards were killed, while attempting to save their
royal mistress. I took my seat in one of the little parlor
carriages that had been used in days of yore for the royal
children, while my friend H. G. Chapman drew me
across the room. The superb apartments are not now in
use. Silence is written upon these walls, although upon
them are suspended the portraits of men of whom the
world has heard.

Paintings representing Napoleon in nearly all his battles are here seen; and, wherever you see the emperor,
there you will also find Murat, with his white plume
waving above. Callot's painting of the battle of Ma-
rengo, Hue's of the retaking of Genoa, and Bouchat's
of the 18th Brumaire, are of the highest order; while
David has transmitted his fame to posterity by his
splendid painting of the coronation of Napoleon and Josephine in Notre Dame. When I looked upon the many
beautiful paintings of the last-named artist that adorn
the halls of Versailles, I did not wonder that his fame
should have saved his life when once condemned and
sentenced to death during the reign of terror. The guillotine was robbed of its intended victim; but the world
gained a great painter. As Boswell transmitted his own
name to posterity with his life of Johnson, so has David

left his with the magnificent paintings that are now suspended upon the walls of the palaces of the Louvre, the Tuileries, St. Cloud, Versailles, and even the little Elysee.

After strolling from room to room, we found ourselves in the Salle du Sacre, Diane, Salon de Mars, de Mercure, and D'Apollon. I gazed with my eyes turned to the ceiling till I was dizzy. The Salon de la Guerre is covered with the most beautiful representations that the mind of man could conceive, or the hand accomplish. Louis XIV. is here in all his glory. No Marie Antoinette will ever do the honors in these halls again.

After spending a whole day in the palace, and several mornings in the gardens, I finally bade adieu to the bronze statue of Louis XIV. that stands in front of the palace, and left Versailles, probably forever.

I am now on the point of quitting the French metropolis. I have occupied the last two days in visiting places of note in the city. I could not resist the inclination to pay a second visit to the Louvre. Another hour was spent in strolling through the Italian Hall, and viewing the master workmanship of Raphael, the prince of painters. Time flies, even in such a place as the Louvre, with all its attractions; and, before I had seen half that I wished, a ponderous clock near by reminded me of an engagement, and I reluctantly tore myself from the splendors of the place.

During the rest of the day I visited the Jardin des Plantes, and spent an hour and a half pleasantly in

walking among plants, flowers, and, in fact, everything
that could be found in any garden in France. From
this place we paid our respects to the Bourse, or Exchange, one of the most superb buildings in the city.
The ground floor and sides of the Bourse are of fine
marble, and the names of the chief cities in the world are
inscribed on the medallions which are under the upper
cornice. The interior of the edifice has a most splendid
appearance as you enter it.

The cemetery of Père la Chaise was too much talked
of by many of our party at the hotel for me to pass it
by; so I took it, after the Bourse. Here lie many of
the great marshals of France, the resting-place of each
marked by the monument that stands over it, except one,
which is marked only by a weeping willow and a plain
stone at its head. This is the grave of Marshal Ney. I
should not have known that it was his, but some unknown
hand had written, with black paint, " Bravest of the
Brave," on the unlettered stone that stands at the head
of the man who followed Napoleon through nearly all his
battles, and who was shot, after the occupation of Paris
by the allied army. Peace to his ashes! During my
ramble through this noted place, I saw several who were
hanging fresh wreaths of "everlasting flowers" on the
tombs of the departed.

A ride in an omnibus down the Boulevards, and away
up the Champs Elysees, brought me to the Arc de Tri-
omphe; and, after ascending a flight of one hundred and
sixty-one steps, I was overlooking the city of statuary.

This stupendous monument was commenced by Napoleon in 1806; and in 1811 it had only reached the cornice of the base, where it stopped, and it was left for Louis Philippe to finish. The first stone of this monument was laid on the 15th of August, 1806, the birth-day of the man whose battles it was intended to commemorate. A model of the arch was erected for Napoleon to pass through as he was entering the city with Maria Louisa, after their marriage. The inscriptions on the monument are many, and the different scenes here represented are all of the most exquisite workmanship. The genius of War is summoning the obedient nations to battle. Victory is here crowning Napoleon after his great success in 1810. Fame stands here recording the exploits of the warrior, while conquered cities lie beneath the whole. But it would take more time than I have at command to give anything like a description of this magnificent piece of architecture.

That which seems to take most with Peace Friends is the portion representing an old man taming a bull for agricultural labor; while a young warrior is sheathing his sword, a mother and children sitting at his feet, and Minerva, crowned with laurels, stands shedding her protecting influence over them. The erection of this regal monument is wonderful, to hand down to posterity the triumphs of the man whom we first hear of as a student in the military school at Brienne; whom in 1784 we see in the Ecole Militaire, founded by Louis XV. in 1751; whom again we find at No. 5 Quai de Court, near Rue

de Mail; and in 1794 as a lodger at No. 19 Rue de la
Michandère. From this he goes to the Hotel Mirabeau,
Rue du Dauphin, where he resided when he defeated his
enemies on the 13th Vendemaire. The Hotel de la Co-
lonade, Rue Neuve des Capuchins, is his next residence,
and where he was married to Josephine. From this hotel
he removed to his wife's dwelling in the Rue Chanteriene,
No. 52. In 1796 the young general started for Italy,
where his conquests paved the way for the ever-memorable 18th Brumaire, that made him Dictator of France.
Napoleon was too great now to be satisfied with private
dwellings, and we next trace him to the Elysee, St. Cloud,
Versailles, the Tuileries, Fontainebleau, and, finally, came
his decline, which I need not relate to you.

After visiting the Gobelins, passing through its many
rooms, seeing here and there a half-finished piece of
tapestry, and meeting a number of the members of the
late Peace Congress, who, like myself, had remained behind to see more of the beauties of the French capital
than could be seen during the Convention week, I
accepted an invitation to dine with a German gentleman
at the Palais Royal, and was soon revelling amid the
luxuries of the table. I was glad that I had gone to the
Palais Royal, for here I had the honor of an introduction
to M. Beranger, the poet; and, although I had to converse with him through an interpreter, I enjoyed his
company very much. "The people's poet," as he is
called, is apparently about seventy years of age, bald on
the top of the head, and rather corpulent, but of active

look, and in the enjoyment of good health. Few writers in France have done better service to the cause of political and religious freedom than Pierre Jean de Beranger. He is the dauntless friend and advocate of the downtrodden poor and oppressed, and has often incurred the displeasure of the government by the arrows that he has thrown into their camp. He felt what he wrote ; it came straight from his heart, and went directly to the hearts of the people. He expressed himself strongly opposed to slavery, and said, "I don't see how the Americans can reconcile slavery with their professed love of freedom." Dinner out of the way, a walk through the different apartments, and a stroll over the court, and I bade adieu to the Palais Royal, satisfied that I should partake of many worse dinners than I had helped to devour that day.

Few nations are more courteous than the French. Here, the stranger, let him come from what country he may, and be ever so unacquainted with the people and language, is sure of a civil reply to any question that he may ask. With the exception of the egregious blunder I have mentioned of the cabman driving me to the Elysee, I was not laughed at once while in France.

CHAPTER VIII.

"There was not, on that day, a speck to stain
The azure heavens ; the blessed sun alone,
In unapproachable divinity,
Careered rejoicing in the field of light."
SOUTHEY.

THE sun had just appeared from behind a cloud and
was setting, and its reflection upon the domes and spires
of the great buildings in Paris made everything appear
lovely and sublime, as the train, with almost lightning
speed, was bringing me from the French metropolis.   I
gazed with eager eyes to catch a farewell glance of the
tops of the regal palaces through which I had passed
during a stay of fifteen days in the French capital.

A pleasant ride of four hours brought us to Boulogne,
where we rested for the night.   The next morning I was
up at an early hour, and out viewing the town.   Boulogne could present but little attraction after a fortnight
spent in seeing the lions of Paris.   A return to the hotel,
and breakfast over, we stepped on board the steamer, and
were soon crossing the channel.   Two hours more, and I
was safely seated in a railway carriage, *en route* to the

English metropolis. We reached London at mid-day, where I was soon comfortably lodged at 22 Cecil-street, Strand. As it was three o'clock, I lost no time in seeking out a dining saloon, which I had no difficulty in finding in the Strand. It being the first house of the kind I had entered in London, I was not a little annoyed at the politeness of the waiter. The first salutation I had, after seating myself in one of the stalls, was, "Ox tail, sir; gravy soup; carrot soup, sir; roast beef; roast pork; boiled beef; roast lamb; boiled leg of mutton, sir, with caper sauce; jugged hare, sir; boiled knuckle of veal and bacon; roast turkey and oyster sauce; sucking pig, sir; curried chicken; harrico mutton, sir." These, and many other dishes, which I have forgotten, were called over with a rapidity that would have done credit to one of our Yankee pedlers in crying his wares in a New England village. I was so completely taken by surprise, that I asked for a "bill of fare," and told him to leave me. No city in the world furnishes a cheaper, better, and quicker meal for the weary traveller, than a London eating-house.

    *   *   *   *   *   *

A few days after my arrival in London, I received an invitation from John Lee, Esq., LL.D., whom I had met at the Peace Congress in Paris, to pay him a visit at his seat, near Aylesbury; and as the time was "fixed" by the doctor, I took the train on the appointed day, on my way to Hartwell House.

I had heard much of the aristocracy of England, and

must confess that I was not a little prejudiced against
them.   On a bright sunshiny day, between the hours of
twelve and two, I found myself seated in a carriage, my
back turned upon Aylesbury, the vehicle whirling rapidly
over the smooth macadamised road, and I on my first
visit to an English gentleman.   Twenty minutes' ride,
and a turn to the right, and we were amid the fine old
trees of Hartwell Park; one having suspended from its
branches the national banners of several different countries, among them the " Stars· and Stripes."   I felt
glad that my own country's flag had a place there,
although Campbell's lines —

> " United States, your banner wears
>   Two emblems, — one of fame ;
> Alas ! the other that it bears
>   Reminds us of your shame !
> The white man's liberty in types
>   Stands blazoned by your stars ;
> But what 's the meaning of your stripes ? —
>   They mean your Negro-scars " —

were at the time continually running through my mind.
Arrived at the door, and we received what every one
does who visits Dr. Lee — a hearty welcome.   I was immediately shown into a room with a lofty ceiling, hung
round with fine specimens of the Italian masters, and told
that this was my apartment.   Hartwell House stands in
an extensive park, shaded with trees that made me think
of the oaks and elms in an American forest, and many
of whose limbs had been trimmed and nursed with the
best of care.   This was for several years the residence of

John Hampden the patriot, and more recently that of
Louis XVIII., during his exile in this country. The
house is built on a very extensive scale, and is orna·
mented in the interior with carvings in wood of many of
the kings and princes of bygone centuries. A room
some sixty feet by twenty-five contains a variety of
articles that the doctor has collected together — the whole
forming a museum that would be considered a sight in
the Western States of America.

The morning after my arrival at Hartwell I was up at
an early hour — in fact, before any of the servants —
wandering about through the vast halls, and trying to
find my way out; in which I eventually succeeded, but
not, however, without aid. It had rained the previous
night, and the sun was peeping through a misty cloud as
I strolled through the park, listening to the sweet voices
of the birds that were fluttering in the tops of the trees,
and trimming their wings for a morning flight. The
silence of the night had not yet been broken by the voice
of man; and I wandered about the vast park unannoyed,
except by the dew from the grass that wet my slippers.
Not far from the house I came abruptly upon a beautiful
little pond of water, where the gold-fish were flouncing
about, and the gentle ripples glittering in the sunshine
looked like so many silver minnows playing on the surface.

While strolling about with pleasure, and only regret-
ting that my dear daughters were not with me to enjoy
the morning's walk, I saw the gardener on his way to

the garden. I followed him, and was soon feasting my
eyes upon the richest specimens of garden scenery.
There were the peaches hanging upon the trees that were
fastened to the wall; vegetables, fruit and flowers, were
there in all their bloom and beauty ; and even the variegated geranium of a warmer clime was there in its hot-
house home, and seemed to have forgotten that it was in
a different country from its own. Dr. Lee shows great
taste in the management of his garden. I have seldom
seen a more splendid variety of fruits and flowers in the
Southern States of America than I saw at Hartwell
House.

I should, however, state that I was not the only guest
at Hartwell during my stay. Dr. Lee had invited
several others of the American delegation to the Peace
Congress, and two or three of the French delegates, who
were on a visit to England, were enjoying the doctor's
hospitality. Dr. Lee is a stanch friend of Temperance,
as well as of the cause of universal freedom. Every
year he treats his tenantry to a dinner, and I need not
add that these are always conducted on the principle of
total abstinence.

During the second day we visited several of the cottages of the work-people, and in these I took no little
interest. The people of the United States know nothing
of the real condition of the laboring classes of England.
The peasants of Great Britain are always spoken of as
belonging to the soil. I was taught in America that the
English laborer was no better off than the slave upon a

Carolina rice-field. I had seen the slaves in Missouri huddled together, three, four, and even five families in a single room, not more than fifteen by twenty-five feet square, and I expected to see the same in England. But in this I was disappointed. After visiting a new house that the doctor was building, he took us into one of the cottages that stood near the road, and gave us an opportunity of seeing, for the first time, an English peasant's cot. We entered a low, whitewashed room, with a stone floor that showed an admirable degree of cleanness. Before us was a row of shelves filled with earthen dishes and pewter spoons, glittering as if they had just come from under the hand of a woman of taste. A "Cobden loaf" of bread, that had just been left by the baker's boy, lay upon an oaken table which had been much worn away with the scrubbing-brush; while just above lay the old family Bible, that had been handed down from father to son, until its possession was considered of almost as great value as its contents. A half-open door, leading into another room, showed us a clean bed; the whole presenting as fine a picture of neatness, order and comfort, as the most fastidious taste could wish to see. No occupant was present, and therefore I inspected everything with a greater degree of freedom. " In front of the cottage was a small grass-plot, with here and there a bed of flowers, cheated out of its share of sunshine by the tall holly that had been planted near it." As I looked upon the home of the laborer, my thoughts were with my enslaved countrymen. What a

difference, thought I, there is between the tillers of the
soil in England and America! There could not be
a more complete refutation of the assertion that the
English laborer is no better off than the American slave,
than the scenes that were then before me. I called the
attention of one of my American friends to a beautiful
rose near the door of the cot, and said to him, "The law
that will protect that flower will also guard and protect
the hand that planted it." He knew that I had drank
deep of the cup of slavery, was aware of what I meant,
and merely nodded his head in reply. I never experienced hospitality more genuine, and yet more unpretending, than was meted out to me while at Hartwell. And
the favorable impression made on my own mind by the
distinguished proprietor of Hartwell Park was nearly as
indelible as my humble name that the doctor had en-
graven in a brick, in a vault beneath the Observatory in
Hartwell House.

On my return to London I accepted an invitation to
join a party on a visit to Windsor Castle; and, taking the
train at the Waterloo Bridge Station, we were soon passing through a pleasant part of the country. Arrived
at the castle, we committed ourselves into the hands of
the servants, and were introduced into Her Majesty's
State Apartments, Audience Chamber, Vandyck Room,
Waterloo Chambers, Gold Pantry, and many others
whose names I have forgotten. In wandering about the
different apartments I lost my company, and in trying to
find them passed through a room in which hung a mag-

nificent portrait of Charles I., by Vandyck. The hum
and noise of my companions had ceased, and I had the
scene and silence to myself. I looked in vain for the
king's evil genius (Cromwell), but he was not in the
same room. The pencil of Sir Peter Lely has left a
splendid full-length likeness of James II. George IV. is
suspended from a peg in the wall, looking as if it was
fresh from the hands of Sir Thomas Lawrence, its admirable painter. I was now in St. George's Hall, and I
gazed upward to view the beautiful figures on the ceiling until my neck was nearly out of joint. Leaving this
room, I inspected with interest the ancient *keep* of the
castle. In past centuries this part of the palace was
used as a prison. Here James the First of Scotland
was detained a prisoner for eighteen years. I viewed the
window through which the young prince had often looked
to catch a glimpse of the young and beautiful Lady Jane,
daughter of the Earl of Somerset, with whom he was
enamored.

From the top of the Round Tower I had a fine view
of the surrounding country. Stoke Park, once the
residence of that great friend of humanity and civilization, William Penn, was among the scenes that I beheld
with pleasure from Windsor Castle. Four years ago,
when in the city of Philadelphia, and hunting up the
places associated with the name of this distinguished
man, and more recently when walking over the farm
once occupied by him, examining the old malt-house
which is now left standing, because of the veneration

with which the name of the man who built it is held, I
had no idea that I should ever see the dwelling which he
had occupied in the Old World. Stoke Park is about
four miles from Windsor, and is now owned by the Right
Hon. Henry Labouchere.

The castle, standing as it does on an eminence, and
surrounded by a beautiful valley covered with splendid
villas, has a most magnificent appearance. It rears its
massive towers and irregular walls over and above every
other object. How full this old palace is of material for
thought ! How one could ramble here alone, or with
one or two congenial companions, and enjoy a recapitula-
tion of its history ! But an engagement to be at Croydon in the evening cut short my stay at Windsor, and
compelled me to return to town in advance of my party.

*   *   *   *   *   *

Having met with John Morland, Esq., at Paris, he gave
me an invitation to visit Croydon, and deliver a lecture
on American Slavery; and last evening, at eight o'clock,
I found myself in a fine old building in the town, and
facing the first English audience that I had seen in the
sea-girt isle. It was my first welcome in England.
The assembly was an enthusiastic one, and made still
more so by the appearance of George Thompson, Esq.,
M. P., upon the platform. It is not my intention to
give accounts of my lectures or meetings in these pages.
I therefore merely say that I left Croydon with a good
impression of the English, and Heath Lodge with a

feeling that its occupant was one of the most benevolent of men.

The same party with whom I visited Windsor being supplied with a card of admission to the Bank of England, I accepted an invitation to be one of the company. We entered the vast building at a little past twelve o'clock. The sun threw into the large halls a brilliancy that seemed to light up the countenances of the almost countless number of clerks, who were at their desks, or serving persons at the counters. As nearly all my countrymen who visit London pay their respects to this noted institution, I shall sum up my visit to it by saying that it surpassed my highest idea of a bank. But a stroll through this monster building of gold and silver brought to my mind an incident with which I was connected a year after my escape from slavery.

In the autumn of 1835, having been cheated out of the previous summer's earnings by the captain of the steamer in which I had been employed running away with the money, I was, like the rest of the men, left without any means of support during the winter, and therefore had to seek employment in the neighboring towns. I went to the town of Monroe, in the State of Michigan, and while going through the principal street looking for work, I passed the door of the only barber in the town, whose shop appeared to be filled with persons waiting to be shaved. As there was but one man at work, and as I had, while employed in the steamer, occasionally shaved a gentleman who could not perform that office himself, it occurred to me that I might get employment here as a journeyman barber. I therefore made immediate application for work, but the barber told me he did not need a hand. But I was not to be put off so easily, and, after making several offers to work cheap, I frankly told him that if he would not employ me I would get a room near to him, and set up an opposition establishment. This threat, however, made no impression on the barber; and, as I was leaving, one of the men who were waiting to be shaved said, "If you want a room in which to commence business, I have one on the opposite side of the street." This man followed me out; we went over, and I looked at the room. He strongly urged me to set up, at the same time promising to give me his influence. I took the room, purchased an old table, two chairs, got a pole with a red stripe painted around it, and the next day opened, with a sign over the door, "Fashionable Hair-dresser from New York, Emperor of the West." I need not add that my enterprise was very annoying to the "shop over the way,"—especially my sign, which happened to be the most expensive part of the concern. Of course, I had to tell all who came in that my neighbor on the opposite side did not keep clean towels, that his razors were dull, and, above all, he had never been to New York to see the fashions. Neither had I. In a few weeks I had the entire business of the town, to the great discomfiture of the other barber.

At this time, money matters in the Western States

were in a sad condition. Any person who could raise a small amount of money was permitted to establish a bank, and allowed to issue notes for four times the sum raised. This being the case, many persons borrowed money merely long enough to exhibit to the bank inspectors, and the borrowed money was returned, and the bank left without a dollar in its vaults, if, indeed, it had a vault about its premises. The result was, that banks were started all over the Western States, and the country flooded with worthless paper. These were known as the "Wild-cat Banks." Silver coin being very scarce, and the banks not being allowed to issue notes for a smaller amount than one dollar, several persons put out notes from six to seventy-five cents in value; these were called "Shinplasters." The Shinplaster was in the shape of a promissory note, made payable on demand. I have often seen persons with large rolls of these bills, the whole not amounting to more than five dollars. Some weeks after I had commenced business on my "own hook," I was one evening very much crowded with customers; and, while they were talking over the events of the day, one of them said to me, "Emperor, you seem to be doing a thriving business. You should do as other business men, issue your Shinplasters." This, of course, as it was intended, created a laugh; but with me it was no laughing matter, for from that moment I began to think seriously of becoming a banker. I accordingly went a few days after to a printer, and he, wishing to get the job of printing, urged me to put out my notes, and showed me some specimens of engravings that he had just received from Detroit. My head being already filled with the idea of a bank, I needed but little persuasion to set the thing finally afloat. Before I left the printer the notes were partly in type, and I studying how I should keep the public from counterfeiting them. The next day my Shinplasters were handed to me, the whole amount being twenty dollars, and, after being duly signed, were ready for circulation. At first my notes did not take well; they were too new, and viewed with a suspicious eye. But through the assistance of my customers, and a good deal of exertion on my own part, my bills were soon in circulation; and nearly all the money received in return for my notes was spent in fitting up and decorating my shop.

Few bankers get through this world without their difficulties, and I was not to be an exception. A short time after my money had been out, a party of young men, either wishing to pull down my vanity, or to try the soundness of my bank, determined to give it "a run." After collecting together a number of my bills, they came one at a time to demand other money for them, and I, not being aware of what was going on, was taken by surprise. One day, as I was sitting at my table, strapping some new razors I had just got with the avails of my "Shinplasters," one of the men entered and said, "Emperor, you will oblige me if you will give me some other money for these notes of yours." I immediately cashed the notes with the most worthless of the

Wild-cat money that I had on hand, but which was a lawful tender. The young man had scarcely left, when a second appeared, with a similar amount, and demanded payment. These were cashed, and soon a third came with his roll of notes. I paid these with an air of triumph, although I had but half a dollar left. I began now to think seriously what I should do, or how to act, provided another demand should be made. While I was thus engaged in thought, I saw the fourth man crossing the street, with a handful of notes, evidently my "Shin-plasters." I instantaneously shut the door, and, looking out of the window, said, "I have closed business for the day; come to-morrow, and I will see you." In looking across the street, I saw my rival standing in his shop-door, grinning and clapping his hands at my apparent downfall. I was completely "done *Brown*" for the day. However, I was not to be "used up" in this way; so I escaped by the back door, and went in search of my friend who had first suggested to me the idea of issuing notes. I found him, told him of the difficulty I was in, and wished him to point out a way by which I might extricate myself. He laughed heartily, and then said, "You must act as all bankers do in this part of the country." I inquired how they did, and he said, "When your notes are brought to you, you must redeem them, and then send them out and get other money for them, and with the latter you can keep cashing your own Shin-plasters." This was indeed a new idea to me. I immediately commenced putting in circulation the notes which

I had just redeemed, and my efforts were crowned with so much success that, before I slept that night, my "Shinplasters" were again in circulation, and my bank once more on a sound basis.

As I saw the clerks shovelling out the yellow coin upon the counters of the Bank of England, and men coming in and going out with weighty bags of the precious metal in their hands or on their shoulders, I could not but think of the great contrast between the monster institution within whose walls I was then standing and the Wild-cat banks of America!

CHAPTER IX.

" We might as soon describe a dream
As tell where falls each golden beam ;
As soon might reckon up the sand,
Sweet Weston ! on thy sea-beat strand,
As count each beauty there."

MISS MITFORD.

I HAVE devoted the past ten days to sight-seeing in
the metropolis, the first two of which were spent in the
British Museum. After procuring a guide-book at the
door as I entered, I seated myself on the first seat that
caught my eye, arranged as well as I could in my mind
the different rooms, and then commenced in good earnest.
The first part I visited was the gallery of antiquities,
through to the north gallery, and thence to the Lycian
room. This place is filled with tombs, bas-reliefs, statues,
and other productions of the same art. Venus, seated,
and smelling a lotus-flower which she held in her hand,
and attended by three Graces, put a stop to the rapid
strides that I was making through this part of the hall.
This is really one of the most precious productions of the
art that I have ever seen. Many of the figures in this

room are very much mutilated; yet one can linger here for hours with interest. A good number of the statues are of uncertain date; they are of great value as works of art, and more so as a means of enlightening much that has been obscure with respect to Lycia, an ancient and celebrated country of Asia Minor.

In passing through the eastern zoological gallery, I was surrounded on every side by an army of portraits suspended upon the walls; and among these was the Protector. The people of one century kicks his bones through the streets of London, another puts his portrait in the British Museum, and a future generation may possibly give him a place in Westminster Abbey. Such is the uncertainty of the human character. Yesterday, a common soldier; to-day, the ruler of an empire; to-morrow, suspended upon the gallows. In an adjoining room I saw a portrait of Baxter, which gives one a pretty good idea of the great nonconformist. In the same room hung a splendid modern portrait, without any intimation in the guide-book of who it represented, or when it was painted. It was so much like one whom I had seen, and on whom my affections were placed in my younger days, that I obtained a seat from an adjoining room and rested myself before it. After sitting half an hour or more, I wandered to another part of the building, but only to return again to my "first love," where I remained till the throng had disappeared, one after another, and the officer reminded me that it was time to close.

It was eight o'clock before I reached my lodgings.

Although fatigued by the day's exertions, I again re-
sumed the reading of Roscoe's "Leo X.," and had nearly
finished seventy-three pages, when the clock on St. Martin's Church apprised me that it was two. He who
escapes from slavery at the age of twenty years, without
any education, as did the writer of this, must read when
others are asleep, if he would catch up with the rest of
the world. "To be wise," says Pope, "is but to know
how little can be known." The true searcher after truth
and knowledge is always like a child; although gaining
strength from year to year, he still "learns to labor and
to wait." The field of labor is ever expanding before
him, reminding him that he has yet more to learn;
teaching him that he is nothing more than a child in
knowledge, and inviting him onward with a thousand
varied charms. The son may take possession of the
father's goods at his death, but he cannot inherit with
the property the father's cultivated mind. He may put
on the father's old coat, but that is all; the immortal
mind of the first wearer has gone to the tomb. Property
may be bequeathed, but knowledge cannot. Then let
him who would be useful in his day and generation be
up and doing. Like the Chinese student who learned
perseverance from the woman whom he saw trying to
rub a crow-bar into a needle, so should we take the
experience of the past to lighten our feet through the
paths of the future.

The next morning, at ten, I was again at the door of
the great building; was soon within its walls seeing what

time would not allow of the previous day.   I spent some
hours in looking through glass cases, viewing specimens
of minerals such as can scarcely be found in any place
out of the British Museum.   During this day I did not
fail to visit the great library.   It is a spacious room,
surrounded with large glass cases filled with volumes
whose very look tells you that they are of age.   Around,
under the cornice, were arranged a number of old, black-
looking portraits, in all probability the authors of some
of the works in the glass cases beneath.   About the
room were placed long tables, with stands for reading and
writing, and around these were a number of men busily
engaged in looking over some chosen author.   Old men
with gray hairs, young men with moustaches, some in
cloth, others in fustian,— indicating that men of different
rank can meet here.   Not a single word was spoken
during my stay; all appearing to enjoy the silence that
reigned throughout the great room.   This is indeed a
retreat from the world.   No one inquires who the man is
that is at his side, and each pursues in silence his own
researches.   The racing of pens over the sheets of paper
was all that disturbed the stillness of the occasion.

From the library I strolled to other rooms, and feasted
my eyes on what I had never before seen.   He who goes
over this immense building cannot do so without a feeling
of admiration for the men whose energy has brought
together this vast and wonderful collection of things, the
like of which cannot be found in any other museum in
the world.   The reflection of the setting sun against a

mirror in one of the rooms told me that night was approaching, and I had but a moment in which to take another look at the portrait that I had seen on the previous day, and then bade adieu to the museum.

Having published the narrative of my life and escape from slavery, and put it into the booksellers' hands, and seeing a prospect of a fair sale, I ventured to take from my purse the last sovereign to make up a small sum to remit to the United States, for the support of my daughters, who are at school there. Before doing this, however, I had made arrangements to attend a public meeting in the city of Worcester, at which the mayor was to preside. Being informed by the friends of the slave there that I would in all probability sell a number of copies of my book, and being told that Worcester was only ten miles from London, I felt safe in parting with all but a few shillings, feeling sure that my purse would soon be again replenished. But you may guess my surprise, when I learned that Worcester was above a hundred miles from London, and that I had not retained money enough to defray my expenses to the place. In my haste and wish to make up the ten pounds to send to my children, I had forgotten that the payment for my lodgings would be demanded before I should leave town. Saturday morning came; I paid my lodging-bill, and had three shillings and fourpence left; and out of this sum I was to get three dinners, as I was only served with breakfast and tea at my lodgings.

Nowhere in the British empire do the people witness

as dark days as in London.   It was on Monday morning, in the fore part of October, as the clock on St. Martin's Church was striking ten, that I left my lodgings, and turned into the Strand.   The street-lamps were yet burning, and the shops were all lighted, as if day had not made its appearance.   This great thoroughfare, as usual at this time of the day, was thronged with business men going their way, and women sauntering about for pleasure or for the want of something better to do.   I passed down the Strand to Charing Cross, and looked in vain to see the majestic statue of Nelson upon the top of the great shaft.   The clock on St. Martin's Church struck eleven, but my sight could not penetrate through the dark veil that hung between its face and me.   In fact, day had been completely turned into night; and the brilliant lights from the shop-windows almost persuaded me that another day had not appeared.   A London fog cannot be described.   To be appreciated, it must be seen, or, rather, felt, for it is altogether impossible to be clear and lucid on such a subject.   It is the only thing which gives you an idea of what Milton meant when he talked of darkness visible.   There is a kind of light, to be sure ; but it only serves as a medium for a series of optical illusions ; and, for all useful purposes of vision, the deepest darkness that ever fell from the heavens is infinitely preferable.   A man perceives a coach a dozen yards off, and a single stride brings him among the horses' feet ; he sees a gas-light faintly glimmering (as he thinks) at a distance, but scarcely has he advanced a step or two towards it, when he becomes convinced of its actual station by finding his head rattling against the post; and as for attempting, if you get once mystified, to distinguish one street from another, it is ridiculous to think of such a thing.

Turning, I retraced my steps, and was soon passing through the massive gates of Temple Bar, wending my way to the city, when a beggar-boy at my heels accosted me for a half-penny to buy bread. I had scarcely served the boy, when I observed near by, and standing close to a lamp-post, a colored man, and from his general appearance I was satisfied that he was an American. He eyed me attentively as I passed him, and seemed anxious to speak. When I had got some distance from him I looked back, and his eyes were still upon me. No longer able to resist the temptation to speak with him, I returned, and, commencing conversation with him, learned a little of his history, which was as follows : He had, he said, escaped from slavery in Maryland, and reached New York ; but not feeling himself secure there, he had, through the kindness of the captain of an English ship, made his way to Liverpool; and not being able to get employment there, he had come up to London. Here he had met with no better success, and having been employed in the growing of tobacco, and being unaccustomed to any other work, he could not get labor in England. I told him he had better try to get to the West Indies ; but he informed me that he had not a single penny, and that he had had nothing to eat that day.

By this man's story I was moved to tears, and, going to a neighboring shop, I took from my purse my last shilling, changed it, and gave this poor brother fugitive one half. The poor man burst into tears as I placed the sixpence in his hand, and said, "You are the first friend I have met in .London." I bade him farewell, and left him with a feeling of regret that I could not place him beyond the reach of want. I went on my way to the city, and while going through Cheapside a streak of light appeared in the east, that reminded me that it was not night. In vain I wandered from street to street, with the hope that I might meet some one who would lend me money enough to get to Worcester. Hungry and fatigued I was returning to my lodgings, when the great clock of St. Paul's Church, under whose shadow I was then passing, struck four. A stroll through Fleet-street and the Strand, and I was again pacing my room. On my return, I found a letter from Worcester had arrived in my absence, informing me that a party of gentlemen would meet me the next day on my reaching that place, and saying, "Bring plenty of books, as you will doubtless sell a large number." The last sixpence had been spent for postage-stamps, in order to send off some letters to other places, and I could not even stamp a letter in answer to the one last from Worcester. The only vestige of money about me was a smooth farthing that a little girl had given to me at the meeting at Croydon, saying, "This is for the slaves." I was three thousand miles from home, with but a single farthing in my

pocket! Where on earth is a man without money more
destitute? The cold hills of the Arctic regions have not
a more inhospitable appearance than London to the
stranger with an empty pocket. But whilst I felt de-
pressed at being in such a sad condition, I was conscious
that I had done right in remitting the last ten pounds to
America. It was for the support of those whom God
had committed to my care, and whom I love as I can no
others. I had no friend in London to whom I could
apply for temporary aid. My friend, Mr. T——, was
out of town, and I did not know his address.

The dark day was rapidly passing away,—the clock
in the hall had struck six. I had given up all hopes of
reaching Worcester the next day, and had just rung the
bell for the servant to bring me some tea, when a gentle
tap at the door was heard; the servant entered, and informed me that a gentleman below was wishing to see
me. I bade her fetch a light and ask him up. The
stranger was my young friend, Frederick Stevenson, son
of the excellent minister of the Borough-Road Chapel.
I had lectured in this chapel a few days previous; and
this young gentleman, with more than ordinary zeal and
enthusiasm for the cause of bleeding humanity, and respect for me, had gone amongst his father's congregation and sold a number of copies of my book, and had
come to bring me the money. I wiped the silent tear
from my eyes as the young man placed the thirteen half-
crowns in my hand. I did not let him know under what
obligation I was to him for this disinterested act of kind-

ness. He does not know to this day what aid he has
rendered to a stranger in a strange land, and I feel that
I am but discharging in a trifling degree my debt of
gratitude to this young gentleman, in acknowledging my
obligation to him.   As the man who called for bread and
cheese, when feeling in his pocket for the last threepence
to pay for it, found a sovereign that he was not aware he
possessed, countermanded the order for the lunch, and
bade them bring him the best dinner they could get; so
I told the servant, when she brought the tea, that I had
changed my mind, and should go out to dine.   With the
means in my pocket of reaching Worcester the next day,
I sat down to dinner at the Adelphi, with a good cut of
roast beef before me, and felt myself once more at home.
Thus ended a dark day in London.

CHAPTER X.

" When I behold, with deepe astonishment,
    To famous Westminster how there resorte,
Living in brass or stoney monument,
    The princes and the worthies of all sorte ;
Doe not I see reformde nobilitie,
    Without contempt, or pride, or ostentation,
And looke upon offenselesse majesty,
    Naked of pomp or earthly domination ?
And how a play-game of a painted stone
    Contents the quiet now and silent sprites,
Whome all the world which late they stood upon
    Could not content nor quench their appetites.
Life is a frost of cold felicitie,
    And death the thaw of all our vanitie."

FOR some days past the sun has not shown his face;
clouds have obscured the sky, and the rain has fallen in
torrents, which has contributed much to the general
gloom. However, I have spent the time in as agreeable
a manner as I well could. Yesterday I fulfilled an engagement to dine with a gentleman at the Whittington
Club. One who is unacquainted with the club system as
carried on in London can scarcely imagine the con-
veniences they present. Every member appears to be

at home, and all seem to own a share in the club.
There is a free-and-easy way with those who frequent
clubs, and a license given there, that is unknown in the
drawing-room of the private mansion.   I met the gentleman at the club at the appointed hour, and after his
writing my name in the visitors' book, we proceeded to
the dining-room, where we partook of a good dinner.

We had been in the room but a short time, when a
small man, dressed in black, with his coat buttoned up
to the chin, entered the saloon, and took a seat at the
table hard by.   My friend, in a low whisper, informed
me that this person was one of the French refugees.   He
was apparently not more than thirty years of age, and
exceedingly good-looking,— his person being slight, his
feet and hands very small and well-shaped, especially his
hands, which were covered with kid gloves, so tightly
drawn on that the points of the finger-nails were visible
through them.   His face was mild and almost womanly
in its beauty, his eyes soft and full, his brow open and
ample, his features well defined, and approaching to the
ideal Greek in contour; the lines about his mouth were
exquisitely sweet, and yet resolute in expression; his
hair was short — his having no moustache gave him
nothing of the look of a Frenchman; and I was not a
little surprised when informed that the person before me
was Louis Blanc.   I could scarcely be persuaded to believe that one so small, so child-like in stature, had
taken a prominent part in the revolution of 1848.   He
held in his hand a copy of *La Presse*, and as soon as he

was seated opened it and began to devour its contents. The gentleman with whom I was dining was not acquainted with him, but at the close of our dinner he procured me an introduction through another gentleman.

As we were returning to our lodgings, we saw in Exeter-street, Strand, one of those exhibitions that can be seen in almost any of the streets in the suburbs of the metropolis, but which is something of a novelty to those from the other side of the Atlantic. This was an exhibition of "Punch and Judy." Everything was in full operation when we reached the spot. A puppet appeared, eight or ten inches from the waist upwards, with an enormous face, huge nose, mouth widely grinning, projecting chin, cheeks covered with grog-blossoms, a large protuberance on his back, another on his chest; yet with these deformities he appeared uncommonly happy. This was Mr. Punch. He held in his right hand a tremendous bludgeon, with which he amused himself by rapping on the head every one who came within his reach. This exhibition seems very absurd, yet not less than one hundred were present — children, boys, old men, and even gentlemen and ladies, were standing by, and occasionally greeting the performer with the smile of approbation. Mr. Punch, however, was not to have it all his own way, for another and better sort of Punch-like exhibition appeared a few yards off, that took away Mr. Punch's audience, to the great dissatisfaction of that gentleman. This was an exhibition called the Fantoccini, and far superior to any of the

street performances which I have yet seen.   The curtain
rose and displayed a beautiful theatre in miniature, and
most gorgeously painted.   The organ which accompanied
it struck up a hornpipe, and a sailor, dressed in his blue
jacket, made his appearance, and commenced keeping
time with the utmost correctness.   This figure was not
so long as Mr. Punch, but much better looking.   At the
close of the hornpipe the little sailor made a bow, and
tripped off, apparently conscious of having deserved the
undivided applause of the bystanders.   The curtain
dropped; but in two or three minutes it was again up, and
a rope was discovered extended on two cross pieces for
dancing upon.   The tune was changed to an air in
which the time was marked; a graceful figure appeared,
jumped upon the rope with its balance-pole, and displayed all the manœuvres of an expert performer on the
tight-rope.   Many who would turn away in disgust from
Mr. Punch will stand for hours and look at the performances of the Fantoccini.   If people, like the Vicar of
Wakefield, will sometimes "allow themselves to be
happy," they can hardly fail to have a hearty laugh at
the drolleries of the Fantoccini.   There may be degrees
of absurdity in the manner of wasting our time, but there
is an evident affectation in decrying these humble and
innocent exhibitions, by those who will sit till two or
three in the morning to witness a pantomime at a theatre
royal.

     *   *   *   *   *   *

An autumn sun shone brightly through a remarkably

transparent atmosphere this morning, which was a most
striking contrast to the weather we had had during the
past three days ; and I again set out to see some of the
lions of the city, commencing with the Tower of London.
Every American, on returning home from a visit to the
Old World, speaks with pride of the places he saw while
in Europe ; and of the many resorts of interest he has
read of, few have made a more lasting impression upon
his memory than the Tower of London.   The stories of
the imprisoning of kings and queens, the murdering of
princes, the torturing of men and women, without regard
to birth, education or station, and of the burning and re-
building of the old pile, have all sunk deep into his
heart.   A walk of twenty minutes, after being set down
at the bank by an omnibus, brought me to the gate of the
Tower.   A party of friends who were to meet me there
had not arrived ; so I had an opportunity of inspecting the
grounds, and taking a good view of the external appearance of the old and celebrated building.   The Tower is
surrounded by a high wall, and around this a deep ditch
partly filled with stagnated water.   The wall encloses
twelve acres of ground, on which stand the several
towers, occupying, with their walks and avenues, the
whole space.   The most ancient part of the building is
called the " White Tower," so as to distinguish it from
the parts more recently built.   Its walls are seventeen
feet in thickness, and ninety-two in height, exclusive of
the turrets, of which there are four.   My company
arrived, and we entered the Tower through four massive

gates, the innermost one being pointed out as the
"Water, or Traitors' Gate," so called from the fact that
it opened to the river, and through it the criminals were
usually brought to the prison within.   But this passage
is now closed up.   We visited the various apartments in
the old building.   The room in the Bloody Tower where
the infant princes were put to death by the command of
their uncle, Richard III., also the recess behind the
gate where the bones of the young princes were concealed, were shown to us.   The warden of the prison, who
showed us through, seemed to have little or no veneration for Henry VIII.; for he often cracked a joke or
told a story at the expense of the murderer of Anne
Boleyn.   The old man wiped the tear from his eye as he
pointed out the grave of Lady Jane Grey.   This was
doubtless one of the best as well as most innocent of
those who lost their lives in the Tower; young, virtuous
and handsome, she became a victim to the ambition of
her own and her husband's relations.   I tried to count
the names on the wall in "Beauchamp's Tower," but
they were too numerous.   Anne Boleyn was imprisoned
here.   The room in the "Brick Tower" where Lady
Jane Grey was imprisoned was pointed out as a place of
interest.   We were next shown into the "White Tower."
We passed through a long room filled with many things
having a warlike appearance; and among them a
number of equestrian figures, as large as life, and clothed
in armor and trappings of the various reigns from
Edward I. to James II., or from 1272 to 1685.   Eliza-

beth, or the " Maiden Queen," as the warden called her,
was the most imposing of the group ; she was on a cream-
colored charger.   We left the Maiden Queen, to examine
the cloak upon which General Wolf died at the storming
of Quebec.   In this room Sir Walter Raleigh was imprisoned, and here was written his " History of the
World."   In his own hand, upon the wall, is written,
" Be thou faithful unto death, and I will give thee a
crown of life."   His Bible is still shown, with these
memorable lines written in it by himself a short time
before his death :

> " Even such is Time, that takes on trust,
> Our youth, our joy, our all we have,
> And pays us but with age and dust ;
> Who in the dark and silent grave,
> When we have wandered all our ways,
> Shuts up the story of our days."

Spears, battle-axes, pikes, helmets, targets, bows and
arrows, and many instruments of torture, whose names I
did not learn, grace the walls of this room.   The block
on which the Earl of Essex and Anne Boleyn were be-
headed was shown among other objects of interest.   A
view of the " Queen's Jewels " closed our visit to the
Tower.   The gold staff of St. Edward, and the Baptis-
mal Font used at the royal christenings, made of solid
silver, and more than four feet high, were among the
jewels here exhibited.   The Sword of Justice was there,
as if to watch the rest of the valuables.   However, this

was not the sword that Peter used. Our acquaintance
with De Foe, Sir Walter Raleigh and Chaucer, through
their writings, and the knowledge that they had been
incarcerated within the walls of the bastile that we were
just leaving, caused us to look back again and again upon
its dark-gray turrets.

I closed the day with a look at the interior of St.
Paul's Cathedral. A service was just over, and we met
a crowd coming out as we entered the great building.
"Service is over, and tuppence for all that wants to
stay," was the first sound that caught our ears. In the
Burlesque of "Esmeralda," a man is met in the belfry
of the Notre Dame at Paris, and, being asked for money
by one of the vergers, says,

> " I paid three pence at the door,
>   And since I came in a great deal more ;
>   Upon my honor, you have emptied my purse, —
>   St. Paul's Cathedral could not do worse."

I felt inclined to join in this sentiment before I left
the church. A fine statue of " Surly Sam " Johnson
was one of the first things that caught our eyes on looking around. A statue of Sir Edward Packenham, who
fell at the battle of New Orleans, was on the opposite
side of the great hall. As we had walked over the
ground where the general fell, we viewed his statue
with more than ordinary interest. We were taken from
one scene of interest to another, until we found ourselves
in the "Whispering Gallery." From the dome we had

a splendid view of the metropolis of the world. A scaffold was erected up here to enable an artist to take sketches, from which a panorama of London was painted. The artist was three years at work. The painting is now exhibited at the Colosseum; but the brain of the artist was turned, and he died insane. Indeed, one can scarcely conceive how it could be otherwise. You in America have no idea of the immensity of this building. Pile together half a dozen of the largest churches in New York or Boston, and you will have but a faint representation of St. Paul's Cathedral.

*   *   *   *   *   *

I have just returned from a stroll of two hours through Westminster Abbey. We entered the building at a door near Poet's Corner, and, naturally enough, looked around for the monuments of the men whose imaginative powers have contributed so much to instruct and amuse mankind. I was not a little disappointed in the few I saw. In almost any church-yard you may see monuments and tombs far superior to anything in Poets' Corner. A few only have monuments. Shakspeare, who wrote of man to man, and for man to the end of time, is honored with one. Addison's monument is also there; but the greater number have nothing more erected to their memories than busts or medallions. Poets' Corner is not splendid in appearance, yet I observed visitors lingering about it, as if they were tied to the spot by love and veneration for some departed friend. All seemed to regard it as classic ground. No sound louder than a whisper was heard during the whole time, except the verger treading over the marble floor with a light step. There is great pleasure in sauntering about the tombs of those with whom we are familiar through their writings; and we tear ourselves from their ashes, as we would from those of a bosom friend. The genius of these men spreads itself over the whole panorama of nature, giving us one vast and varied picture, the color of which will endure to the end of time. None can portray like the poet the passions of the human soul. The statue of Addison, clad in his dressing-gown, is not far from that of Shakspeare. He looks as if he had just left the study, after finishing some chosen paper for the *Spectator*. This memento of a great man was the work of the British public. Such a mark of national respect was but justice to the one who had contributed more to purify and raise the standard of English literature than any man of his day. We next visited the other end of the same transept, near the northern door. Here lie Mansfield, Chatham, Fox, the second William Pitt, Grattan, Wilberforce and a few other statesmen. But, above all, is the stately monument of the Earl of Chatham. In no other place so small do so many great men lie together. To these men, whose graves strangers from all parts of the world wish to view, the British public are in a great measure indebted for England's fame. The high preëminence which England has so long enjoyed and maintained in the scale of empire has constantly been the boast and pride of the English people. The warm panegyrics that have been lavished on her constitution and laws, the songs chanted to celebrate her glory, the lustre of her arms, as the glowing theme of her warriors, the thunder of her artillery in proclaiming her moral prowess, her flag being unfurled to every breeze and ocean, rolling to her shores the tribute of a thousand realms, show England to be the greatest nation in the world, and speak volumes for the great departed, as well as for those of the living present. One requires no company, no amusements, no books, in such a place as this. Time and death have placed within those walls sufficient to occupy the mind, if one should stay here a week.

On my return, I spent an hour very pleasantly in the Royal Academy, in the same building as the National Gallery. Many of the paintings here are of a fine order. Oliver Cromwell looking upon the headless corpse of King Charles I. appeared to draw the greatest number of spectators. A scene from "As You Like It" was one of the best executed pieces we saw. This was "Rosalind, Celia and Orlando." The artist did himself and the subject great credit. Kemble, in Hamlet, with that ever-memorable skull in his hand, was one of the pieces which we viewed with no little interest. It is strange that Hamlet is always represented as a thin, lean man, when the Hamlet of Shakspeare was a fat, John Bull kind of a man.

But the best piece in the gallery was "Dante meditating the episode of Francesca da Rimini and Paolo Malatesta, S'Inferno, Canto V." Our first interest for

the great Italian poet was created by reading Lord Byron's poem, "The Lament of Dante." From that hour
we felt like examining everything connected with the
poet. The history of poets, as well as painters, is written in their works. The best written life of Goldsmith
is to be found in his poem of "The Traveller," and his
novel of "The Vicar of Wakefield." Boswell could not
have written a better life of himself than he has done in
giving the Biography of Dr. Johnson. It seems clear
that no one can be a great poet without having been
sometime during life a lover, and having lost the object
of his affection in some mysterious way. Burns had his
Highland Mary, Byron his Mary, and Dante was not
without his Beatrice. Whether there ever lived such a
person as Beatrice seems to be a question upon which
neither of his biographers has thrown much light.
However, a Beatrice existed in the poet's mind, if not
on earth. His attachment to Beatrice Portinari, and
the linking of her name with the immortality of his
great poem, left an indelible impression upon his future
character. The marriage of the object of his affections
to another, and her subsequent death, and the poet's
exile from his beloved Florence, together with his death
amongst strangers, all give an interest to the poet's
writings which could not be heightened by romance
itself. When exiled and in poverty, Dante found a
friend in the father of Francesca. And here, under the
roof of his protector, he wrote his great poem. The
time the painter has chosen is evening. Day and night

meet in mid-air: one star is alone visible. Sailing in vacancy are the shadows of the lovers. The countenance of Francesca is expressive of hopeless agony. The delineations are sublime, the conception is of the highest order, and the execution admirable. Dante is seated in a marble vestibule, in a meditating attitude, the face partly concealed by the right hand upon which it is resting. On the whole, it is an excellently painted piece, and causes one to go back with a fresh relish to the Italian's celebrated poem.

In coming out we stopped a short while in the upper room of the gallery, and spent a few minutes over a painting representing Mrs. Siddons in one of Shakspeare's characters. This is by Sir Joshua Reynolds, and is only one of the many pieces that we have seen of this great artist. His genius was vast and powerful in its grasp, his fancy fertile, and his inventive faculty inexhaustible in its resources. He displayed the very highest powers of genius by the thorough originality of his conceptions, and by the entirely new path that he struck out in art. Well may Englishmen be proud of his name. And as time shall step between his day and those that follow after him, the more will his works be appreciated. We have since visited his grave, and stood over his monument in St. Paul's.

CHAPTER XI.

To give implicit credence to each tale
    Of monkish legends, — relics to order ;
To think God honored by the cowl or veil,
    Regardless who, or what, the emblem wore,
Indeed is mockery, mummery, nothing more :
    But if cold Scepticism usurp the place
That Superstition held in days of yore,
    We may not be in much more hopeful case
Than if we still implored the Virgin Mary's grace.

                                    BARTON.

SOME days since, I left the metropolis to fulfil a few
engagements to visit provincial towns; and after a ride
of nearly eight hours, we were in sight of the ancient
city of York. It was night, the moon was in her zenith,
and there seemed nothing between her and the earth but
glittering cold. The moon, the stars, and the innumerable gas-lights, gave the city a panoramic appearance.
Like a mountain starting out of a plain, there stood the
cathedral in its glory, looking down upon the surrounding buildings, with all the appearance of a Gulliver
standing over the Lilliputians. Night gave us no opportunity to view the minster. However, we were up the
next morning before the sun, and walking round the

cathedral with a degree of curiosity seldom excited within us. It is thought that a building of the same dimensions would take fifty years to complete it at the present time, even with all the improvements of the nineteenth century, and would cost no less than the enormous sum of two millions of pounds sterling. From what I had heard of this famous cathedral, my expectations were raised to the highest point; but it surpassed all the idea that I had formed of it. On entering the building, we lost all thought of the external appearance by the matchless beauty of the interior. The echo produced by the tread of our feet upon the floor as we entered, resounding through the aisles, seemed to say, "Put off your shoes, for the place whereon you tread is holy ground." We stood with hat in hand, and gazed with wonder and astonishment down the incomparable vista of more than five hundred feet. The organ, which stands near the centre of the building, is said to be one of the finest in the world. A wall, in front of which is a screen of the most gorgeous and florid architecture, and executed in solid stone, separates the nave from the service choir. The beautiful workmanship of this makes it appear so perfect, as almost to produce the belief that it is tracery-work of wood. We ascended the rough stone steps through a winding stair to the turrets, where we had such a view of the surrounding country as can be obtained from no other place. On the top of the centre and highest turret is a grotesque figure of a fiddler; rather a strange-looking object, we thought, to occupy the most elevated pinnacle on the house of God. All dwellings in the neighborhood appear like so many dwarfs crouching at the feet of the minster; while its own vastness and beauty impress the observer with feelings of awe and sublimity. As we stood upon the top of this stupendous mountain of ecclesiastical architecture, and surveyed the picturesque hills and valleys around, imagination recalled the tumult of the sanguinary battles fought in sight of the edifice. The rebellion of Octavius near three thousand years ago, his defeat and flight to the Scots, his return and triumph over the Romans, and being crowned king of all Britain; the assassination of Oswald, King of the Northumbrians; the flaying alive of Osbert; the crowning of Richard III.; the siege by William the Conqueror; the siege by Cromwell, and the pomp and splendor with which the different monarchs had been received in York, all appeared to be vividly before me. While we were thus calling to our aid our knowledge of history, a sweet peal from the lungs of the ponderous organ below cut short our stay among the turrets, and we descended to have our organ of tune gratified, as well as to finish the inspection of the interior.

I have heard the sublime melodies of Handel, Haydn and Mozart, performed by the most skilful musicians; I have listened with delight and awe to the soul-moving compositions of those masters, as they have been chanted in the most magnificent churches; but never did I hear such music, and played upon such an instrument, as that sent forth by the great organ in the Cathedral of York.

The verger took much delight in showing us the horn that was once mounted with gold, but is now garnished with brass. We viewed the monuments and tombs of the departed, and then spent an hour before the great north window. The design on the painted glass, which tradition states was given to the church by five virgin sisters, is the finest thing of the kind in Great Britain. I felt a relief on once more coming into the open air, and again beholding Nature's own sunlight. The splendid ruin of St. Mary's Abbey, with its eight beautiful light Gothic windows, next attracted our attention. A visit to the castle finished our stay in York; and as we were leaving the old city we almost imagined that we heard the chiming of the bells for the celebration of the first Christian Sabbath, with Prince Arthur as the presiding genius.

    *   *   *   *   *   *

England stands preeminently the first government in the world for freedom of speech and of the press. Not even in our own beloved America can the man who feels himself oppressed speak as he can in Great Britain. In some parts of England, however, the freedom of thought is tolerated to a greater extent than in others; and of the places favorable to reforms of all kinds, calculated to elevate and benefit mankind, Newcastle-on-Tyne doubtless takes the lead. Surrounded by innumerable coalmines, it furnishes employment for a large laboring population, many of whom take a deep interest in the passing events of the day, and, consequently, are a reading class. The public debater or speaker, no matter what may be his subject, who fails to get an audience in other towns, is sure of a gathering in the Music Hall, or Lecture Room, in Newcastle.

Here I first had an opportunity of coming in contact with a portion of the laboring people of Britain. I have addressed large and influential meetings in New-castle and the neighboring towns, and the more I see and learn of the condition of the working-classes of England, the more I am satisfied of the utter fallacy of the state-ments often made that their condition approximates to that of the slaves of America. Whatever may be the disad-vantages that the British peasant labors under, he is free; and if he is not satisfied with his employer, he can make choice of another. He also has the right to educate his children; and he is the equal of the most wealthy person before an English court of justice. But how is it with the American slave? He has no right to him-self; no right to protect his wife, his child, or his own person. He is nothing more than a living tool. Be-yond his field or workshop he knows nothing. There is no amount of ignorance he is not capable of. He has not the least idea of the face of this earth, nor of the history or constitution of the country in which he dwells. To him the literature, science and art, the progressive history and the accumulated discoveries of by-gone ages, are as if they had never been. The past is to him as yesterday, and the future scarcely more than to-mor-row. Ancestral monuments he has none; written documents, fraught with cogitations of other times, he has none; and any instrumentality calculated to awaken and expound the intellectual activity and comprehension of a present or approaching generation, he has none. His condition is that of the leopard of his own native Africa. It lives, it propagates its kind; but never does it indicate a movement towards that all but angelic intelligence of man. The slave eats, drinks and sleeps, all for the benefit of the man who claims his body as his property. Before the tribunals of his country he has no voice. He has no higher appeal than the mere will of his owner. He knows nothing of the inspired Apostles through their writings. He has no Sabbath, no church, no Bible, no means of grace,— and yet we are told that he is as well off as the laboring classes of England. It is not enough that the people of my country should point to their Declaration of Independence, which declares that "all men are created equal." It is not enough that they should laud to the skies a constitution containing boasting declarations in favor of freedom. It is not enough that they should extol the genius of Washington, the patriotism of Henry, or the enthusiasm of Otis. The time has come when nations are judged by the acts of the present, instead of the past. And so it must be with America. In no place in the United Kingdom has the American slave warmer friends than in Newcastle.

*　　*　　*　　*　　*　　*

I am now in Sheffield, and have just returned from a visit to James Montgomery, the poet. In company with

James Wall, Esq., I proceeded to the Mount, the residence of Mr. Montgomery; and our names being sent in,
we were soon in the presence of the "Christian poet." He
held in his left hand the *Eclectic Review* for the month,
and with the right gave me a hearty shake, and bade me
"Welcome to Old England." He was anything but like
the portraits I had seen of him, and the man I had in
my mind's eye. I had just been reading his "Pelican
Island," and I eyed the poet with no little interest. He
is under the middle size; his forehead high and well
formed, the top of which was a little bald; his hair of a
yellowish color, his eyes rather small and deep-set, the
nose long and slightly acquiline, his mouth rather small,
and not at all pretty. He was dressed in black, and a
large white cravat entirely hid his neck and chin; his
having been afflicted from childhood with salt-rheum
was doubtless the cause of his chin being so completely
buried in the neckcloth. Upon the whole, he looked
more like one of our American Methodist parsons than
any one I have seen in this country. He entered freely
into conversation with us. He said he should be glad to
attend my lecture that evening, but that he had long
since quit going out at night. He mentioned having
heard William Lloyd Garrison some years before, and
with whom he was well pleased. He said it had long
been a puzzle to him how Americans could hold slaves
and still retain their membership in the churches. When
we rose to leave, the old man took my hand between his
two, and with tears in his eyes said, "Go on your Chris-

tian mission, and may the Lord protect and prosper you! Your enslaved countrymen have my sympathy, and shall have my prayers." Thus ended our visit to the bard of Sheffield. Long after I had quitted the presence of the poet, the following lines of his were ringing in my ears:

> "Wanderer, whither dost thou roam?
> Weary wanderer, old and gray,
> Wherefore hast thou left thine home,
> In the sunset of thy day?
> Welcome, wanderer, as thou art,
> All my blessings to partake;
> Yet thrice welcome to my heart,
> For thine injured people's sake.
> Wanderer, whither wouldst thou roam?
> To what region far away?
> Bend thy steps to find a home,
> In the twilight of thy day,
> Where a tyrant never trod,
> Where a slave was never known —
> But where Nature worships God
> In the wilderness alone."

Mr. Montgomery seems to have thrown his entire soul into his meditations on the wrongs of Switzerland. The poem which we have just quoted is unquestionably one of his best productions, and contains more of the fire of enthusiasm than all his other works. We feel a reverence almost amounting to superstition for the poet who deals with nature. And who is more capable of understanding the human heart than the poet? Who has better known the human feelings than Shakspeare; better

painted than Milton the grandeur of virtue; better
sighed than Byron over the subtle weaknesses of Hope?
Who ever had a sounder taste, a more exact intellect,
than Dante? or who has ever tuned his harp more in
favor of freedom than our own Whittier?

CHAPTER XII.

" How changed, alas ! from that revered abode,
    Graced by proud majesty in ancient days,
  When monks recluse these sacred pavements trod,
    And taught the unlettered world its Maker's praise !

KEATS.

In passing through Yorkshire, we could not resist the
temptation it offered to pay a visit to the extensive and
interesting ruin of Kirkstall Abbey, which lies embosomed in a beautiful recess of Airedale, about three miles
from Leeds. A pleasant drive over a smooth road
brought us abruptly in sight of the Abbey. The tran-
quil and pensive beauty of the desolate monastery, as it
reposes in the lap of pastoral luxuriance, and amidst the
touching associations of seven centuries, is almost beyond
description, when viewed from where we first beheld it.
After arriving at its base, we stood for some moments
under the mighty arches that lead into the great hall,
gazing at its old gray walls frowning with age. At the
distance of a small field, the Aire is seen gliding past
the foot of the lawn on which the ruin stands, after it
has left those precincts, sparkling over a weir with a

pleasing murmur.   We could fully enter into the feelings of the poet when he says:

> " Beautiful fabric ! even in decay
>   And desolation, beauty still is thine ;
> As the rich sunset of an autumn day,
>   When gorgeous clouds in glorious hues combine
> To render homage to its slow decline,
>   Is more majestic in its parting hour :
> Even so thy mouldering, venerable shrine
>   Possesses now a more subduing power
> Than in thine earlier sway, with pomp and pride thy dower."

The tale of "Mary, the Maid of the Inn," is supposed, and not without foundation, to be connected with
this abbey.   "Hark to Rover," the name of the house
where the key is kept, was, a century ago, a retired inn
or pot-house, and the haunt of many a desperate high-
wayman and poacher.   The anecdote is so well known
that it is scarcely necessary to relate it.   It, however, is
briefly this :

"One stormy night, as two travellers sat at the inn,
each having exhausted his news, the conversation was
directed to the abbey, the boisterous night, and Mary's
heroism; when a bet was at last made by one of them,
that she would not go and bring back from the nave a
slip of the alder-tree growing there.   Mary, however,
did go ; but, having nearly reached the tree, she heard a
low, indistinct dialogue; at the same time, something
black fell and rolled towards her, which afterwards
proved to be a hat.   Directing her attention to the place
whence the conversation proceeded, she saw, from behind

a pillar, two men carrying a murdered body: they passed near the place where she stood, a heavy cloud was swept from off the face of the moon, and Mary fell senseless — one of the murderers was her intended husband! She was awakened from her swoon, but — her reason had fled forever." Mr. Southey wrote a beautiful poem founded on this story, which will be found in his published works. We spent nearly three hours in wandering through these splendid ruins. It is both curious and interesting to trace the early history of these old piles, which become the resort of thousands, nine tenths of whom are unaware either of the classic ground on which they tread, or of the peculiar interest thrown around the spot by the deeds of remote ages.

During our stay in Leeds, we had the good fortune to become acquainted with Wilson Armistead, Esq. This gentleman is well known as an able writer against slavery. His most elaborate work is "A Tribute for the Negro." This is a volume of five hundred and sixty pages, and is replete with facts refuting the charges of inferiority brought against the negro race. Few English gentlemen have done more to hasten the day of the slave's liberation than Wilson Armistead.

A few days after, I paid a visit to Newstead Abbey, the far-famed residence of Lord Byron. I posted from Hucknall over to Newstead one pleasant morning, and, being provided with a letter of introduction to Colonel Wildman, I lost no time in presenting myself at the door of the abbey. But, unfortunately for me, the colonel

was at Mansfield, in attendance at the Assizes — he being one of the county magistrates. I did not, however,
lose the object of my visit, as every attention was paid
in showing me about the premises. I felt as every one
must who gazes for the first time upon these walls, and
remembers that it was here, even amid the comparative
ruins of a building once dedicated to the sacred cause of
Religion and her twin sister, Charity, that the genius of
Byron was first developed; here that he paced with
youthful melancholy the halls of his illustrious ancestors,
and trode the walks of the long-banished monks. The
housekeeper — a remarkably good-looking and polite
woman — showed us through the different apartments,
and explained in the most minute manner every object
of interest connected with the interior of the building.
We first visited the Monk's Parlor, which seemed to
contain nothing of note, except a very fine-stained window — one of the figures representing St. Paul, surmounted by a cross. We passed through Lord Byron's
Bed-room, the Haunted Chamber, the Library and the
Eastern Corridor, and halted in the Tapestry Bed-room,
which is truly a magnificent apartment, formed by the
Byrons for the use of King Charles II. The ceiling is
richly decorated with the Byron arms. We next visited
the grand Drawing-room, probably the finest in the
building. This saloon contains a large number of splendid portraits, among which is the celebrated portrait of
Lord Byron, by Phillips. In this room we took into

our hand the skull-cup, of which so much has been written, and that has on it:

> " Start not — nor deem my spirit fled ;
>   In me behold the only skull
> From which, unlike a living head,
>   Whatever flows is never dull.

> " I lived, I loved, I quaffed like thee ;
>   I died — let earth my bones resign :
> Fill up — thou canst not injure me ;
>   The worm hath fouler lips than thine.

> " Better to hold the sparkling grape,
>   Than nurse the earth-worm's slimy brood ;
> And circle in the goblet's shape
>   The drink of gods, than reptile's food.

> " Where once my wit, perchance, hath shone,
>   In aid of others let me shine ;
> And when, alas ! our brains are gone,
>   What nobler substitute than wine ?

> " Quaff while thou canst — another race,
>   When thou and thine like thee are sped,
> May rescue thee from earth's embrace,
>   And rhyme and revel with the dead.

> " Why not ? since through life's little day
>   Our heads such sad effects produce ;
> Redeemed from worms and wasting clay,
>   This chance is theirs, to be of use.''

Leaving this noble room, we descended by a few polished oak steps into the West Corridor, from which we entered the grand Dining Hall, and through several other rooms, until we reached the Chapel. Here we

were shown a stone coffin which had been found near the
high altar, when the workmen were excavating the vault
intended by Lord Byron for himself and his dog. The
coffin contained the skeleton of an abbot, and also the
identical skull from which the cup of which I have
made mention was made. We then left the building,
and took a stroll through the grounds. After passing a
pond of cold crystal water, we came to a dark wood, in
which are two leaden statues of Pan, and a female satyr
— very fine specimens as works of art. We here inspected the tree whereon Byron carved his own name
and that of his sister, with the date, all of which are still
legible. However, the tree is now dead, and we were
informed that Colonel Wildman intended to have it cut
down, so as to preserve the part containing the inscription. After crossing an interesting and picturesque part
of the gardens, we arrived within the precincts of the
ancient chapel, near which we observed a neat marble
monument, and which we supposed to have been erected
to the memory of some of the Byrons; but, on drawing
near to it, we read the following inscription :

"Near this spot are deposited the Remains of one who possessed Beauty without
    Vanity, Strength without Insolence, Courage without Ferocity, and all the Virtues
    of Man without his Vices. This Praise, which would be unmeaning Flattery if in-
    scribed over human ashes, is but a just tribute to the Memory of BOATSWAIN, a
    Dog, who was born at Newfoundland, May, 1803, and died at Newstead Abbey,
    Nov. 18, 1808.

        " When some proud son of man returns to earth,
          Unknown to glory, but upheld by birth,
          The sculptured art exhausts the pomp of woe,
          And storied urns record who rests below ;

When all is done, upon the tomb is seen
Not what he was, but what he should have been.
But the poor dog, in life the firmest friend,
The first to welcome, foremost to defend,
Whose honest heart is still his master's own,
Who labors, fights, lives, breathes for him alone,
Unhonored falls, unnoticed all his worth,
Denied in heaven the soul he held on earth ;
While man, vain insect ! hopes to be forgiven,
And claims himself a sole, exclusive heaven.
O, man ! thou feeble tenant of an hour,
Debased by slavery, or corrupt by power,
Who knows thee well must quit thee with disgust,
Degraded mass of animated dust ;
Thy love is lust, thy friendship all a cheat,
Thy smiles hypocrisy, thy words deceit !
By nature vile, ennobled but by name,
Each kindred brute might bid thee blush for shame.
Ye, who perchance behold this simple urn,
Pass on — it honors none you wish to mourn :
To mark a friend's remains these stones arise ;
I never knew but one,— and here he lies.''

By a will which his lordship executed in 1811, he directed that his own body should be buried in a vault in the garden, near his faithful dog. This feeling of affection to his dumb and faithful follower, commendable in itself, seems here to have been carried beyond the bounds of reason and propriety.

In another part of the grounds we saw the oak-tree planted by the poet himself. It has now attained a goodly size, considering the growth of the oak, and bids fair to become a lasting memento to the noble bard, and to be a shrine to which thousands of pilgrims will resort in future ages, to do homage to his mighty genius. This tree promises to share in after times the celebrity of Shakspeare's mulberry, and Pope's willow. Near by, and in the tall trees, the rooks were keeping up a tremendous noise. After seeing everything of interest connected with the great poet, we entered our chaise, and left the premises. As we were leaving, I turned to take a farewell look at the abbey, standing in solemn grandeur; the long ivy clinging fondly to the rich tracery of a former age. Proceeding to the little town of Hucknall we entered the old gray parish church, which has for ages been the last resting-place of the Byrons, and where repose the ashes of the poet, marked by a neat marble slab, bearing the following inscription :

In the vault beneath,
where many of his Ancestors and his Mother are
Buried,
lie the remains of
GEORGE GORDON NOEL BYRON,
Lord Byron, of Rochdale,
in the County of Lancaster,
the author of " Childe Harold's Pilgrimage."
He was born in London, on the
22nd of January, 1788.
He died at Missolonghi, in Western Greece, on the
19th of April, 1824,
Engaged in the glorious attempt to restore that
country to her ancient grandeur and renown.

His Sister, the Honorable
Augusta Maria Leigh,
placed this Tablet to his Memory.

From an Album that is kept for visitors to register their names in, I copied the following lines, composed by William Howitt, immediately after the interment :

> " Rest in thy tomb, young heir of glory, rest !
> Rest in thy rustic tomb, which thou shalt make
> A spot of light upon thy country's breast,
> Known, honored, haunted ever for thy sake.
> Thither romantic pilgrims shall betake
> Themselves from distant lands.   When we are still
> In centuries of sleep, thy fame shall wake,
> And thy great memory with deep feelings fill
> These scenes which thou hast trod, and hallow every hill.''

This closed my visit to the interesting scenes associated with Byron's strange and eventful history — scenes that ever acquire a growing charm as the lapse of years softens the errors of the man, and confirms the genius of the poet.

The following lines, written by Byron in early life, were realized in his death in a fore' n land :

> " When Time or soon or late shall bring
> The dreamless sleep that lulls the dead,
> Oblivion ! may thy languid limb
> Wave gently o'er my dying bed !
>
> " No band of friends or heirs be there,
> To weep, or wish the coming blow :
> No maiden, with dishevelled hair,
> To feel, or feign, decorous woe.
>
> " But silent let me sink to Earth,
> With no officious mourners near ;
> I would not mar one hour of mirth,
> Nor startle friendship with a tear.''

CHAPTER XIII.

" Now, this once gorgeous edifice, if reared
    By piety, which sought with honest aim
The glory of the Lord, should be revered
    Even for that cause, by those who seek the same.
Perchance the builders erred ; but who shall blame
    Error, nor feel that they partake it too ?
Then judge with charity, whate'er thy name,
    Be thou a Pagan, Protestant, or Jew ;
Nor with a scornful glance these Papal reliques view."

BARTON.

It was on a lovely morning that I found myself on
board the little steamer *Wye*, passing out of Bristol
harbor. In going down the river, we saw on our right
the stupendous rocks of St. Vincent towering some four
or five hundred feet above our heads. By the swiftness
of our fairy steamer, we were soon abreast of Cook's
Folly, a singular tower, built by a man from whom it
takes its name, and of which the following romantic story
is told : "Some years since a gentleman, of the name
of Cook, erected this tower, which has since gone by the
name of ' Cook's Folly.' A son having been born, he
was desirous of ascertaining, by means of astrology, if he
would live to enjoy his property. Being himself a firm

believer, like the poet Dryden, that certain information might be obtained from the above science, he caused the child's horoscope to be drawn, and found, to his dismay, that in his third, sixteenth, or twenty-first year, he would be in danger of meeting with some fearful calamity or sudden death, to avert which he caused the turret to be constructed, and the child placed therein. Secure, as he vainly thought, there he lived, attended by a faithful servant, their food and fuel being conveyed to them by means of a pulley-basket, until he was old enough to wait upon himself. On the eve of his twenty-first year his parent's hopes rose high, and great were the rejoicings prepared to welcome the young heir to his home. But, alas! no human skill could avert the dark fate which clung to him. The last night he had to pass alone in the turret, a bundle of fagots was conveyed to him as usual, in which lay concealed a viper, which clung to his hand. The bite was fatal; and, instead of being borne in triumph, the dead body of his only son was the sad spectacle which met the sight of his father."

We crossed the channel, and soon entered the mouth of that most picturesque of rivers, the Wye. As we neared the town of Chepstow the old castle made its appearance, and a fine old ruin it is. Being previously provided with a letter of introduction to a gentleman in Chepstow, I lost no time in finding him out. This gentleman gave me a cordial reception, and did what Englishmen seldom ever do, lent me his saddle-horse to ride to the abbey. While lunch was in preparation I took a stroll through the castle which stood near by. We entered the castle through the great doorway, and were soon treading the walls that had once sustained the cannon and the sentinel, but were now covered with weeds and wild-flowers. The drum and fife had once been heard within these walls — the only music now is the cawing of the rook ʻand daw. We paid a hasty visit to the various apartments, remaining longest in those of most interest. The room in which Martin the Regicide was imprisoned nearly twenty years was pointed out to to us. The Castle of Chepstow is still a magnificent pile, towering upon the brink of a stupendous cliff, on reaching the top of which, we had a splendid view of the surrounding country. Time, however, compelled us to retrace our steps, and, after partaking of a lunch, we mounted a horse for the first time in ten years, and started for Tintern Abbey. The distance from Chepstow to the abbey is about five miles, and the road lies along the banks of the river. The river is walled in on either side by hills of much beauty, clothed from base to summit with the richest verdure. I can conceive of nothing more striking than the first appearance of the abbey. As we rounded a hill, all at once we saw the old ruin standing before us in all its splendor. This celebrated ecclesiastical relic of the olden time is doubtless the finest ruin of its kind in Europe. Embosomed amongst hills, and situated on the banks of the most fairy-like river in the world, its beauty can scarcely be surpassed. We halted at the " Beaufort Arms," left our horse, and sallied forth to view the abbey. The sun was pouring a flood of light upon the old gray walls, lighting up its dark recesses, as if to give us a better opportunity of viewing it. I gazed with astonishment and admiration at its many beauties, and especially at the superb Gothic windows over the entrance-door. The beautiful Gothic pillars, with here and there a representation of a praying priest, and mailed knights, with saints and Christian martyrs, and the hundreds of Scriptural representations, all indicate that this was a place of considerable importance in its palmy days. The once stone floor had disappeared, and we found ourselves standing on a floor of unbroken green grass, swelling back to the old walls, and looking so verdant and silken that it seemed the very floor of fancy. There are more romantic and wilder places than this in the world, but none more beautiful. The preservation of these old abbeys should claim the attention of those under whose charge they are, and we felt like joining with the poet, and saying—

> " O ye who dwell
> Around yon ruins, guard the precious charge
> From hands profane ! O save the sacred pile—
> O'er which the wing of centuries has flown
> Darkly and silently, deep-shadowing all
> Its pristine honors — from the ruthless grasp
> Of future violation ! "

In contemplating these ruins more closely, the mind insensibly reverts to the period of feudal and regal oppression, when structures like that of Tintern Abbey necessarily became the scenes of stirring and highly-important events. How altered is the scene! Where were formerly magnificence and splendor, the glittering array of priestly prowess, the crowded halls of haughty bigots, and the prison of religious offenders, there is now but a heap of mouldering ruins. The oppressed and the oppressor have long since lain down together in the peaceful grave. The ruin, generally speaking, is unusually perfect, and the sculpture still beautifully sharp. The outward walls are nearly entire, and are thickly clad with ivy. Many of the windows are also in a good state of preservation; but the roof has long since fallen in. The feathered songsters were fluttering about, and pouring forth their artless lays as a tribute of joy; while the lowing of the herds, the bleating of flocks, and the hum of bees upon the farm near by, all burst upon the ear, and gave the scene a picturesque sublimity that can be easier imagined than described. Most assuredly Shakspeare had such ruins in view when he exclaimed,

> "The cloud-capped towers, the gorgeous palaces,
> The solemn temples, the great globe itself,
> Yes, all which it inherit, shall dissolve,
> And, like the baseless fabric of a vision,
> Leave not a wreck behind."

In the afternoon we returned to Bristol, and I spent the greater part of the next day in examining the interior of Redcliffe Church. Few places in the west of England have greater claims upon the topographer and historian than the church of St. Mary's, Redcliffe. Its antiquity, the beauty of its architecture, and, above all, the interesting circumstances connected with its history, entitle it to peculiar notice. It is also associated with the enterprise of genius; for its name has been blended with the reputation of Rowley, of Canynge, and of Chatterton, and no lover of poetry and admirer of art can visit it without a degree of enthusiasm. And, when the old building shall have mouldered into ruins, even these will be trodden with veneration, as sacred to the recollection of genius of the highest order. Ascending a winding stair, we were shown into the treasury room. The room forms an irregular octagon, admitting light through narrow, unglazed apertures, upon the broken and scattered fragments of the famous Rowleian chests, that, with the rubble and dust of centuries, cover the floor. It is here creative fancy pictures forth the sad image of the spirit of the spot — the ardent boy, flushed and fed by hope, musing on the brilliant deception he had conceived, whose daring attempt has left his name unto the intellectual world as a marvel and a mystery.

That a boy under twelve years of age should write a series of poems, imitating the style of the fifteenth century, and palm these poems off upon the world as the work of a monk, is indeed strange; and that these should become the object of interesting contemplation to the literary world, and should awaken inquiries, and exercise the talents of a Southey, a Bryant, a Miller, a Mathias, and others, savors more of romance than reality. I had visited the room in a garret in High Holborn where this poor boy died; I had stood over a grave in the burial-ground of Shoe-Lane Work-house, which was pointed out to me as the last rest-ing-place of Chatterton; and now I was in the room where, it was alleged, he obtained the manuscripts that gave him such notoriety. We descended and viewed other portions of the church. The effect of the chancel, as seen behind the pictures, is very singular, and sug-gestive of many swelling thoughts. We look at the great east window — it is unadorned with its wonted painted glass; we look at the altar-screen beneath, on which the light of day again falls, and behold the injuries it has received at the hands of time. There is a dreary mournfulness in the scene which fastens on the mind, and is in unison with the time-worn mouldering frag-ments that are seen all around us. And this dreariness is not removed by our tracing the destiny of man on the storied pavements or on the graven brass, that still bears upon its surface the names of those who obtained the world's regard years back. This old pile is not only an ornament to the city, but it stands a living monument to the genius of its founder. Bristol has long sustained a high position, as a place from which the American abo-litionists have received substantial encouragement in their arduous labors for the emancipation of the slaves of that land; and the writer of this received the best evidence that in this respect the character of the people had not been exaggerated, especially as regards the

"Clifton Ladies' Anti-Slavery Society." From Bristol I paid a hasty visit to the Scotch capital.

Edinburgh is the most picturesque of all the towns which I have visited since my arrival in the father-land. Its situation has been compared to that of Athens; but it is said that the modern Athens is superior to the ancient. I was deeply impressed with the idea that I had seen the most beautiful of cities, after beholding those fashionable resorts, Paris and Versailles. I have seen nothing in the way of public grounds to compare with the gardens of Versailles, or the Champs Elysces, at Paris; and as for statuary, the latter place is said to take the lead of the rest of the world.

The general appearance of Edinburgh prepossesses one in its favor. The town, being built upon the brows of a large terrace, presents the most wonderful perspective. Its first appearance to a stranger, and the first impression, can scarcely be but favorable. In my first walk through the town I was struck with the difference in the appearance of the people from the English. But the difference between the Scotch and the Americans is very great. The cheerfulness depicted in the countenances of the people here, and their free-and-easy appearance, is very striking to a stranger. He who taught the sun to shine, the flowers to bloom, the birds to sing, and blesses us with rain, never intended that his creatures should look sad. There is a wide difference between the Americans and any other people which I have seen. The

Scotch are healthy and robust, unlike the long-faced, sickly-looking Americans.

While on our journey from London to Paris, to attend the Peace Congress, I could not but observe the marked difference between the English and American delegates. The former looked as if their pockets had been filled with sandwiches, made of good bread and roast beef; while the latter appeared as if their pockets had been filled with Holloway's pills and Mrs. Kidder's cordial.

I breakfasted this morning in a room in which the poet Burns, as I was informed, had often sat. The conversation here turned upon Burns. The lady of the house pointed to a scrap of poetry which was in a frame hanging on the wall, written, as she said, by the poet, on hearing the people rejoicing in a church over the intelligence of a victory. I copied it, and will give it to you:

> " Ye hypocrites ! are these your pranks,
> To murder men and give God thanks?
> For shame ! give o'er, proceed no further ;
> God won't accept your thanks for murder."

The fact that I was in the room where Scotland's great national poet had been a visitor caused me to feel that I was on classic, if not hallowed ground. On returning from our morning visit, we met a gentleman with a colored lady on each arm. C—— remarked, in a very dry manner, "If they were in Georgia, the slaveholders would make them walk in a more hurried gait than they do." I said to my friend that, if he meant the pro-

slavery prejudice would not suffer them to walk peace-
ably through the streets, they need go no further than
the pro-slavery cities of New York and Philadelphia.
When walking through the streets, I amused myself by
watching C——'s countenance; and, in doing so, imagined
I saw the changes experienced by every fugitive slave in
his first month's residence in this country. A sixteen
months' residence has not yet familiarized me with the
change.

*   *   *   *   *   *

I remained in Edinburgh a day or two, which gave me
an opportunity of seeing some of the lions in the way of
public buildings, &c., in company with our friend C ——.
I paid a visit to the Royal Institute, and inspected the
very fine collection of paintings, statues, and other productions of art. The collection in the Institute is not to
be compared to the British Museum at London, or the
Louvre at Paris, but is probably the best in Scotland.
Paintings from the hands of many of the masters, such
as Sir A. Vandyke, Tiziano, Vercellio and Van Dellen,
were hanging on the wall, and even the names of Ru-
bens and Titian were attached to some of the finer specimens. Many of these represent some of the nobles and
distinguished families of Rome, Athens, Greece, &c. A
beautiful one, representing a group of the Lomellini
family of Genoa, seemed to attract the attention of most
of the visitors.

In visiting this place, we passed close by the monument of Sir Walter Scott. This is the most exquisite

thing of the kind that I have seen since coming to this
country.   It is said to be the finest monument in Europe.
There sits the author of "Waverley," with a book and
pencil in hand, taking notes.   A beautiful dog is seated
by his side.   Whether this is meant to represent his
favorite dog, Camp, at whose death the poet shed so
many tears, we were not informed; but I was of opinion
that it might be the faithful Percy, whose monument
stands in the grounds at Abbotsford.   Scott was an admirer of the canine tribe.   One may form a good idea
of the appearance of this distinguished writer when living, by viewing this remarkable statue.   The statue is
very beautiful, but not equal to the one of Lord Byron,
which was executed to be placed by the side of Johnson,
Milton and Addison, in Poets' Corner, Westminster
Abbey; but the vestry not allowing it a place there, it
now stands in one of the colleges at Cambridge.   While
viewing the statue of Byron, I thought he, too, should
have been represented with a dog by his side; for he, like
Scott, was remarkably fond of dogs; so much so that he
intended to have his favorite, Boatswain, interred by his
side.

We paid a short visit to the monuments of Burns and
Allan Ramsay, and the renowned old Edinburgh Castle.
The castle is now used as a barrack for infantry.   It is
accessible only from the High Street, and must have been
impregnable before the discovery of gunpowder.   In the
wars with the English, it was twice taken by stratagem :
once in a very daring manner, by climbing up the most

inaccessible part of the rock upon which it stands, and where a foe was least expected, and putting the guard to death ; and at another time, by a party of soldiers disguising themselves as merchants, and obtaining admission inside the castle gates. They succeeded in preventing the gates from being closed until reinforced by a party of men under Sir Wm. Douglas, who soon overpowered the occupants of the castle.

We could not resist the temptation held out to see the palace of Holyrood. It was in this place that the beautiful but unfortunate Mary Queen of Scots resided for a number of years. On reaching the palace, we were met at the door by an elderly-looking woman, with a red face, garnished with a pair of second-hand curls, the whole covered with a cap having the widest border that I had seen for years. She was very kind in showing us about the premises, especially as we were foreigners, no doubt expecting an extra fee for politeness. The most interesting of the many rooms in this ancient castle is the one which was occupied by the queen, and where her Italian favorite, Rizzio, was murdered.

But by far the most interesting object which we visited while in Edinburgh was the house where the celebrated Reformer, John Knox, resided. It is a queer-looking old building, with a pulpit on the outside, and above the door are the nearly obliterated remains of the following inscription: " Lufe. God. Above. Al. And. your. Nichbour. As you. Self." This was probably traced under the immediate direction of the great Reformer.

Such an inscription put upon a house of worship at the present day would be laughed at. I have given it to you, punctuation and all, just as it stands.

The general architecture of Edinburgh is very imposing, whether we regard the picturesque disorder of the buildings in the Old Town, or the symmetrical proportions of the streets and squares in the New. But on viewing this city, which has the reputation of being the finest in Europe, I was surprised to find that it had none of those sumptuous structures which, like St. Paul's, or Westminster Abbey, York Minster, and some other of the English provincial cathedrals, astonish the beholder alike by their magnitude and their architectural splendor. But in no city which I have visited in the kingdom is the general standard of excellence better maintained than in Edinburgh.

CHAPTER XIV.

" I was a traveller then upon the moor ;
    I saw the hare that raced about with joy ;
    I heard the woods and distant waters roar,
    Or heard them not, as happy as a boy."
                                WORDSWORTH.

I AM glad once more to breathe an atmosphere uncontaminated by the fumes and smoke of a city with its population of three hundred thousand inhabitants. In company with my friend C——, I left Glasgow on the afternoon of the 23d inst., for Dundee, a beautiful town situated on the banks of the river Tay. One like myself, who has spent the best part of an eventful life in cities, and who prefers, as I do, a country to a town life, feels a greater degree of freedom when surrounded by forest trees, or country dwellings, and looking upon a clear sky, than when walking through the thronged thoroughfares of a city, with its dense population, meeting every moment a new or strange face, which one has never seen before, and never expects to see again.

Although I had met with one of the warmest public receptions with which I have been greeted since my arrival in the country, and had had an opportunity of shaking hands with many noble friends of the slave, whose names I had often seen in print, yet I felt glad to see the tall chimneys and smoke of Glasgow receding in the distance, as our " iron-horse " was taking us with almost lightning speed from the commercial capital of Scotland.

The distance from Glasgow to Dundee is some seventy or eighty miles, and we passed through the finest country which I have seen in this portion of the queen's dominions. We passed through the old town of Stirling, which lies about thirty miles distant from Glasgow, and is a place much frequented by those who travel for pleasure. It is built on the brow of a hill, and the castle from which it most probably derived its name may be seen from a distance. Had it not been for a " professional " engagement the same evening at Dundee, I would most assuredly have halted to take a look at the old building.

The castle is situated or built on an isolated rock, which seems as if nature had thrown it there for that purpose. It was once the retreat of the Scottish kings, and famous for its historical associations. Here the " Lady of the Lake," with the magic ring, sought the monarch to intercede for her father ; here James II. murdered the Earl of Douglas ; here the beautiful but unfortunate Mary was made queen ; and here John Knox, the Reformer, preached the coronation sermon of James VI. The Castle Hill rises from the valley of the Forth, and makes an imposing and picturesque appearance. The windings of the noble river, till lost in the distance, present pleasing contrasts, scarcely to be surpassed.

The speed of our train, after passing Stirling, brought before us, in quick succession, a number of fine villas and farm-houses. Every spot seemed to have been arrayed by nature for the reception of the cottage of some happy family. During this ride we passed many sites where the lawns were made, the terraces defined and levelled, the groves tastefully clumped, the ancient trees, though small when compared to our great forest oaks, were beautifully sprinkled here and there, and in everything the labor of art seemed to have been anticipated by nature. Cincinnatus could not have selected a prettier situation for a farm than some which presented themselves during this delightful journey. At last we arrived at the place of our destination, where our friends were in waiting for us.

As I have already forwarded to you a paper containing an account of the Dundee meeting, I shall leave you to judge from these reports the character of the demonstration. Yet I must mention a fact or two connected with our first evening's visit to this town. A few hours after our arrival in the place, we were called upon by a gentleman whose name is known wherever the English language is spoken — one whose name is on the tongue of every student and school-boy in this country and America, and what lives upon their lips will live and be loved forever.

We were seated over a cup of strong tea, to revive our

spirits for the evening, when our friend entered the room, accompanied by a gentleman, small in stature, and apparently seventy-five years of age, yet he appeared as active as one half that age. Feeling half drowsy from riding in the cold, and then the sudden change to a warm fire, I was rather inclined not to move on the entrance of the stranger. But the name of Thomas Dick, LL.D., roused me in a moment from my lethargy; I could scarcely believe that I was in the presence of the " Christian Philosopher." Dr. Dick is one of the men to whom the age is indebted. I never find myself in the presence of one to whom the world owes so much, without feeling a thrilling emotion, as if I were in the land of spirits. Dr. Dick had 'come to our lodgings to see and congratulate William and Ellen Craft upon their escape from the republican Christians of the United States; and as he pressed the hand of the " white slave," and bid her " welcome to British soil," I saw the silent tear stealing down the cheek of this man of genius. How I wished that the many slaveholders and pro-slavery professed Christians of America, who have read and pondered the philosophy of this man, could have been present! Thomas Dick is an abolitionist — one who is willing that the world should know that he hates the " peculiar institution." At the meeting that evening, Dr. Dick was among the most prominent. But this was not the only distinguished man who took part on that occasion.

Another great mind was on the platform, and entered

his solemn protest in a manner long to be remembered by those present. This was the Rev. George Gilfillan, well known as the author of the "Portraits of Literary Men." Mr. Gilfillan is an energetic speaker, and would have been the lion of the evening, even if many others who are more distinguished as platform orators had been present. I think it was Napoleon who said that the enthusiasm of others abated his own. At any rate, the spirit with which each speaker entered upon his duty for the evening abated my own enthusiasm for the time being. The last day of our stay in Dundee, I paid a visit, by invitation, to Dr. Dick, at his residence in the little village of Broughty Ferry. We found the great astronomer in his parlor waiting for us. From the parlor we went to the new study, and here I felt more at ease, for I went to see the philosopher in his study, and not in his drawing-room. But even this room had too much the look of nicety to be an author's *sanctum ;* and I inquired and was soon informed by Mrs. Dick, that I should have a look at the "*old study.*"

During a sojourn of eighteen months in Great Britain, I have had the good fortune to meet with several distinguished literary characters, and have always managed, while at their places of abode, to see the table and favorite chair. William and Ellen Craft were seeing what they could see through a microscope, when Mrs. Dick returned to the room, and intimated that we could now see the old literary workshop. I followed, and was soon in a room about fifteen feet square, with but one window, which óccupied one side of the room. The walls of the other three sides were lined with books, and many of these looked the very personification of age. I took my seat in the "*old arm-chair;*" and here, thought I, is the place and the seat in which this distinguished man sat while weaving the radiant wreath of renown which now, in his old age, surrounds him, and whose labors will be more appreciated by future ages than the present.

I took a farewell of the author of the "Solar System," but not until I had taken a look through the great telescope in the observatory. This instrument, through which I tried to see the heavens, was not the one invented by Galileo, but an improvement upon the original. On leaving this learned man, he shook hands with us, and bade us "God speed" in our mission; and I left the philosopher, feeling I had not passed an hour more agreeably with a literary character since the hour which I spent with the poet Montgomery a few months since. And, by-the-by, there is a resemblance between the poet and the philosopher. In becoming acquainted with great men I have become a convert to the opinion that a big nose is an almost necessary appendage to the form of a man with a giant intellect. If those whom I have seen be a criterion, such is certainly the case. But I have spun out this too long, and must close.

CHAPTER XV.

"Proud relic of the mighty dead !
    Be mine with shuddering awe to tread
        Thy roofless weedy hall,
    And mark, with fancy's kindling eye,
    The steel-clad ages, gliding by,
        Thy feudal pomp recall."

                                        KEATS.

I CLOSED my last in the ancient town of Melrose, on the banks of the Tweed, and within a stone's throw of the celebrated ruins from which the town derives its name. The valley in which Melrose is situated, and the surrounding hills, together with the monastery, have so often been made a theme for the Scottish bards, that this has become the most interesting part of Scotland. Of the many gifted writers who have taken up the pen, none have done more to bring the Eildon Hills and Melrose Abbey into note than the author of "Waverley." But who can read his writings without a regret that he should have so woven fact and fiction together that it is almost impossible to discriminate between the one and the other ?

We arrived at Melrose in the evening, and proceeded

to the chapel where our meeting was to be held, and where our friends, the Crafts, were warmly greeted. On returning from the meeting we passed close by the ruins of Melrose, and, very fortunately, it was a moonlight night. There is considerable difference of opinion among the inhabitants of the place as regards the best time to view the abbey. The author of the "Lay of the Last Minstrel" says :

> " If thou wouldst view fair Melrose aright,
> Go visit it by the pale moonlight :
> For the gay beams of lightsome day
> Gild but to flout the ruins gray."

In consequence of this admonition, I was informed that many persons remain in town to see the ruins by moonlight. Aware that the moon did not send its rays upon the old building every night in the year, I asked the keeper what he did on dark nights. He replied that he had a large lantern, which he put upon the end of a long pole, and with this he succeeded in lighting up the ruins. This good man labored hard to convince me that his invention was nearly, if not quite as good, as nature's own moon. But having no need of an application of his invention to the abbey, I had no opportunity of judging of its effect. I thought, however, that he had made a moon to some purpose, when he informed me that some nights, with his pole and lantern, he earned his four or five shillings. Not being content with a view by "moonlight alone," I was up the next morning before the sun,

and paid my respects to the abbey. I was too early for
the keeper, and he handed me the key through the window, and I entered the ruins alone. It is one labyrinth
of gigantic arches and dilapidated halls, the ivy growing
and clinging wherever it can fasten its roots, and the
whole as fine a picture of decay as imagination could
create. This was the favorite resort of Sir Walter Scott,
and furnished him much matter for the "Lay of the
Last Minstrel." He could not have selected a more fitting place for solitary thought than this ancient abode
of monks and priests. In passing through the cloisters
I could not but remark the carvings of leaves and
flowers, wrought in stone in the most exquisite manner,
looking as fresh as if they were just from the hands of
the artist. The lapse of centuries seems not to have
made any impression upon them, or changed their appearance in the least. I sat down among the ruins of the
abbey. The ground about was piled up with magnificent fragments of stone, representing various texts of
Scripture, and the quaint ideas of the priests and monks
of that age. Scene after scene swept through my fancy
as I looked upon the surrounding objects. I could
almost imagine I saw the bearded monks going from hall
to hall, and from cell to cell. In visiting these dark
cells, the mind becomes oppressed by a sense of the
utter helplessness of the victims who once passed over
the thresholds and entered these religious prisons. There
was no help or hope but in the will that ordered their
fate. How painful it is to gaze upon these walls, and to

think how many tears were shed by their inmates, when this old monastery was in its glory! I ascended to the top of the ruin by a circuitous stairway, whose stone steps were worn deep from use by many who, like myself, had visited them to gratify a curiosity. From the top of the abbey I had a splendid view of the surrounding hills and the beautiful valley through which flow the Gala Water and Tweed. This is unquestionably the most splendid specimen of Gothic architectural ruin in Scotland. But any description of mine conveys but a poor idea to the fancy. To be realized, it must be seen.

During the day, we paid a visit to Abbotsford, the splendid mansion of the late Sir Walter Scott, Bart. This beautiful seat is situated on the banks of the Tweed, just below its junction with the Gala Water. It is a dreary-looking spot, and the house from the opposite side of the river has the appearance of a small, low castle. In a single day's ride through England one may see half a dozen cottages larger than Abbotsford house. I was much disappointed in finding the premises undergoing repairs and alterations, and that all the trees between the house and the river had been cut down. This is to be regretted the more, because they were planted, nearly every one of them, by the same hand that waved its wand of enchantment over the world. The fountain had been removed from where it had been placed by the hands of the poet to the centre of the yard; and even a small stone that had been placed over the favorite dog

"Percy" had been taken up and thrown among some loose stones. One visits Abbotsford because of the genius of the man that once presided over it. Everything connected with the great poet is of interest to his admirers, and anything altered or removed tends to diminish that interest. We entered the house, and were conducted through the great hall, which is hung all round with massive armor of all descriptions, and other memorials of ancient times. The floor is of white and black marble. In passing through the hall, we entered a narrow arched room, stretching quite across the building, having a window at each end. This little or rather narrow room is filled with all kinds of armor, which is arranged with great taste. We were next shown into the dining-room, whose roof is of black oak, richly carved. In this room is a painting of the head of Queen Mary, in a charger, taken the day after the execution. Many other interesting portraits grace the walls of this room. But by far the finest apartment in the building is the drawing-room, with a lofty ceiling, and furnished with antique ebony furniture. After passing through the library, with its twenty thousand volumes, we found ourselves in the study, and I sat down in the same chair where once sat the poet: while before me was the table upon which were written the "Lady of the Lake," "Waverley," and other productions of this gifted writer. The clothes last worn by the poet were shown to us. There was the broad-skirted blue coat, with its large buttons, the plaid trousers, the heavy shoes, the black vest and white hat.

These were all in a glass case, and all looked the poet
and novelist.   But the inside of the buildings had undergone alterations, as well as the outside.   In passing
through the library, we saw a granddaughter of the poet.
She was from London, and was only on a visit of a few
days.   She looked pale and dejected, and seemed as if
she longed to leave this secluded spot and return to the
metropolis.   She looked for all the world like a hot-house
plant.   I don't think the Scotch could do better than to
purchase Abbotsford, while it has some imprint of the
great magician, and secure its preservation ; for I am sure
that, a hundred years hence, no place will be more frequently visited in Scotland than the home of the late
Sir Walter Scott.   After sauntering three hours about
the premises, I left, but not without feeling that I had
been well paid for my trouble in visiting Abbotsford.

    In the afternoon of the same day, in company with
the Crafts, I took a drive to Dryburgh Abbey.   It is a
ruin of little interest, except as being the burial-place of
Scott.   The poet lies buried in St. Mary's Aisle.   His
grave is in the left transept of the cross, and close to
where the high altar formerly stood.   Sir Walter Scott
chose his own grave, and he could not have selected a
sunnier spot if he had roamed the wide world over.   A
shaded window breaks the sun as it falls upon his grave.
The ivy is creeping and clinging wherever it can, as if it
would shelter the poet's grave from the weather.   The
author lies between his wife and eldest son, and there is
only room enough for one grave more, and the son's wife
has the choice of being buried here.

The four o'clock train took us to Hawick; and after a pleasant visit in this place, and the people registering their names against American slavery, and the Fugitive Bill in particular, we set out for Carlisle, passing through the antique town of Langholm. After leaving the latter place, we had to travel by coach. But no matter how one travels here, he travels at a more rapid rate than in America. The distance from Langholm to Carlisle, twenty miles, occupied only two and a half hours in the journey. It was a cold day, and I had to ride on the outside, as the inside had been taken up. We changed horses and took in and put out passengers with a rapidity which seems almost incredible. The road was as smooth as could be imagined.

We bid farewell to Scotland, as we reached the little town of Gretna Green. This town, being on the line between England and Scotland, is noted as the place where a little cross-eyed, red-faced blacksmith, by the name of Priestly, first set up his own altar to Hymen, and married all who came to him, without regard to rank or station, and at prices to suit all. It was worth a ride through this part of the country, if for no other purpose than to see the town where more clandestine marriages have taken place than in any other part of the world. A ride of eight or nine miles brought us in sight of the Eden, winding its way slowly through a beautiful valley, with farms on either side, covered with sheep and cattle. Four very tall chimneys, sending forth dense columns of black smoke, announced to us that we were

near Carlisle. I was really glad of this, for Ulysses
was never more tired of the shores of Ilion than I of the
top of that coach.

We remained over night at Carlisle, partaking of the
hospitality of the prince of bakers, and left the next
day for the lakes, where we had a standing invitation to
pay a visit to a distinguished literary lady. A cold ride
of about fifty miles brought us to the foot of Lake Windermere, a beautiful sheet of water, surrounded by mountains that seemed to vie with each other which should
approach nearest the sky. The margin of the lake is
carved out and built up into terrace above terrace, until
the slopes and windings are lost in the snow-capped peaks
of the mountains. It is not surprising that such men as
Southey, Coleridge, Wordsworth, and others, resorted to
this region for inspiration. After a coach ride of five
miles (passing on our journey the " Dove's Nest," home
of the late Mrs. Hemans), we were put down at the
door of the Salutation Hotel, Ambleside, and a few
minutes after found ourselves under the roof of the
authoress of " Society in America." I know not how
it is with others, but, for my own part, I always form an
opinion of the appearance of an author whose writings I
am at all familiar with, or a statesman whose speeches I
have read. I had pictured in my own mind a tall, stately-
looking lady of about sixty years, as the authoress of
" Travels in the East ; " and for once I was right, with
the single exception that I had added on too many years
by twelve. The evening was spent in talking about the

United States ; and William Craft had to go through the narrative of his escape from slavery. When I retired for the night, I found it almost impossible to sleep. The idea that I was under the roof of the authoress of " The Hour and the Man," and that I was on the banks of the sweetest lake in Great Britain, within half a mile of the residence of the late poet Wordsworth, drove sleep from my pillow. But I must leave an account of my visit to the Lakes for a future chapter.

When I look around and see the happiness here, even among the poorer classes, and that too in a country where the soil is not at all to be compared with our own, I mourn for our down-trodden countrymen, who are plundered, oppressed and made chattels of, to enable an ostentatious aristocracy to vie with each other in splendid extravagance.

CHAPTER XVI.

"Why weeps the Muse for England? What appears
In England's case to move the Muse to tears?
From side to side of her delightful isle
Is she not clothed with a perpetual smile?
Can nature add a charm, or art confer
A new-found luxury, not seen in her?"
                                        COWPER.

MY last left me under the hospitable roof of Harriet
Martineau. I had long had an invitation to visit this
distinguished friend of our race, and as the invitation
was renewed during my tour through the north, I did
not feel disposed to decline it, and thereby lose so favorable an opportunity of meeting with one who had written so much in behalf of the oppressed of our land.
About a mile from the head of Lake Windermere, and
immediately under Wonsfell, and encircled by mountains
on all sides except the south-west, lies the picturesque
little town of Ambleside; and the brightest spot in the
place is "The Knoll," the residence of Miss Martineau.

We reached "The Knoll" a little after night-fall,
and a cordial shake of the hand by Miss M., who was
waiting for us, trumpet in hand, soon assured us that we
had met with a warm friend.

It is not my intention to lay open the scenes of domestic life at "The Knoll," nor to describe the social parties of which my friends and I were partakers during our sojourn within the hospitable walls of this distinguished writer; but the name of Miss M. is so intimately connected with the Anti-slavery movement by her early writings, and those have been so much admired by the friends of the slave in the United States, that I deem it not at all out of place for me to give my readers some idea of the authoress of "Political Economy," "Travels in the East," "The Hour and the Man," &c.

The dwelling is a cottage of moderate size, built after Miss M.'s own plan, upon a rise of land, from which it derives the name of "The Knoll." The library is the largest room in the building, and upon the walls of it were hung some beautiful engravings and a continental map. On a long table, which occupied the centre of the room, were the busts of Shakspeare, Newton, Milton, and a few other literary characters of the past. One side of the room was taken up with a large case, filled with a choice collection of books; and everything indicated that it was the home of genius and of taste.

The room usually occupied by Miss M., and where we found her on the evening of our arrival, is rather small, and lighted by two large windows. The walls of this room were also decorated with prints and pictures, and on the mantel-shelf were some models in terra cotta of Italian groups. On a circular table lay casts, medallions, and some very choice water-color drawings. Under the south window stood a small table covered with newly-opened letters, a portfolio, and several new books, with here and there a page turned down, and one with a paper-knife between its leaves, as if it had only been half read. I took up the last-mentioned, and it proved to be the "Life and Poetry of Hartley Coleridge," son of S. T. Coleridge. It was just from the press, and had, a day or two before, been forwarded to her by the publisher. Miss M. is very deaf, and always carries in her left hand a trumpet; and I was not a little surprised on learning from her that she had never enjoyed the sense of smell, and only on one occasion the sense of taste, and that for a single moment. Miss M. is loved with a sort of idolatry by the people of Ambleside, and especially the poor, to whom she gives a course of lectures every winter gratuitously. She finished her last course the day before our arrival. She was much pleased with Ellen Craft, and appeared delighted with the story of herself and husband's escape from slavery, as related by the latter, during the recital of which I several times saw the silent tear stealing down her cheek, and which she tried in vain to hide from us.

When Craft had finished, she exclaimed, " I would that every woman in the British empire could hear that tale as I have, so that they might know how their own sex was treated in that boasted land of liberty." It seems strange to the people of this country, that one so white and so ladylike as Mrs. Craft should have been a slave, and forced to leave the land of her nativity and seek an asylum in a foreign country.

The morning after our arrival I took a stroll by a circuitous pathway to the top of Loughrigg Fell. At the foot of the mount I met a peasant, who very kindly offered to lend me his donkey, upon which to ascend the mountain. Never having been upon the back of one of these long-eared animals, I felt some hesitation about trusting myself upon so diminutive looking a creature. But, being assured that if I would only resign myself to his care, and let him have his own way, I would be perfectly safe, I mounted, and off we set. We had, however, scarcely gone fifty rods, when, in passing over a narrow part of the path and overlooking a deep chasm, one of the hind feet of the donkey slipped, and with an involuntary shudder I shut my eyes to meet my expected doom; but, fortunately, the little fellow gained his foothold, and in all probability saved us both from a premature death. After we had passed over this dangerous place I dismounted; and, as soon as my feet had once more gained terra firma, I resolved that I would never again yield my own judgment to that of any one, not even to a donkey.

It seems as if nature had amused herself in throwing these mountains together. From the top of Loughrigg Fell the eye loses its power in gazing upon the objects below. On our left lay Rydal Mount, the beautiful seat of the late poet Wordsworth; while to the right, and away in the dim distance, almost hidden by the native trees, was the cottage where once resided Mrs. Hemans. And below us lay Windermere, looking more like a river than a lake, and which, if placed by the side of our own Ontario, Erie or Huron, would be lost in the fog. But here it looks beautiful in the extreme, surrounded as it is by a range of mountains that have no parallel in the United States for beauty. Amid a sun of uncommon splendor, dazzling the eye with the reflection upon the water below, we descended into the valley, and I was soon again seated by the fireside of our hospitable hostess. In the afternoon of the same day we took a drive to the " Dove's Nest," the home of the late Mrs. Hemans.

We did not see the inside of the house, on account of its being occupied by a very eccentric man, who will not permit a woman to enter the house; and it is said that he has been known to run when a female had unconsciously intruded herself upon his premises. As our company was in part composed of ladies, we had to share their fate, and therefore were prevented from seeing the interior of the " Dove's Nest." The exhibitor of such a man would be almost sure of a prize at the Great Exhibition.

At the head of Grassmere Lake, and surrounded by a few cottages, stands an old, gray, antique-looking parish church, venerable with the lapse of centuries, and the walls partly covered with ivy, and in the rear of which is the parish burial-ground. After leaving the " Dove's Nest," and having a pleasant ride over the hills and between the mountains, and just as the sun was disappear-

ing behind them, we arrived at the gate of Grassmere
Church; and, alighting and following Miss M., we soon
found ourselves standing over a grave, marked by a single stone, and that, too, very plain, with a name deeply
cut. This announced to us that we were standing over
the grave of William Wordsworth. He chose his own
grave, and often visited the spot before his death. He
lies in the most sequestered spot in the whole grounds;
and the simplicity and beauty of the place were enough to
make one in love with it, to be laid so far from the bustle
of the world, and in so sweet a place. The more one
becomes acquainted with the literature of the Old World,
the more he must love her poets. Among the teachers
of men, none are more worthy of study than the poets;
and, as teachers, they should receive far more credit than
is yielded to them. No one can look back upon the lives
of Dante, Shakspeare, Milton, Goethe, Cowper, and
many others that we might name, without being reminded
of the sacrifices which they made for mankind, and which
were not appreciated until long after their deaths. We
need look no further than our own country to find men
and women wielding the pen practically and powerfully
for the right. It is acknowledged on all hands, in this
country, that England has the greatest dead poets, and
America the greatest living ones. The poet and the true
Christian have alike a hidden life. Worship is the vital
element of each. Poetry has in it that kind of utility
which good men find in their Bible, rather than such
convenience as bad men often profess to draw from it.

It ennobles the sentiments, enlarges the affections, kindles the imagination, and gives to us the enjoyment of a life in the past, and in the future, as well as in the present. Under its light and warmth, we wake from our torpidity and coldness, to a sense of our capabilities. This impulse once given, a great object is gained. Schiller has truly said, "Poetry can be to a man what love is to a hero. It can neither counsel him, nor smite him, nor perform any labor for him; but it can bring him up to be a hero, can summon him to deeds, and arm him with strength for all he ought to be." I have often read with pleasure the sweet poetry of our own Whitfield, of Buffalo, which has appeared from time to time in the columns of the newspapers. I have always felt ashamed of the fact that he should be compelled to wield the razor instead of the pen for a living. Meaner poets than James M. Whitfield are now living by their compositions; and were he a white man he would occupy a different position.

Near the grave of Wordsworth is that of Hartley Coleridge. This name must be lifted up as a beacon, with all its pleasant and interesting associations; it must be added to the list in which some names of brighter fame are written — Burns, Byron, Campbell, and others their compeers. They had all the rich endowment of genius, and might, in achieving fame for themselves, have gained glory for God, and great good for man. But they looked "upon the wine when it was red," and gave life and fame, and their precious gifts, and God's blessing, for its false and ruinous joys. We would not drag forth their names that we may gloat over their infirmities. We pity them for their sad fall. We acknowledge the strength of their temptations, and, walking backwards, would throw a mantle over their frailties. But these men are needed, also, as warnings. The moral world must have its light-houses. Thousands of young men are running down upon the same rocks on which they were cast away. If the light of their genius has made them conspicuous, let us then use their conspicuity, and throw a ray from them, as from a beacon, far out upon the dim and perilous sea.

Hartley Coleridge was the eldest son of Samuel Taylor Coleridge, poet and metaphysician. He had some of his father's gifts, particularly his captivating conversational power, and his propensity for novel and profound speculation. He had also his father's infirmity of purpose. In the case of the son, the reason, as the world is now informed in a biography written by his brother, was that he early became the slave of intemperate habits, from which no aspirations of his own heart, no struggles with the enslaving appetite, and no efforts of sympathizing and sorrowful friends, could ever deliver him. He gained a fellowship in Oriel College, Oxford, and forfeited it in consequence of these habits. He then cast himself, as a literary adventurer, into the wild vortex of London life; failed sadly in all his projects; drank deep of the treacherous wine-cup, often to his own shame and the chagrin of his friends, from whom he would sometimes hide himself in places where restraint was unknown and shame forgotten, that he might be delivered from their reproachful pity. In the end, he betook himself to a cottage near Grassmere, and where, on the 6th of January, 1849, he died, not, we trust, without penitence and faith in the Redeemer of guilty and wretched men.

Hartley Coleridge tells us, in one of his confessions, that his first resort to wine was for the purpose of seeking relief from the sting of defeated ambition. This temptation was necessarily brief in its duration; for time would gradually extract this sting from his sensitive mind and heart. This, therefore, was not the doorway of the path which led him down to the gulf. The " wine parties " of Oxford were the scenes in which Hartley Coleridge was betrayed and lost. We have but a momentary glimpse of these things in the biography; but that glimpse is sufficient. It reveals to us what in popular language is called a gay scene, but which to us, and in reality, is sombre as death. In the midst of it there sits a bright-eyed, enthusiastic, impetuous young man, heated with repeated draughts of wine, urged by his fellow-revellers to drink deeper, yielding readily to their solicitations, and pouring forth all the while a stream of continuous and sparkling discourse, which fascinated his companions by its wit, its facility and its beauty. Alas! how many of those companions, it may be, are with him in graves where men can only weep and be silent!

It has often been said, and with much truth, that there is no more dangerous gift for a young man than

to be able to sing a good song. It is equally dangerous,
we think, to be known as a good talker. The gift of
rapid, brilliant, mirth-moving speech, is a perilous possession. The dullards, for whose amusement this gift is
so often invoked, know well that to ply its possessor
with wine is the readiest way to bring out its power.
But in the end the wine destroys the intellect, and the
man of wit degenerates into a buffoon, and dies a drunkard. Such is the brief life and history of many a young
man, who, behind the stained-glass windows of the
fashionable *restaurant*, or in the mirrored and cushioned
rooms of the club-house, was hailed as the " prince of
good fellows," and the rarest of wits. The laughing
applauders pass on, each in his own way, and he who
made them sport is left to struggle in solitude with the
enemy they have helped to fasten upon him. Let every
young man who longs for these gifts, and envies their
possessors, remember " poor Hartley Coleridge." Let
them be warned by the fate of one who was caught in
the toils they are weaving around themselves, and perished therein, leaving behind him the record of a life of
unfulfilled purposes, and of great departures from the
path of duty and peace.

After remaining a short time, and reading the epitaphs
of the departed, we again returned to "The Knoll."
Nothing can be more imposing than the beauty of English park scenery, and especially in the vicinity of the
Lakes. Magnificent lawns that extend like sheets of
vivid green, with here and there a sprinkling of fine

trees, heaping up rich piles of foliage, and then the forest with the hare, the deer, and the rabbit, "bounding away to the covert, or the pheasant suddenly bursting upon the wing — the artificial stream, the brook taught to wind in natural meanderings, or expand into the glassy lake, with the yellow leaf sleeping upon its bright waters, and occasionally a rustic temple or sylvan statue grown green and dark with age," give an air of sanctity and picturesque beauty to English scenery that is unknown in the United States. The very laborer with his thatched cottage and narrow slip of ground-plot before the door, the little flower-bed, the woodbine trimmed against the wall, and hanging its blossoms about the windows, and the peasant seen trudging home at nightfall with the avails of the toil of the day upon his back — all this tells us of the happiness both of rich and poor in this country. And yet there are those who would have the world believe that the laborer of England is in a far worse condition than the slaves of America. Such persons know nothing of the real condition of the working classes of this country. At any rate, the poor here, as well as the rich, are upon a level, as far as the laws of the country are concerned. The more one becomes acquainted with the English people, the more one has to admire them. They are so different from the people of our own country. Hospitality, frankness and good humor, are always to be found in an Englishman. After a ramble of three days about the Lakes, we mounted the coach, bidding Miss Martineau farewell, and quitted the lake district.

CHAPTER XVII.

"And there are dresses splendid but fantastical,
  Masks of all times and nations, Turks and Jews,
And Harlequins and Clowns with feats gymnastical ;
  Greeks, Romans, Yankee-doodles, and Hindoos."

PRESUMING that you will expect from me some account of the great World's Fair, I take my pen to give you my own impressions, although I am afraid that anything which I may say about this "lion of the day" will fall far short of a description. On Monday last, I quitted my lodgings at an early hour, and started for the Crystal Palace. The day was fine, such as we seldom experience in London, with a clear sky, and invigorating air, whose vitality was as rousing to the spirits as a blast from the "horn of Astolpho." Although it was not yet ten o'clock when I entered Piccadilly, every omnibus was full, inside and out, and the street was lined with one living stream, as far as the eye could reach, all wending their way to the "Glass House." No metropolis in the world presents such facilities as London for the reception of the Great Exhibition now collected within its walls. Throughout its myriads of veins the stream of industry and toil pulses with sleepless energy. Every one seems to feel that this great capital of the world is the fittest place wherein they might offer homage to the dignity of toil. I had already begun to feel fatigued by my pedestrian excursions as I passed "Apsley House," the residence of the Duke of Wellington, and emerged into Hyde Park.

I had hoped that on getting into the Park I would be out of the crowd that seemed to press so heavily in the street. But in this I was mistaken. I here found myself surrounded by and moving with an overwhelming mass, such as I had never before witnessed. And, away in the distance, I beheld a dense crowd, and above every other object was seen the lofty summit of the Crystal Palace. The drive in the Park was lined with princely-looking vehicles of every description. The drivers in their bright red and gold uniforms, the pages and footmen in their blue trousers and white silk stockings, and the horses dressed up in their neat, silver-mounted harness, made the scene altogether one of great splendor. I was soon at the door, paid my shilling, and entered the building at the south end of the transept. For the first ten or twenty minutes, I was so lost in astonishment, and absorbed in pleasing wonder, that I could do nothing but gaze up and down the vista of the noble building. The Crystal Palace resembles in some respects the interior of the cathedrals of this country. One long avenue from east to west is intercepted by a transept, which divides the building into two nearly equal parts. This is the greatest building the world ever saw, before which the Pyramids of Egypt, and the Colossus of Rhodes must hide their diminished heads. The palace was not full at any time during the day, there being only sixty-four thousand persons present. Those who love to study the human countenance in all its infinite varieties can find ample scope for the indulgence of their taste, by a visit to the World's Fair. All countries are there represented — Europeans, Asiatics, Americans and Africans, with their numerous subdivisions. Even the exclusive Chinese, with his hair braided, and hanging down his back, has left the land of his nativity, and is seen making long strides through the Crystal Palace, in his wooden-bottomed shoes. Of all places of curious costumes and different fashions, none has ever yet presented such a variety as this Exhibition. No dress is too absurd to be worn in this place.

There is a great deal of freedom in the Exhibition. The servant who walks behind his mistress through the Park feels that he can crowd against her in the Exhibition. The queen and the day laborer, the prince and the merchant, the peer and the pauper, the Celt and the Saxon, the Greek and the Frank, the Hebrew and the Russ, all meet here upon terms of perfect equality. This amalgamation of rank, this kindly blending of interests, and forgetfulness of the cold formalities of ranks and grades, cannot but be attended with the very best results. I was pleased to see such a goodly sprinkling of my own countrymen in the Exhibition — I mean colored men and women — well-dressed, and moving about with their fairer brethren. This, some of our pro-slavery Americans did not seem to relish very well. There was no help for it. As I walked through the American part of the Crystal Palace some of our Virginia neighbors eyed me closely and with jealous looks, especially as an English lady was leaning on my arm. But their sneering looks did not disturb me in the least. I remained the longer in their department, and criticized the bad appearance of their goods the more. Indeed, the Americans, as far as appearance goes, are behind every other country in the Exhibition. The "Greek Slave" is the only production of art which the United States has sent. And it would have been more to their credit had they kept that at home. In so vast a place as the Great Exhibition one scarcely knows what to visit first, or what to look upon last. After wandering about through the building for five hours, I sat down in one of the galleries and looked at the fine marble statue of Virginius, with the knife in his hand and about to take the life of his beloved and beautiful daughter, to save her from the hands of Appius Claudius. The admirer of genius will linger for hours among the great variety of statues in the long avenue. Large statues of Lords Eldon and Stowell, carved out of solid marble, each weighing above twenty tons, are among the most gigantic in the building.

I was sitting with my four hundred paged guide-book before me, and looking down upon the moving mass, when my attention was called to a small group of gentlemen standing near the statue of Shakspeare, one of whom wore a white coat and hat, and had flaxen hair, and trousers rather short in the legs. The lady by my side, and who had called my attention to the group, asked if I could tell what country this odd-looking gentleman was from. Not wishing to run the risk of a mistake, I was about declining to venture an opinion, when the reflection of the sun against a mirror, on the opposite side, threw a brilliant light upon the group, and especially on the face of the gentleman in the white coat, and I immediately recognized under the brim of the white hat the features of Horace Greeley, Esq., of the New York *Tribune*. His general appearance was as much out of the English style as that of the Turk whom I had seen but a moment before, in his bag-like trousers, shuffling along in his slippers. But oddness in dress is one of the characteristics of the Great Exhibition.

Among the many things in the Crystal Palace, there are some which receive greater attention than others, around which may always be seen large groups of the visitors. The first of these is the Koh-i-noor, the " Mountain of Light." This is the largest and most valuable diamond in the world, said to be worth two million pounds sterling. It is indeed a great source of attraction to those who go to the Exhibition for the first time, but it is doubtful whether it obtains such admiration afterwards. We saw more than one spectator turn away with the idea that, after all, it was only a piece of glass.

After some jamming, I got a look at the precious jewel; and although in a brass-grated cage, strong enough to hold a lion, I found it to be no larger than the third of a hen's egg. Two policemen remain by its side day and night.

The finest thing in the Exhibition is the "Veiled Vestal," a statue of a woman carved in marble, with a veil over her face, and so neatly done that it looks as if it had been thrown over after it was finished. The Exhibition presents many things which appeal to the eye and touch the heart, and altogether it is so decorated and furnished as to excite the dullest mind, and satisfy the most fastidious.

England has contributed the most useful and substantial articles; France, the most beautiful; while Russia, Turkey and the West Indies, seem to vie with each other in richness. China and Persia are not behind. Austria has also contributed a rich and beautiful stock. Sweden, Norway, Denmark, and the smaller states of Europe, have all tried to outdo themselves in sending goods to the World's Fair. In machinery, England has no competitor. In art, France is almost alone in the Exhibition, setting aside England.

In natural productions and provisions, America stands alone in her glory. There lies her pile of canvassed hams; whether they were wood or real, we could not tell. There are her barrels of salt beef and pork, her beautiful white lard, her Indian-corn and corn-meal, her rice and tobacco, her beef-tongues, dried peas, and a few bags of cotton. The contributors from the United States seemed to have forgotten that this was an exhibition of art, or they most certainly would not have sent provisions. But the United States takes the lead in the contributions, as no other country has sent in provisions. The finest thing contributed by our countrymen is a large piece of silk with an eagle painted upon it, surrounded by stars and stripes.

After remaining more than five hours in the great temple, I turned my back upon the richly-laden stalls, and left the Crystal Palace. On my return home I was more fortunate than in the morning, inasmuch as I found a seat for my friend and myself in an omnibus. And even my ride in the close omnibus was not without interest. For I had scarcely taken my seat, when my friend, who was seated opposite me, with looks and gesture informed me that we were in the presence of some distinguished person. I eyed the countenances of the different persons, but in vain, to see if I could find any one who by his appearance showed signs of superiority over his fellow-passengers. I had given up the hope of selecting the person of note, when another look from my friend directed my attention to a gentleman seated in the corner of the omnibus. He was a tall man, with strongly-marked features, hair dark and coarse. There was a slight stoop of the shoulder — that bend which is almost always a characteristic of studious men. But he wore upon his countenance a forbidding and disdainful frown, that seemed to tell one that he thought himself better than those about him. His dress did not indicate a man of high rank; and had we been in America, I would have taken him for an Ohio farmer.

While I was scanning the features and general appearance of the gentleman, the omnibus stopped and put down three or four of the passengers, which gave me an opportunity of getting a seat by the side of my friend, who, in a low whisper, informed me that the gentleman whom I had been eying so closely was no less a person than Thomas Carlyle. I had read his "Hero-worship," and "Past and Present," and had formed a high opinion of his literary abilities. But his recent attack upon the emancipated people of the West Indies, and his laborious article in favor of the reëstablishment of the lash and slavery, had created in my mind a dislike for the man, and I almost regretted that we were in the same omnibus. In some things Mr. Carlyle is right: but in many he is entirely wrong. As a writer, Mr. Carlyle is often monotonous and extravagant. He does not exhibit a new view of nature, or raise insignificant objects into importance; but generally takes commonplace thoughts and events, and tries to express them in stronger and statelier language than others. He holds no communion with his kind, but stands alone, without mate or fellow. He is like a solitary peak, all access to which is cut off. He exists not by sympathy, but by antipathy. Mr. Carlyle seems chiefly to try how he shall display his own powers, and astonish mankind, by starting new trains of speculation, or by expressing old ones

so as not to be understood. He cares little what he
says, so as he can say it differently from others. To
read his works, is one thing ; to understand them, is another. If any one thinks that I exaggerate, let him sit
for an hour over " Sartor Resartus," and if he does not
rise from its pages, place his three or four dictionaries on
the shelf, and say I am right, I promise never again to
say a word against Thomas Carlyle. He writes one
page in favor of reform, and ten against it. He would
hang all prisoners to get rid of them ; yet the inmates of
the prisons and " workhouses are better off than the
poor." His heart is with the poor; yet the blacks of
the West Indies should be taught that if they will not
raise sugar and cotton by their own free will, " Quashy
should have the whip applied to him." He frowns upon
the reformatory speakers upon the boards of Exeter Hall ;
yet he is the prince of reformers. He hates heroes and
assassins; yet Cromwell was an angel, and Charlotte
Corday a saint. He scorns everything, and seems to be
tired of what he is by nature, and tries to be what he is
not.

CHAPTER XVIII.

" The time shall come, when, free as seas or wind,
  Unbounded Thames shall flow for all mankind
  Whole nations enter with each swelling tide,
  And seas but join the regions they divide ;
  Earth's distant ends our glories shall behold,
  And the New World launch forth to meet the Old."

POPE.

THE past six weeks have been of a stirring nature in this great metropolis. It commenced with the Peace Congress, the proceedings of which have long since reached you. And although that event has passed off, it may not be out of place here to venture a remark or two upon its deliberations.

A meeting upon the subject of peace, with the support of the monied and influential men who rally around the peace standard, could scarcely have been held in Exeter Hall without creating some sensation. From all parts of the world flocked delegates to this practical protest against war. And among those who took part in the proceedings were many men whose names alone would, even on ordinary occasions, have filled the great hall. The speakers were chosen from among the representatives of the various countries, without regard to dialect or complexion; and the only fault which seemed to be found with the committee's arrangement was, that in their desire to get foreigners and Londoners, they forgot the country delegates, so that none of the large provincial towns were at all represented in the Congress, so far as speaking was concerned. Manchester, Leeds, Newcastle, and all the important towns in Scotland and Ireland, were silenced in the great meeting. I need not say that this was an oversight of the committee, and one, too, that has done some injury. Such men as the able chairman of the late Anti-Corn-Law League cannot be forgotten in such a meeting, without giving offence to those who sent him, especially when the committee brought forward, day after day, the same speakers, chosen from amongst the metropolitan delegation. However, the meeting was a glorious one, and will long be remembered with delight as a step onward in the cause of peace. Burritt's Brotherhood Bazaar followed close upon the heels of the Peace Congress; and this had scarcely closed, when that ever-memorable meeting of the American fugitive slaves took place in the Hall of Commerce.

The temperance people made the next reformatory move. This meeting took place in Exeter Hall, and was made up of delegates from the various towns in the kingdom. They had come from the North, East, West and South. There was the quick-spoken son of the Emerald Isle, with his pledge suspended from his neck; there, too, the Scot, speaking his broad dialect; also the representatives from the provincial towns of England and Wales, who seemed to speak anything but good English.

The day after the meeting had closed in Exeter Hall, the country societies, together with those of the metropolis, assembled in Hyde Park, and then walked to the Crystal Palace. Their number while going to the Exhibition was variously estimated at from fifteen thousand to twenty thousand, and was said to have been the largest gathering of teetotallers ever assembled in London. They consisted chiefly of the working classes, their wives and children — clean, well-dressed and apparently happy: their looks indicating in every way those orderly habits which, beyond question, distinguish the devotees of that cause above the common laborers of this country. On arriving at the Exhibition, they soon distributed themselves among the departments, to revel in its various wonders, eating their own lunch, and drinking from the Crystal Fountain.

And, now I am at the world's wonder, I will remain here until I finish this sheet. I have spent fifteen days in the Exhibition, and have conversed with those who have spent double that number amongst its beauties, and the general opinion appears to be that six months would not be too long to remain within its walls to enable one to examine its laden stalls. Many persons make the Crystal Palace their home, with the exception of night. I have seen them come in the morning, visit the dressing-room, then go to the refreshment-room, and sit down

to breakfast as if they been at their hotel.   Dinner and
tea would be taken in turn.

The Crystal Fountain is the great place of meeting in
the Exhibition.   There you may see husbands looking for
lost wives, wives for stolen husbands, mothers for their
lost children, and towns-people for their country friends;
and, unless you have an appointment at a certain place at
an hour, you might as well prowl through the streets of
London to find a friend as in the Great Exhibition.
There is great beauty in the "Glass House."   Here, in
the transept, with the glorious sunlight coming through
that wonderful glass roof, may the taste be cultivated
and improved, the mind edified, and the feelings chas-
tened.   Here, surrounded by noble creations in marble
and bronze, and in the midst of an admiring throng, one
may gaze at statuary which might fitly decorate the
house of the proudest prince in Christendom.

He who takes his station in the gallery, at either end,
and looks upon that wondrous nave, or who surveys the
matchless panorama around him from the intersection
of the nave and transept, may be said, without presump-
tion or exaggeration, to see all the kingdoms of this
world and the glory of them.   He sees not only a greater
collection of fine articles, but also a greater as well as
more various assemblage of the human race, than ever
before was gathered under one roof.

One of the beauties of this great international gathering is, that it is not confined to rank or grade.   The
million toilers from mine, and factory, and workshop,

and loom, and office, and field, share with their more wealthy neighbors the feast of reason and imagination spread out in the Crystal Palace.

It is strange, indeed, to see so many nations assembled and represented on one spot of British ground.   In short, it is one great theatre, with thousands of performers, each playing his own part.   England is there, with her mighty engines toiling and whirring, indefatigable in her enterprises to shorten labor.   India spreads her glitter and paint.   France, refined and fastidious, is there every day, giving the last touch to her picturesque group; and the other countries, each in its turn doing what it can to show off.   The distant hum of thousands of good-humored people, with occasionally a national anthem from some gigantic organ, together with the noise of the machinery, seems to send life into every part of the Crystal Palace.

When you get tired of walking you can sit down and write your impressions, and there is the "post" to receive your letter; or, if it be Friday or Saturday, you may, if you choose, rest yourself by hearing a lecture from Professor Anstead; and then, before leaving, take your last look, and see something that you have not before seen.   Everything which is old in cities, new in colonial life, splendid in courts, useful in industry, beautiful in nature, or ingenious in invention, is there represented.   In one place we have the Bible translated into one hundred and fifty languages; in another, we have saints and archbishops painted on glass; in another, old palaces, and the altars of a John Knox, a Baxter, or some other divines of olden time. In the old Temple of Delphi we read that every state of the civilized world had its separate treasury, where Herodotus, born two thousand years before his time, saw and observed all kinds of prodigies in gold and silver, brass and iron, and even in linen. The nations all met there on one common ground, and the peace of the earth was not a little promoted by their common interest in the sanctity and splendor of that shrine. As long as the Exhibition lasts, and its memory endures, we hope and trust that it may shed the same influence. With this hasty scrap I take leave of the Great Exhibition.

CHAPTER XIX.

" And gray walls moulder round, on which dull time
   Feeds, like slow fire upon a hoary brand ;
And one keen pyramid, with wedge sublime,
   Stands o'er the dust of him who planned."

SHELLEY.

I HAVE just finished a short visit to the far-famed city of Oxford, which has not unaptly been styled the City of Palaces. Aside from this being one of the principal seats of learning in the world, it is distinguished alike for its religious and political changes in times past. At one time it was the seat of Popery; at another, the uncompromising enemy of Rome. Here the tyrant Richard the Third held his court; and when James the First and his son Charles the First found their capital too hot to hold them, they removed to their loyal city of Oxford. The writings of the great republicans were here committed to the flames. At one time Popery sent Protestants to the stake and fagot; at another, a Papist king found no favor with the people. A noble monument now stands where Cranmer, Ridley and Latimer, proclaimed their sentiments and faith, and sealed them with their blood. And now we read upon the town treasurer's book — "For three loads of wood, one load of fagots, one post, two chains and staples, to burn Ridley and Latimer, £1 5s. 1d." Such is the information one gets by looking over the records of books written three centuries ago.

It was a beautiful day on which I arrived at Oxford, and, instead of remaining in my hotel, I sallied forth to take a survey of the beauties of the city. I strolled into Christ Church Meadows, and there spent the evening in viewing the numerous halls of learning which surround that splendid promenade. And fine old buildings they are: centuries have rolled over many of them, hallowing the old walls, and making them gray with age. They have been for ages the chosen homes of piety and philosophy. Heroes and scholars have gone forth from their studies here into the great field of the world, to seek their fortunes, and to conquer and be conquered. As I surveyed the exterior of the different colleges, I could here and there see the reflection of the light from the window of some student, who was busy at his studies, or throwing away his time over some trashy novel, too many of which find their way into the trunks or carpet-bags of the young men on setting out for college. As I looked upon the walls of these buildings I thought, as the rough stone is taken from the quarry to the finisher, there to be made into an ornament, so was the young mind brought here to be cultivated and developed. Many a poor, unobtrusive young man, with the appearance of little or no ability, is here moulded into a hero, a scholar, a tyrant, or a friend of humanity. I never look upon these monuments of education without a feeling of regret that so few of our own race can find a place within their walls. And, this being the fact, I see more and more the need of our people being encouraged to turn their attention more seriously to self-education, and thus to take a respectable position before the world, by virtue of their own cultivated minds and moral standing.

Education, though obtained by a little at a time, and that, too, over the midnight lamp, will place its owner in a position to be respected by all, even though he be black. I know that the obstacles which the laws of the land and of society place between the colored man and education in the United States are very great, yet if *one* can break through these barriers more can; and if our people would only place the right appreciation upon education, they would find these obstacles are easier to be overcome than at first sight appears. A young man once asked Carlyle what was the secret of success. His reply was, "Energy; whatever you undertake, do it with all your might." Had it not been for the possession of energy, I might now have been working as a servant for some brainless fellow who might be able to command my labor with his money, or I might have been yet toiling in chains and slavery. But thanks to energy, not only for my being to-day in a land of freedom, but also for my dear girls being in one of the best seminaries in France, instead of being in an American school, where the finger of scorn would be pointed at them by those whose superiority rests entirely upon their having a whiter skin.

Oxford is, indeed, one of the finest located places in the kingdom, and every inch of ground about it seems hallowed by interesting associations. The university, founded by the good King Alfred, still throws its shadow upon the side-walk ; and the lapse of ten centuries seems to have made but little impression upon it. Other seats of learning may be entitled to our admiration, but Oxford claims our veneration. Although the lateness of the night compelled me, yet I felt an unwillingness to tear myself from the scene of such surpassing interest. Few places in any country as noted as Oxford is are without some distinguished person residing within their precincts ; and, knowing that the city of palaces was not an exception to this rule, I resolved to see some of its lions. Here, of course, is the head-quarters of the Bishop of Oxford, a son of the late William Wilberforce, Africa's noble champion. I should have been glad to have seen this distinguished pillar of the church ; but I soon learned that the bishop's residence was out of town, and that he seldom visited the city, except on business. I then determined to see one who, although a lesser dignitary in the church, is, nevertheless, scarcely less known than the Bishop of Oxford. This was the Rev. Dr. Pusey, a divine whose name is known wherever the religion of Jesus is known and taught, and the acknowledged head of the Puseyites. On the second morning of my visit I proceeded to Christ Church Chapel, where the reverend gentleman officiates. Fortunately I had an opportunity of seeing the doctor, and following close in his footsteps to the church. His personal appearance is anything but that of one who is the leader of a growing and powerful party in the church. He is rather under the middle size, and is round-shouldered, or rather stoops. His profile is more striking than his front face, the nose being very large and prominent. As a matter of course, I expected to see a large nose, for all great men have them. He has a thoughtful and somewhat sullen brow, a firm and somewhat pensive mouth, a cheek pale, thin, and deeply furrowed. A monk fresh from the cloisters of Tinterran Abbey, in its proudest days, could scarcely have made a more ascetic and solemn appearance than did Dr. Pusey on this occasion. He is not apparently above forty-five, or, at most, fifty years of age, and his whole aspect renders him an admirable study for an artist. Dr. Pusey's style of preaching is cold and tame, and one looking at him would scarcely believe that such an apparently uninteresting man could cause such an eruption in the church as he has. I was glad to find that a colored young man was among the students at Oxford.

A few months since, I paid a visit to our countryman, Alexander Crummel, who is still pursuing his studies at Cambridge,— a place which, though inferior to Oxford as far as appearance is concerned, is yet said to be greatly its superior as a place of learning. In an hour's walk through the Strand, Regent-street or Piccadilly, in London, one may meet half a dozen colored men, who are inmates of the various colleges in the metropolis. These are all signs of progress in the cause of the sons of Africa. Then let our people take courage, and with that courage let them apply themselves to learning. A determination to excel is the sure road to greatness, and that is as open to the black man as the white. It is that which has accomplished the mightiest and noblest triumphs in the intellectual and physical world. It is that which has made such rapid strides towards civilization, and broken the chains of ignorance and superstition which have so long fettered the human intellect. It was determination which raised so many worthy individuals from the humble walks of society, and from poverty, and placed them in positions of trust and renown. It is no slight barrier that can effectually oppose the determination of the will; — success must ultimately crown its efforts. " The world shall hear of me," was the exclamation of one whose name has become as familiar as household words. A Toussaint once labored in the sugar-field with his spelling-book in his pocket, amid the combined efforts of a nation to keep him in ignorance. His name is now recorded among the list of statesmen of the past. A Soulouque was once a slave, and knew not how to read. He now sits upon the throne of an empire.

In our own country there are men who once held the plough, and that too without any compensation, who are now presiding at the editor's table. It was determination that brought out the genius of a Franklin, and a

Fulton, and that has distinguished many of the American statesmen, who, but for their energy and determination, would never have had a name beyond the precincts of their own homes.

It is not always those who have the best advantages, or the greatest talents, that eventually succeed in their undertakings: but it is those who strive with untiring diligence to remove all obstacles to success, and who, with unconquerable resolution, labor on until the rich reward of perseverance is within their grasp. Then again let me say to our young men, Take courage. "There is a good time coming." The darkness of the night appears greatest just before the dawn of day.

CHAPTER XX.

" Blush ye not
To boast your equal laws, your just restraints,
Your rights defined, your liberties secured ;
Whilst, with an iron hand, ye crush to earth
The helpless African, and bid him drink
That cup of sorrow which yourselves have dashed,
Indignant, from Oppression's fainting grasp ? "

WILLIAM ROSCOE.

THE love of freedom is one of those natural impulses of the human breast which cannot be extinguished. Even the brute animals of the creation feel and show sorrow and affection when deprived of their liberty. Therefore is a distinguished writer justified in saying, "Man is free, even were he born in chains." The Americans boast, and justly too, that Washington was the hero and model patriot of the American Revolution,— the man whose fame, unequalled in his own day and country, will descend to the end of time, the pride and honor of humanity. The American speaks with pride of the battles of Lexington and Bunker Hill ; and, when standing in Faneuil Hall, he points to the portraits of Otis, Adams, Hancock, Quincy, Warren and Franklin, and tells you that their names will go down to posterity among the world's most devoted and patriotic friends of human liberty.

It was on the first of August, 1851, that a number of men, fugitives from that boasted land of freedom, assembled at the Hall of Commerce in the city of London, for the purpose of laying their wrongs before the British nation, and, at the same time, to give thanks to the God of freedom for the liberation of their West India brethren on the first of August, 1834. Little notice had been given of the intended meeting, yet it seemed to be known in all parts of the city. At the hour of half-past seven, for which the meeting had been called, the spacious hall was well filled, and the fugitives, followed by some of the most noted English Abolitionists, entered the hall, amid the most deafening applause, and took their seats on the platform. The appearance of the great hall at this juncture was most splendid. Besides the committee of fugitives, on the platform there were a number of the oldest and most devoted of the slaves' friends. On the left of the chair sat Geo. Thompson, Esq., M.P.; near him was the Rev. Jabez Burns, D.D., and by his side the Rev. John Stevenson, M.A., Wm. Farmer, Esq., R. Smith, Esq.; while on the other side were Joseph Hume, Esq., M.P., John Lee, LL.D., Sir J. Walmsley, M.P., the Rev. Edward Matthews, John Cunliff, Esq., Andrew Paton, Esq., J. P. Edwards, Esq., and a number of colored gentlemen from the West Indies. The body of the hall was not without its distinguished guests. The

Chapmans and Westons of Boston, U. S., were there. The Estlins and Tribes had come all the way from Bristol to attend the great meeting. The Patons, of Glasgow, had delayed their departure, so as to be present. The Massies had come in from Upper Clapton. Not far from the platform sat Sir Francis Knowles, Bart.; still further back was Samuel Bowly, Esq., while near the door were to be seen the greatest critic of the age, and England's best living poet. Macaulay had laid aside the pen, entered the hall, and was standing near the central door, while not far from the historian stood the newly-appointed Poet Laureate. The author of "In Memoriam" had been swept in by the crowd, and was standing with his arms folded, and beholding for the first time (and probably the last) so large a number of colored men in one room. In different parts of the hall were men and women from nearly all parts of the kingdom, besides a large number who, drawn to London by the Exhibition, had come in to see and hear these oppressed people plead their own cause.

The writer of this sketch was chosen chairman of the meeting, and commenced its proceedings by delivering the following address, which we cut from the columns of the *Morning Advertiser :*

" The chairman, in opening the proceedings, remarked that, although the metropolis had of late been inundated with meetings of various characters, having reference to almost every variety of subjects, yet that the subject

they were called upon that evening to discuss differed
from them all. Many of those by whom he was surrounded, like himself, had been victims to the inhuman
institution of slavery, and were in consequence exiled
from the land of their birth. They were fugitives from
their native land, but not fugitives from justice; and they
had not fled from a monarchical, but from a so-called
republican government. They came from amongst a
people who declared, as part of their creed, that all men
were born free; but who, while they did so, made slaves
of every sixth man, woman and child, in the country.
(Hear, hear.)   He must not, however, forget that one of
the purposes for which they were met that night was to
commemorate the emancipation of their brothers and
sisters in the isles of the sea.   That act of the British
Parliament, and he might add in this case, with peculiar
emphasis, of the British nation, passed on the twelfth
day of August, 1833, to take effect on the first day of
August, 1834, and which enfranchised eight hundred
thousand West Indian slaves, was an event sublime in its
nature, comprehensive and mighty in its immediate in-
fluences and remote consequences, precious beyond expression to the cause of freedom, and encouraging beyond
the measure of any government on earth to the hearts
of all enlightened and just men.   This act was the result
of a long course of philanthropic and Christian efforts on
the part of some of the best men that the world ever produced.   It was not his intention to go into a discussion
or a calculation of the rise and fall of property, or

whether sugar was worth more or less by the act of emancipation. But the abolition of slavery in the West Indies was a blow struck in the right direction, at that most inhuman of all traffics, the slave-trade — a trade which would never cease so long as slavery existed; for where there was a market there would be merchandise; where there was demand there would be a supply; where there were carcasses there would be vultures; and they might as well attempt to turn the water, and make it run up the Niagara river, as to change this law.

"It was often said by the Americans that England was responsible for the existence of slavery there, because it was introduced into that country while the colonies were under the British crown. If that were the case, they must come to the conclusion that, as England abolished slavery in the West Indies, she would have done the same for the American States if she had had the power to do it; and if that was so, they might safely say that the separation of the United States from the mother country was (to say the least) a great misfortune to one sixth of the population of that land. England had set a noble example to America, and he would to heaven his countrymen would follow the example. The Americans boasted of their superior knowledge; but they needed not to boast of their superior guilt, for that was set upon a hill-top, and that, too, so high, that it required not the lantern of Diogenes to find it out. Every breeze from the western world brought upon its wings the groans and cries of the victims of this guilt. Nearly all countries had fixed the seal of disapprobation on slavery; and when, at some future age, this stain on the page of history shall be pointed at, posterity will blush at the discrepancy between American profession and American practice. What was to be thought of a people boasting of their liberty, their humanity, their Christianity, their love of justice, and at the same time keeping in slavery nearly four millions of God's children, and shutting out from them the light of the Gospel, by denying the Bible to the slave! (Hear, hear.)   No education, no marriage, everything done to keep the mind of the slave in darkness.   There was a wish on the part of the people of the Northern States to shield themselves from the charge of slaveholding; but, as they shared in the guilt, he was not satisfied with letting them off without their share in the odium.

"And now a word about the Fugitive Slave Bill. That measure was in every respect an unconstitutional measure.   It set aside the right formerly enjoyed by the fugitive of trial by jury; it afforded to him no protection, no opportunity of proving his right to be free; and it placed every free colored person at the mercy of any unprincipled individual who might wish to lay claim to him. (Hear.)   That law is opposed to the principles of Christianity — foreign alike to the laws of God and man.   It had converted the whole population of the Free States into a band of slave-catchers, and every rood of territory is but so much hunting-ground, over which they might chase the fugitive.   But while they were

speaking of slavery in the United States, they must not
omit to mention that there was a strong feeling in that
land, not only against the Fugitive Slave Law, but also
against the existence of slavery in any form. There
was a band of fearless men and women in the United
States, whose labors for the slave had resulted in good
beyond calculation. This noble and heroic class had
created an agitation in the whole country, until their
principles have taken root in almost every association in
the land, and which, with God's blessing, will, in due
time, cause the Americans to put into practice what they
have so long professed. (Hear, hear.) He wished it to
be continually held up before the country, that the
Northern States are as deeply implicated in the guilt of
slavery as the South. The North had a population of
13,553,328 freemen; the South had a population of
only 6,393,756 freemen; the North has 152 representatives in the House, the South only 81; and it would be
seen by this that the balance of power was with the Free
States. Looking, therefore, at the question in all its
aspects, he was sure that there was no one in this country but who would find out that the slavery of the
United States of America was a system the most aban-
doned and the most tyrannical. (Hear, hear.)"

At the close of this address, the Rev. Edward Matthews, from Bristol, but who had recently returned from
the United States, where he had been maltreated on account of his fidelity to the cause of freedom, was intro-

duced, and made a most interesting speech. The next
speaker was George Thompson, Esq., M.P. ; and we
need only say that his eloquence, which has seldom if
ever been equalled, and never surpassed, exceeded, on this
occasion, the most sanguine expectations of his friends.
All who sat under the thundering anathemas which he
hurled against slavery seemed instructed, delighted, and
animated.   Scarcely any one could have remained un-
moved by the pensive sympathies that pervaded the entire
assembly.   There were many in the meeting who had
never seen a fugitive slave before, and when any of the
speakers would refer to those on the platform the whole
audience seemed moved to tears.   No meeting of the
kind held in London for years created a greater sensation than this gathering of refugees from the " Land of
the free, and the home of the brave."

The Rev. J. Burns, D.D., next made an eloquent
speech, and was followed by J. P. Edwards, Esq.

CHAPTER XXI.

"For 't is the mind that makes the body rich ;
And as the sun breaks through the darkest clouds,
So Honor peereth in the meanest habit."

SHAKSPEARE.

AFTER strolling, for more than two hours, through the beautiful town of Lemington, in which I had that morning arrived, a gentleman, to whom I had a letter of introduction, asked me if I was not going to visit Shakspeare's House. It was only then that I called to mind the fact that I was within a few miles of the birthplace of the world's greatest literary genius. A horse and chaise was soon procured, and I on my way to Stratford. A quick and pleasant ride brought me to the banks of the Avon, and, a short time after, to the little but picturesque town of Stratford. I gave the horse in charge of the man-of-all-work at the inn, and then started for the much-talked-of and celebrated cottage. I found it to be a small, mean-looking house of wood and plaster, the walls of which are covered with names, inscriptions and hieroglyphics, in every language, by people of all nations, ranks and conditions, from the highest to the lowest, who have made their pilgrimage there. The old shattered and worn-out stock of the gun with which Shakspeare shot Sir Thomas Lucy's deer was shown to us. The old-fashioned tobacco-box was also there. The identical sword with which he played Hamlet, the lantern with which Romeo and Juliet were discovered, lay on the table. A plentiful supply of Shakspeare's mulberry-tree was there, and we were asked if we did not want to purchase; but, fearing that it was not the genuine article, we declined. In one of the most gloomy and dilapidated rooms is the old chair in which the poet used to sit. After viewing everything of interest, and paying the elderly young woman (old maid) her accustomed fee, we left the poet's birthplace to visit his grave. We were soon standing in the chancel of the parish church, a large and venerable edifice, mouldering with age, but finely ornamented within, and the ivy clinging around without. It stands in a beautiful situation on the banks of the Avon. Garrick has most truthfully said :

> " Thou soft-flowing Avon, by thy silver stream
> Of things more than mortal sweet Shakspeare would dream ;
> The fairies by moonlight dance round his green bed,
> For hallowed the turf is which pillowed his head."

The picturesque little stream runs murmuring at the foot of the church-yard, disturbed only by the branches of the large elms that stand on the banks, and whose limbs droop down. A flat stone is the only thing that marks the place where the poet lies buried. I copied the following verse from the stone, and which is said to have been written by the bard himself:

> " Good friend, for Jesus' sake, forbeare
> To dig the dust enclosed here :
> Blessed be he that spares these stones,
> And cursed be he that moves my bones."

Above the grave, in a niche in the wall, is a bust of the poet, placed there not long after his death, and which is supposed to bear some resemblance. Shakspeare's wife and daughter lie near him. After beholding everything of any possible interest, we stepped into our chaise and were soon again in Lemington ; which, by the by, is the most beautiful town in all Great Britain, not excepting Cheltenham. In the evening I returned to Coventry, and was partaking of the hospitality of my excellent friend, Joseph Cash, Esq., of Sherburne House, and had stretched myself out on a sofa, with Carlyle's Life of Stirling in my hands, when I was informed that the younger members of the family were preparing to attend a lecture at the Mechanics' Institution. I did not feel inclined to stir from my easy position, after the fatigues of the day ; but, learning that the lecturer was George Dawson, Esq., I resolved to join the company.

The hall was nearly filled when we reached it, which was only a few minutes before the commencement of the lecture. The stamping of feet and clapping of hands — which is the best evidence of an Englishman's impatience — brought before us a thin-faced, spare-made,

wiry-looking man, with rather a dark complexion for an
Englishman, but with prepossessing features. I must
confess that I entered the room with some little prejudice against the speaker, caused by an unfavorable criticism from the pen of George Gilfillan, the essayist.
However, I was happily disappointed. His style is
witty, keen and gentle, with the language of the drawing-room. His smiling countenance, piercing glance
and musical voice, captivated his audience. Mr. Dawson's subject was "The Rise and Spread of the Anglo-
Saxon Race," and he showed that he understood his task.
During his discourse he said:

"The Greeks and Romans sent out colonies; but no
nation but England ever before gave a nation birth. The
Americans are a nation, with no language, no creed, no
grave-yards. Their names are a derivation; and it is
laughable to see the pains an American takes to appear
national. He will soon explain to you that he is not an
Englishman, but a free-born citizen of the U-nited
States, with a pretty considerable contempt for them
British-ers. These notions make an Englishman smile;
the Americans are a nation without being a nation; they
are impressed with an idea that they have characteristics,
— they are odd, not national, and remind one of a long,
slender youth, somewhat sallow, who has just had a new
watch, consequently blasphemes the old one; and as for
the watch his father used, what is it? — a turnip; by
this means he assumes the independent. The American
is independent; he flaunts it in your face, and surprises

you with his galvanic attempts at showing off his nation-
ality. They have, in fact, no literature; we don't want
them to have any, as long as they can draw from the old
country; the feeling is kindly, and should be cherished;
it is like the boy at Christmas coming home to spend the
holidays. Long may they draw inspiration from Shakspeare and Milton, and come again and again to the old
well. Walking down Broadway is like looking at a
page of the Polyglot Bible. America was founded in a
great thought, peopled through liberty; and long may
that country be the noblest thing that England has to
boast of.

"Some people think that we, as a nation, are going
down; that we have passed the millennium; but there is
no reason yet. We have work to do,— gold mines to dig,
railways to construct, &c. &c. When all the work is
done, then, and not till then, will the Saxon folk have
finished their destiny. We have continents to fill yet;
our work is not done till Europe is free. When Emer-
son visited us, he said that England was not an old country, but had the two-fold character of youth and age;
he saw new cities, new docks; a good day's work yet to
be done, and many vast undertakings only just begun.
The coal, the iron and the gold, are ours; we have noble
days in store, but we must labor more than we have yet
done. Talk of going down!—we have hardly arrived at
our meridian. We have our faults; any Frenchman or
German may point them out. We have our duties, and
often waste our precious moments by indulging in one

eternal grumble at what we do, compared to what we
ought to do. A little praise is good sometimes,— we
walk the taller for it, and work the better. Only as
we know our work here, and do it as our fathers did,
shall we promote good; working heartily, and not fal-
tering until the object is gained. The more we add to
the happiness of a people, the more we shall be worthy
of the good gifts of God."

As an orator, Mr. Dawson stands deservedly high;
and was on several occasions applauded to the echo. He
was educated for the ministry in the Orthodox persuasion,
but left it and became a Unitarian, and has since gone a
step further. Mr. Dawson resides in Birmingham,
where he has a fine chapel, and a most intellectual congregation, and is considered the Theodore Parker of
England.

It is indeed strange, the impression which a mind
well cultivated can make upon those about it; and in
this we see more clearly the need of education. In whatever light we view education, it cannot fail to appear the
most important subject that can engage the attention of
mankind. When we contrast the ignorance, the rude-
ness and the helplessness of the savage, with the knowledge, the refinement and the resources of civilized man,
the difference between them appears so wide, that they
can scarcely be regarded as of the same species; yet
compare the infant of the savage with that of the educated and enlightened philosopher, and you will find them
in all respects the same. The same *high, capacious*

powers of the mind lie folded up in both, and in both the organs of sensation adapted to these mental powers are exactly similar. All the difference which is afterwards to distinguish them depends entirely upon their education, energy and self-culture.

CHAPTER XXII.

" Proud pile ! that rearest thy hoary head,
In ruin vast, in silence dread,
O'er Teme's luxuriant vale,
Thy moss-grown halls, thy precincts drear,
To musing Fancy's pensive ear
Unfold a varied tale."

IT was in the latter part of December, and on one of
the coldest nights that I have experienced, that I found
myself seated before the fire, and alone, in the principal
hotel in the town of Ludlow, and within a few minutes'
walk of the famous old castle from which the town derives its name.   A ride of one hundred and fifty miles
by rail, in such uncomfortable carriages as no country
except Great Britain furnishes for the weary traveller,
and twenty miles on the top of a coach, in a drenching
rain, caused me to remain by the fire's side to a later
hour than I otherwise would have done.   "Did you
ring, sir?" asked the waiter, as the clock struck twelve.
" No," I replied; but I felt that this was the servant's
mode of informing me that it was time for me to retire
to bed, and consequently I asked for a candle, and was

shown to my chamber, and was soon in bed. From the weight of the covering on the bed, I felt sure that the extra blanket which I had requested to be put on was there; yet I was shivering with cold. As the sheets began to get warm, I discovered, to my astonishment, that they were damp; indeed, wet. My first thought was to ring the bell for the chambermaid, and have them changed; but, after a moment's consideration, I resolved to adopt a different course. I got out of bed, pulled the sheets off, rolled them up, raised the window, and threw them into the street. After disposing of the wet sheets, I returned to bed and got in between the blankets, and lay there trembling with cold till Morpheus came to my relief. The next morning I said nothing about the uncomfortable night I had experienced, and determined to leave it until they discovered the loss of the sheets. As soon as I had breakfasted, I went out to view the castle. For many years this was one of the strongest baronial fortifications in England. It was from Ludlow Castle that Edward, Prince of Wales, and his brother, were taken to London and put to death in the Tower, by order of their uncle, Richard III., before that villain seized upon the crown. The family of Mortimer for centuries held the castle, and, consequently, ruled Hereford-shire. The castle rises from the point of a headland, and its foundations are ingrafted into a bare gray rock. The front consists of square towers, with high connecting walls. The castle is a complete ruin, and has been for centuries; large trees are still growing in the midst of the old pile, which give it a picturesque appearance. It was here that the exquisite effusion of the youthful genius of Milton — The Masque of Comus — was composed, and performed before His Majesty Charles I., in 1631. Little did the king think that the poet would one day be secretary to the man who should put him to death and rule his kingdom. Although a ruin, this fact is enough to excite interest, and to cause one to venerate the old building, and to do homage to the memory of the divine poet who hallowed it with his immortal strains. From a visitor's book that is kept at the gate-house, I copied the following verses :

> " Here Milton sung ; what needs a greater spell
>   To lure thee, stranger, to these far-famed walls ?
> Though chroniclers of other ages tell
>   That princes oft have graced fair Ludlow's halls,
> Their honors glide along oblivion's stream,
>   And o'er the wreck a tide of ruin drives ;
> Faint and more faint the rays of glory beam
>   That gild their course — the bard alone survives.
> And, when the rude, unceasing shocks of Time
>   In one vast heap shall whelm this lofty pile,
> Still shall his genius, towering and sublime,
>   Triumphant o'er the spoils of grandeur smile ;
> Still in these haunts, true to a nation's tongue,
> Echo shall love to dwell, and say, Here Milton sung."

I lingered long in the room pointed out to me as the one in which Milton wrote his " Comus." The castle was not only visited by the author of " Paradise Lost," but here, amidst the noise and bustle of civil dissensions,

Samuel Butler, the satirical author of "Hudibras," found an asylum. The part of the tower in which it is said he composed his "Hudibras" was shown to us. In looking over the different apartments, we passed through a cell with only one small window through which the light found its way. On a stone, chiselled with great beauty, was a figure in a weeping position, and underneath it some one had written with pencil, in a legible hand:

> "The Muse, too, weeps ; in hallowed hour
> Here sacred Milton owned her power,
> And woke to nobler song."

The weather was exceedingly cold, and made more so by the stone walls partly covered with snow and frost around us; and I returned to the inn. It being near the time for me to leave by the coach for Hereford, I called for my bill. The servant went out of the room; but soon returned, and began stirring up the fire with the poker. I again told him that the coach would shortly be up, and that I wanted my bill. "Yes, sir, in a moment," he replied, and left in haste. Ten or fifteen minutes passed away, and the servant once more came in, walked to the window, pulled up the blinds, and then went out. I saw that something was in the wind; and it occurred to me that they had discovered the loss of the sheets. The waiter soon returned again, and, in rather an agitated manner, said, "I beg your pardon, sir, but the landlady is in the hall, and would like to speak to you." Out I went, and found the finest specimen of an

English landlady that I had seen for many a day.   There
she stood, nearly as thick as she was high, with a red
face, garnished around with curls, that seemed to say,
"I have just been brushed and oiled."   A neat apron
covered a black alpacca dress that swept the ground with
modesty, and a bunch of keys hung at her side.   O,
that smile! such a smile as none but a woman who had
often been before a mirror could put on.   However, I
had studied human nature too successfully not to know
that thunder and lightning were concealed under that
smile; and I nerved myself up for the occasion.   "I am
sorry to have to name it, sir," said she, "but the sheets
are missing off your bed."   "O, yes," I replied; "I took
them off last night."   "Indeed!" exclaimed she; "and
pray what have you done with them?"   "I threw them
out of the window," said I.   "What! into the street?"
"Yes, into the street," I said.   "What did you do that
for?"   "They were wet; and I was afraid that if I left
them in the room they would be put on at night, and
give somebody else a cold."   And here I coughed with
all my might, to remind her that I had suffered from the
negligence of her chambermaid.   The heaving of the
chest and panting for breath which the lady was expe-
riencing at this juncture told me plainly that an explo-
sion was at hand; and the piercing glance of those
wicked-looking black eyes, and the rapid changes that
came over that never-to-be-forgotten face, were enough to
cause the most love-sick man in the world to give up all
ideas of matrimony, and to be contented with being his

own master. "Then, sir," said the landlady, "you will
have to pay for the sheets." "O, yes," replied I; "I
will pay for them; put them in the bill, and I will send
the bill to *The Times*, and have it published, and let
the travelling public know how much you charge for wet
sheets!" and I turned upon my heel and walked into the
room.

A few minutes after, the servant came in and laid
before me the bill. I looked, but in vain, to see how
much I had been charged for my hasty indiscretion the
previous night. No mention was made of the sheets;
and I paid the bill as it stood. The blowing of the coachman's horn warned me that I must get ready; and I put
on my top coat. As I was passing through the hall,
there stood the landlady just where I had left her, looking as if she had not stirred a single peg. And that
smile, that had often cheered or carried consternation to
many a poor heart, was still to be seen. I would rather
have gone without my dinner than to have looked her in
the face, such is my timidity. But common courtesy
demanded that I should at least nod as I passed by; and
therefore I was thrown back upon my manners, and unconsciously found myself giving her one of my best bows.
Whether this bow was the result of my early training
while in slavery, the domestic discipline that I afterwards
experienced in freedom, or the terror with which every
nerve was shaken on first meeting the landlady, I am
still unaware. However, the bow was made and the ice
broken, and the landlady smilingly said, "You do not

know, sir, how much I am grieved at your being put to
so much trouble last night, with those wet sheets; it was
all the fault of the chambermaid, and I have given her
warning, and shall dismiss her a month from to-day.
And I do hope, sir, that if you should ever mention this
circumstance you will not name the house in which it
occurred." How could I do otherwise than to acquiesce
in her wishes? Yes, I promised that I would never
name the inn at which I had caught the rheumatism;
and, therefore, reader, you may ask me, but in vain,—I
will not tell you. One more bow, and out I went, and
mounted the coach. As the driver was pulling up his
reins, and raising his whip in the air, I turned to take a
farewell glance of the inn, when, to my surprise, I beheld the landlady at the door with a white handkerchief
in her hand, and a countenance beaming with smiles that
I still see in my mind's eye. I raised my hat, she nodded, and away went the coach. Although the ride was
a cold and dreary one, I often caught myself smiling
over the fright in which I had put the landlady by
threatening to publish her house.

After a fatiguing stage twenty miles or more, over a
bad road, we reached Hereford, a small city, situated in
a fertile plain, bounded on all sides with orchards, and
watered by the translucent Wye. I spent the greater
part of the next day in seeing the lions of the little city.
I first visited, what most strangers do, the cathedral; a
building partly Gothic and partly Saxon in its architecture, the interior of which is handsome, and contains

an excellent organ, a piece of furniture that often calls more hearers to a place of worship than the preacher. In passing through the cathedral I stood a moment or two over the grave of the poet Phillips, the author of the "Splendid Shilling," "Cider," etc. While in the library the verger showed me a manuscript Bible of Wickliffe's, the first in use, written on vellum in the old black letter, full of abbreviations. He also pointed out some Latin manuscripts, in various parts beautifully illuminated with most ingenious penmanship, the coloring of the figures very bright. After all, there is a degree of pleasure in handling these old and laid-aside books. Hereford is noted for having been the birthplace of several distinguished persons. I was shown the house in which David Garrick was born. From Hereford he was removed to Litchfield and became the pupil of Dr. Johnson, and eventually both master and pupil went to London in search of bread; one became famous as an actor, the other noted as *surly Sam Johnson.* An obscure cottage in Pipe-lane was pointed out as the birthplace of the celebrated Nell Gwynne, who first appeared in London in the pit of Drury-lane Theatre as an apple-girl, and afterwards became an actress, in which position she was seen by King Charles II., who took her to his bed and board, and created her Duchess of St. Albans. However, she had many crooked paths to tread, after becoming an actress, before she captivated the heart of the *Merry Monarch.* The following story of her life, told by herself, is too good to be lost; so I insert it here.

"When I was a poor girl," said the Duchess of St. Albans, "working very hard for my thirty shillings a week, I went down to Liverpool during the holidays, where I was always well received. I was to perform in a new piece, something like those pretty little affecting dramas they get up now at our minor theatres; and in my character I represented a poor, friendless orphan-girl, reduced to the most wretched poverty. A heartless tradesman prosecutes the sad heroine for a heavy debt, and insists on putting her in prison, unless some one will be bail for her. The girl replies, 'Then I have no hope; I have not a friend in the world.' 'What! will no one be bail for you, to save you from going to prison?' asks the stern creditor. 'I have told you I have not a friend on earth,' was the reply. But just as I was uttering the words, I saw a sailor in the upper gallery springing over the railing, letting himself down from one tier to another, until he bounded clear over the orchestra and footlights, and placed himself beside me in a moment. 'Yes, you shall have *one* friend at least, my poor young woman,' said he, with the greatest expression in his honest, sunburnt countenance; 'I will go bail for you to any amount. And as for *you*,' turning to the fright-ened actor, 'if you don't bear a hand and shift your moorings, you lubber, it will be worse for you when I come athwart your bows!' Every creature in the house rose; the uproar was indescribable — peals of

laughter, screams of terror, cheers from his tawny mess-
mates in the gallery, preparatory scrapings of violins
from the orchestra; and, amidst the universal din, there
stood the unconscious cause of it, sheltering me, 'the
poor, distressed young woman,' and breathing defiance
and destruction against my mimic persecutor. He was
only persuaded to relinquish his care of me, by the man-
ager pretending to arrive and rescue me, with a pro-
fusion of theatrical bank-notes."

Hereford was also the birthplace of Mrs. Siddons, the
unequalled tragic actress. The views around Hereford
are very sylvan, and from some points, where the Welsh
mountains are discernible, present something of the magnificent. All this part of the country still shows unmis-
takable evidence that war has had its day here. In those
times the arts and education received no encouragement.
The destructive exploits of conquerors may dazzle for a
while, but the silent labors of the student and the artist,
of the architect and the husbandman, which embellish
the earth, and convert it into a terrestrial paradise,
although they do not shine with so conspicuous a glare,
diversify the picture with milder colors and more beautiful shades.

CHAPTER XXIII.

" To him no author was unknown,
   Yet what he writ was all his own ;
   Horace's wit, and Virgil's state,
   He did not steal, but emulate ;
   And when he would like them appear,
   Their form, but not their clothes, did wear."

                                        DENHAM.

IF there be an individual living who has read the
"Essay on Man," or "The Rape of the Lock," without
a wish to become more acquainted with the writings of
the gifted poet that penned those exquisite poems, I confess that such an one is made of different materials from
myself.

It is possible that I am too great a devotee to authors,
and especially poets ; yet such is my reverence for departed writers, that I would rather walk five miles to see
a poet's grave than to spend an evening at the finest
entertainment that could be got up.

It was on a pleasant afternoon in September, that I
had gone into Surrey to dine with Lord C——, that I
found myself one of a party of nine, and seated at a table

loaded with everything that the heart could wish. Four men-servants, in livery, with white gloves, waited upon the company.

After the different courses had been changed, the wine occupied the most conspicuous place on the table, and all seemed to drink with a relish unappreciated except by those who move in the higher walks of life. My glass was the only one on the table in which the juice of the grape had not been poured. It takes more nerve than most men possess to cause one to decline taking a glass of wine with a lady; and in English society they don't appear to understand how human beings can live and enjoy health without taking at least a little wine. By my continued refusal to drink with first one and then another of the company, I had become rather an object of pity than otherwise.

A lady of the party, and in company with whom I had dined on a previous occasion, and who knew me to be an abstainer, resolved to relieve me from the awkward position in which my principles had placed me, and therefore caused a decanter of raspberry vinegar to be adulterated and brought on the table. A note in pencil from the lady informed me of the contents of the new bottle. I am partial to this kind of beverage, and felt glad when it made its appearance. No one of the party, except the lady, knew of the fraud; and I was able, during the remainder of the time, to drink with any of the company. The waiters, as a matter of course, were in the secret; for they had to make the change while passing the wine from me to the person with whom I drank.

After a while, as is usual, the ladies all rose and left the room. The retiring of the fair sex left the gentlemen in a more free-and-easy position, and consequently the topics of conversation were materially changed, but not for the better. The presence of women is always a restraint in the right direction. An hour after the ladies had gone, the gentlemen were requested to retire to the drawing-room, where we found tea ready to be served up. I was glad when the time came to leave the dining-room, for I felt it a great bore to be compelled to remain at the table *three hours*. Tea over, the wine again brought on, and the company took a stroll through the grounds at the back of the villa. It was a bright moon-light night, and the stars were out, and the air came laden with the perfume of sweet flowers, and there were no sounds to be heard, except the musical splashing of the little cascade at the end of the garden, and the song of the nightingale, that seemed to be in one of the trees near by. How pleasant everything looked, with the flowers creeping about the summer-house, and the windows opening to the velvet lawn, with its modest front, neat trellis-work, and meandering vine! The small smooth fish-pond, and the life-like statues standing or kneeling in different parts of the grounds, gave it the appearance of a very paradise.

"There," said his lordship, "is where Cowley used to sit, under that tree, and read."

This reminded me that I was near Chertsey, where the poet spent his last days; and, as I was invited to spend the night within a short ride of that place, I resolved to visit it the next day. We returned to the drawing-room, and a few moments after the party separated, at ten o'clock.

After breakfast the following morning, I drove over to Chertsey, a pretty little town, with but two streets of any note. In the principal street, and not far from the railway station, stands a low building of wood and plaster, known as the *Porch House*. It was in this cottage that Abraham Cowley, the poet, resided, and died in 1667, in the forty-ninth year of his age. It being the residence of a gentleman who was from home, I did not have an opportunity of seeing the interior of the building, which I much regretted. Having visited Cowley's house, I at once determined to do what I had long promised myself; that was, to see Pope's villa, at Twickenham; and I returned to London, took the Richmond boat, and was soon gliding up the Thames.

I have seldom had a pleasanter ride by water than from London Bridge to Richmond; the beautiful panoramic view which unfolds itself on either side of the river can scarcely be surpassed by the scenery in any country. In the centre of Twickenham stands the house made celebrated from its having been the residence of Alexander Pope. The house is not large, but occupies a beautiful site, and is to be seen to best advantage from the river. The garden and grounds have undergone

some change since the death of the poet. The grotto
leading from the villa to the Thames is in a sad condition.

The following lines, written by Pope soon after finishing this idol of his fancy, show in what estimate he held
it, and should at least have preserved it from decay :

> " Thou who shalt stop where *Thames*' translucent wave
>   Shines a broad mirror through the shadowy cave ;
>   Where lingering drops from mineral roofs distill,
>   And pointed crystals break the sparkling rill ;
>   Unpolished gems no ray on pride bestow,
>   And latent metals innocently glow —
>   Approach !   Great nature studiously behold !
>   And eye the mine without a wish for gold.
>   Approach — but awful !   Lo ! the Ægerian grot,
>   Where, nobly pensive, St. John sate and thought ;
>   Where *British* sighs from dying Wyndham stole,
>   And the bright flame was shot through Marchmont's soul.
>   Let such — such only — tread this sacred floor,
>   Who dare to love their country and be poor."

It is strange that there are some at the present day
who deny that Pope was a poet; but it seems to me that
such either show a want of appreciation of poetry, or
themselves no judge of what constitutes poetry.   Where
can be found a finer effusion than the " Essay on Man"?
Johnson, in his admirable Life of Pope, in drawing a
comparison between him and Dryden, says, " If the
flights of Dryden are higher, Pope continues longer on
the wing; if of Dryden's fire the blaze is brighter, of
Pope is the heat more regular and constant.   Dryden

often surpasses expectation, and Pope never falls below
it; Dryden is read with frequent astonishment, and Pope
with perpetual delight." In speaking of the " Rape of
the Lock," the same great critic remarks that it " stands
forward in the classes of literature, as the most exquisite
example of ludicrous poetry." Another poet and critic
of no mean authority calls him " The sweetest and most
elegant of English poets, the severest chastiser of vice,
and the most persuasive teacher of wisdom." Lord
Byron terms him " the most perfect and harmonious of
poets." How many have quoted the following lines
without knowing that they were Pope's!

> " To look through Nature up to Nature's God."
> " An honest man 's the noblest work of God."
> " Just as the twig is bent, the tree 's inclined."
> " If to her share some female errors fall,
>   Look on her face, and you 'll forget them all."
> " For modes of faith let graceless zealots fight,
>   His can't be wrong whose life is in the right."

Pope was certainly the most independent writer of his
time; a poet who never sold himself, and never lent his
pen to the upholding of wrong. And although a severe
critic, the following verse will show that he did not wish
to bestow his chastisement in a wrong direction:

> " Curst be the verse, how well soe'er it flow,
>   That tends to make one honest man my foe,
>   Give Virtue scandal, Innocence a fear,
>   Or from the soft-eyed virgin steal a tear ! "

No poet's pen was ever more thoroughly used to suppress vice than Pope's; and what he did was done conscientiously, as the following lines will show :

> " Ask you what provocation I have had ?
> The strong antipathy of good to bad.
> When Truth or Virtue an affront endures,
> The affront is mine, my friend, and should be yours."

Pope is not only a poet of a high order, but as yet he is the unsurpassed translator of Homer.

My visit to Pope's villa was a short one, but it was attended with many pleasing incidents. I have derived much pleasure from reading his Iliad and other translations. The verse from the pen of Lord Denham, that heads this chapter, conveys but a faint idea of my estimate of Pope's genius and talents.

CHAPTER XXIV.

"This modest stone, what few vain marbles can,
    May truly say, here lies an honest man:
    A poet, blest beyond the poet's fate,
    Whom heaven kept sacred from the proud and great."
                                                POPE.

WHILE on a recent visit to Dumfries, I lodged in the same house with Robert Burns, the eldest son of the Scottish bard, who is now about sixty-five years old. I also visited the grave of the poet, which is in the church-yard at the lower end of the town. A few days afterwards I arrived at Ayr, and being within three miles of the birth-place of Burns, and having so lately stood over his grave, I felt no little interest in seeing the cottage in which he was born, and the monument erected to his memory; and therefore, after inquiring the road, I started on my pilgrimage. In going up the High Street, we passed the Wallace Tower, a Gothic building, with a statue of the renowned chief, cut by Thom, the famed sculptor of "Tam O'Shanter and Souter Johnny," occupying the highest niche. The Scottish hero is represented not in warlike attitude, but in a thoughtful mood, as if musing over the wrongs of his country. We were soon out of

the town, and on the high road to the "Land of Burns."
On the west side of the road, and about two miles from
Ayr, stands the cottage in which the poet was born; it
is now used as an ale-house or inn. This cottage was
no doubt the fancied scene of that splendid poem, "The
Cottar's Saturday Night." A little further on, and we
were near the old kirk, in the yard of which is the grave
of Burns' father, marked by a plain tombstone, on which
is engraved the following epitaph, from the pen of the
poet:

> "O ye whose cheek the tear of pity stains,
>   Draw near with pious reverence and attend ;
> Here lie the loving husband's dear remains,
>   The tender father, and the generous friend.
> The pitying heart that felt for human woe,
>   The dauntless heart that feared no human pride,
> The friend of man — to vice alone a foe ;
>   ' For e'en his failings leant to Virtue's side.' "

A short distance beyond the church, we caught a sight
of the "Auld Brig" crossing the Doon's classic stream,
along which Tam O'Shanter was pursued by the witches,
his "Gray Mare Meg" losing her tail in the struggle
on the keystone. On the banks of the Doon stands the
beautiful monument, surrounded by a little plat of
ground very tastefully laid out. The edifice is of the
composite order, blending the finest models of Grecian
and Roman architecture. It is about sixty feet high; on
the ground floor there is a circular room lighted by a
cupola of stained glass, in the centre of which stands a

table with relics, and editions of Burns' writings. Amongst these relics is the Bible given by the poet to his Highland Mary. It is bound in two volumes, which are enclosed in a neat oaken box with a glass lid. In both volumes is written " Robert Burns, Mossgiel," in the bard's own hand-writing. In the same room are the original far-famed figures of " Tam O'Shanter and Souter Johnny," chiselled out of solid blocks of free-stone, by the self-taught sculptor, Thom. No one can look at these statues without feeling that the poet has not more graphically described than the sculptor has delineated the jolly couple. Immediately on the banks of the river stands the Shell Palace. This most beauti-ful of little edifices is scarcely less to be admired than the monument itself.

Like its great prototype, the Shell Palace, to be judged of, must be seen. It is not easy to describe even this miniature. Lying in the heart of the Monument scenery, it forms a fitting spot for something dazzlingly beauti-ful ; and it realizes the aspiration. It is a palace of which rare and beautiful shells, gathered in many climes, form the entire surface, internal and external. The erection is twenty feet long, by fourteen and a half feet broad, and fourteen feet high in the roof. It is in form an irregular or oblong octagon — the two sides long, and the three sections at each end, of course, narrow, thus giving, by the cross reflections of no fewer than nine-teen mirrors, an infinite multiplicity of its internal treasures. Of these the shells are the leading feature, and many thousands of the rarest sorts go to make up this conchological wonder. The floor is covered with a very rich carpet, and rugs to match front two unique dwarf grates. The seats, set on imitation granite props, are covered with rich crimson velvet. Opposite the stained-glass entrance-door, in a recess, is a beautiful fountain, surrounded by large ornamental shells, playing from a delightful spring, the jet rising from a rich green vase, in tasteful contrast with the "winking gold-fish," now sporting and now lazily floating round its base. The side walls are inlaid in the most regular and artistic manner with shells, which vary in size, the roof being studded with large ornamental shells, the upward unseen points of which, being bored, act as ventilators, while in the centre of the roof some of the very choicest middle-sized shells are grouped together in the form of flowers, with a very rich and beautiful effect, seldom attained in the choicest bouquets. With so much of the beautiful so very attractively arranged, the mirrors work wonders. The large mirrors at either end show a line of table as far as the eye can carry, and multiply the visitors accordingly — green vases and golden fish presenting themselves anew at every turn. The Doon ran silently past as we entered; but here it meanders round us on every side, and our fairy palace seems the centre of some enchanted island. It is, indeed, a beautiful grotto, and all who have not seen it will, we dare say, on visiting it, not begrudge it the title of the "Shell Palace."

We next visited Newark Castle, about a mile from the
monument. It is remarkable for its antiquity, and for
the splendid view obtained from the balcony on its summit. While standing on this celebrated spot, we saw at
one glance the Frith of Clyde and Bay of Ayr; in
the immediate foreground the cradle-land of Burns, and
the winding Doon; and in the distance the eye wanders
over a vast tract of richly-wooded country, embracing a
panoramic view of portions of at least seven counties,
and the much-admired and celebrated rock, Ailsacraig.
While in the neighborhood, we could not forego the
temptation which presented itself of visiting the scene of
Burns' tender parting with Mary Campbell. It is near
the junction of the water of Fail with the river Ayr,
where the poet met his Mary on a Sunday in the month
of May, and, laying their hands in the stream, vowed,
over Mary's Bible, love while the woods of Montgomery
grew and its waters ran. The death of the girl before
the appointed time of marriage caused the composition of
the following poem, one of Burns' sweetest pieces.

HIGHLAND MARY.

" Ye banks, and braes, and streams around
　　The castle o' Montgomery,
Green be your woods, and fair your flowers,
　　Your waters never drumlie !
There Simmer first unfaulds her robes,
　　And there they langest tarry ;
For there I took the last fareweel
　　O' my sweet Highland Mary.

'How sweetly bloomed the gay green birk,
　　How rich the hawthorn's blossom,
　　As underneath their fragrant shade
　　　I clasped her to my bosom !
　　The golden hours, on angel wings,
　　　Flew o'er me and my dearie :
　　For dear to me as light and life
　　　Was my sweet Highland Mary.

" Wi' mony a vow, and locked embrace,
　　　Our parting was fu' tender ;
　　And, pledging aft to meet again,
　　　We tore oursels asunder ;
　　But, O ! fell Death's untimely frost,
　　　That nipt my flower sae early !
　　Now green 's the sod, and cauld 's the clay,
　　　That wraps my Highland Mary !

" O pale, pale now, those rosy lips,
　　　I aft hae kissed sae fondly !
　　And closed for aye the sparkling glance
　　　That dwalt on me sae kindly !
　　And mouldering now in silent dust
　　　That heart that lo'ed me dearly !
　　But still within my bosom's core
　　　Shall live my Highland Mary."

It was indeed pleasant to walk over the ground once
pressed by the feet of the Scottish bard, and to look
upon the scenes that inspired his youthful breast, and
gave animation to that blaze of genius that burst upon
the world. The classic Doon, the ruins of the old kirk
Alloway, the cottage in which the poet first drew breath,
and other places made celebrated by his pen, all filled us
with a degree of enthusiasm we have seldom experienced.

In every region where the English language is known the songs of Burns give rapture; and from every land, and from climes the most remote, comes the praise of Burns as a poet. In song-writing he surpassed Sir Walter Scott and Lord Byron; for in that department he was above "all Greek, above all Roman fame;" a more than Simonides in pathos, as in his "Highland Mary;" a more than Tyrtæus in fire, as in his "Scots wha ha'e wi' Wallace bled;" and a softer than Sappho in love, as in his —

> " Had we never loved so kindly,
> Had we never loved so blindly,
> Never met or never parted,
> We had ne'er been broken-hearted."

CHAPTER XXV.

"If thou art worn and hard beset
   With sorrows, that thou wouldst forget ;
   If thou wouldst read a lesson, that would keep
   Thy heart from fainting and thy soul from sleep, —
   Go to the Colosseum."   LONGFELLOW.

IT was in the middle of May, when London is usually
inundated with strangers from the country, who come up
to attend the anniversaries, that a party of friends called
on me with a request that I would accompany them to
some of the lions of the metropolis. We started for
the Thames Tunnel, one of the wonders of London. The
idea of making a thoroughfare under the largest river in
England was a project that could scarcely have been
carried out by any except a most enterprising people.
We faintly heard the clock on St. Paul's striking eleven,
as the Woolwich boat put us down at the Tunnel; which
we entered, after paying the admission fee of one penny.
After descending one hundred steps, we found ourselves
under the river, and looking towards the faint glimmer
of light that showed itself on the Surrey side. There
are two arches, one of which is closed up, with here and

there a stall, loaded with old maps, books, and views of the Tunnel. Lamps, some six or eight yards apart, light up the otherwise dark and dismal place. Signs of frequent repairs show that they must ever be on the watch to keep the water out. An hour spent in the Tunnel satisfied us all, and we left in the direction of the Tower, a description of which will be found in another chapter. Some of our party seemed bent on going next to the Colosseum, and to the Colosseum we went. On arriving at the doors, and entering a long, capacious passage, our eyes became quite dazzled by the gleams of colored light which shone upon them, both directly and reflectedly. The effect was heightened by the beautiful designs which figured on the walls, and by the graceful forms of the many statues which lined the path. In fact, the strength of the sense of sight became much greater, because the ear, which, all the day before, had listened to the busy hum of bustle and activity, now ceased to hear aught but a silent whisper or a wondering " O," — no echo had even the foot-fall from the luxuriant softness of the carpeting.

Following up this fairy viaduct, we merged into a spacious circularly-formed apartment, on the downy couches of which reclined many an enraptured group; while nimble fingers and enticing lips caused sweet harmonious strains to chase each other from niche to niche, and among marbled figures within that charming temple.

Ascending a narrow flight of stairs, we landed on a balcony, from which we viewed the principal spectacle

exhibited — and, O, it was a grand one ! We found ourselves, as it were, upon the summit of some high building
in the centre of the French metropolis, and there, all
brilliant with gas-lights, and favored by the shining
moon, Paris lay spread far out beneath us, though the
canvas on which the scene was painted was but half a
dozen feet from where we gazed in wonder. The moon
herself seemed actually in the heavens. Nay, bets were
laid that she had risen since we entered. Nothing can
surpass the uniformity of appearance which every spire,
and house, and wood, and river — yea, which every
shop-window, ornamented, presented. All seemed natural,
from the twinkling of the stars above us, to the monkey
of the organ-man in the market-place below. Reader, if
ever thou hast occasion to go to London, leave it not till
thou hast seen the Colosseum.

Mustering our forces to return together, the cry was
raised "A man a-wanting ! " It seems there is an appa-
ratus constructed in an apartment leading from the
balcony, by which parties may, with a great degree of
suddenness, be raised or lowered from or to the music-
room. Our friend, at all times anxious to make the
most of a shilling, followed some parties into the "ascen-
sion-room," as it is called, and took his seat beside
them, expecting that on the withdrawal of a curtain
he should witness something which his companions
would miss. A bell sounded, and suddenly our expect-
ant found himself some twenty feet lower, and obliged
to follow the example of his co-descendants still further,

by furnishing the attendant with such a gratuity as became an imitator of the Queen Elizabeth.

To another, but extremely different, of nature's imitations, we now turned our steps. After traversing one or two passages, the lights of which became more dim as we advanced, we reached a cavern's mouth. Here our progress was arrested by an iron grating. Our inquisitive friend, however, soon discovered that this obstacle could be removed,— it being, in fact, similar to those revolving barriers (we forget the name given in the "trade") placed at the entrance to the Great Exhibition. Like them, too, they checked all egress, and, to the further astonishment of the man of prying propensity, we were soon called upon for so many extra sixpences, indicated by this tell-tale gateway as being the number of persons who had entered since the keeper left.

The damp and dripping stones, with their coat of foggy green,— the exclusion of every sound from without,— the stunted measure of our speech,— the sharp clank of our footsteps,— and the frowning gloom of every corner of this retreat, soon gave evidence of the excellence of the design and entire structure, in the impression which it raised that, in reality, we were in some secluded rendezvous of smugglers, or of outlaws. Yea, the question was put by one who had seldom crossed the Cree, Was Meg Merrilies' one like this? while a party who had explored Ben Lomond and its neighborhood was asked if from it there could not be formed some notion of that which bears the name of the chief, Rob Roy.

Relieved alike from depressing atmosphere and cloudy thoughts, we retired to a projecting window, from which to view the "Swiss cottage," as it is called. Upon the verge of a tremendous precipice is seen a lonely cot. All communication with it is cut off, save by the rugged trunk of a withered tree which spans an opposite projection. Under this unstable bridge gush torrents of foaming water, lashed down from the heights beyond. Yet morn and eve does an industrious peasant leave and return to his romantic home across this dangerous way. See now, as he returns from his toil, he paces cautiously along; and yonder, at the further end, stand wife and little ones waiting to greet him when he crosses. O! happy man, to live where thus thou 'rt called to venture much and oft for those thou lovest, and be as oft rewarded by renewed tokens of their affection and most tender attachment!

Through openings in the walls we witnessed, also, the representation of mines and manufactures in full operation; and then, as we withdrew, we passed through artificial walks adorned with every kind of fantastical structure, and at some points of which, from the position of reflecting-glasses, we viewed in them hundreds of the very objects of which we could, with the unaided eye, see but one.

> "Passing we looked, and, looking, grieved to pass
> From the fair (?) figures smiling in the glass."

CHAPTER XXVI.

" The treasures of the deep are not so precious
  As are the concealed comforts of a man
  Locked up in woman's love.   I scent the air
  Of blessings, when I come but near the house.
  What a delicious breath marriage sends forth ! . . .
  The violet bed 's not sweeter."
                                        MIDDLETON.

DURING a sojourn of five years in Europe, I have
spent many pleasant hours in strolling through old
church-yards, and reading the epitaphs upon the tomb-
stones of the dead.   Part of the pleasure was derived
from a wish for solitude; and no place offers as quiet
walks as a village burial-ground.   And the curious epitaphs that are to be seen in a church-yard six or eight
hundred years old are enough to cause a smile, even in
so solemn a place as a grave-yard.   While walking
through Horsleydown church, in Cumberland, a short
time since, I read an inscription over a tomb which I
copied, and shall give in this chapter, although at the
risk of bringing down upon my devoted head the indignation of the fair sex.   Domestic enjoyment is often
blasted by an intermixture of foibles with virtues of a

superior kind; and if the following shall prove a warning to wives, I shall be fully compensated for my trouble.

Here lie the bodies of
THOMAS BOND, and MARY his wife.
She was temperate, chaste and charitable ;
But
She was proud, peevish and passionate.
She was an affectionate wife and a tender mother ;
But
Her husband and child, whom she loved, seldom saw her
countenance without a disgusting frown,
Whilst she received visitors, whom she despised, with an
endearing smile.
Her behavior was discreet toward strangers ;
But
imprudent in her family.
Abroad, her conduct was influenced by good-breeding ;
But
at home, by ill-temper.
She was a professed enemy to flattery, and was
Seldom known to praise or commend ;
But
the talents in which she principally excelled were
difference of opinion, and discovering
flaws and imperfections.
She was an admirable economist,
and, without prodigality,
dispensed plenty to every person in her family ;
But
would sacrifice their eyes to a farthing candle.
She sometimes made her husband happy with her good qualities ;
But
Much more frequently miserable with her many failings ;
Insomuch, that, in thirty years' cohabitation, he often
lamented that, maugre her virtues,

He had not, in the whole, enjoyed two years
of matrimonial comfort.
At length,
finding that she had lost the affections of her
husband, as well as the regard of her neighbors, family
disputes having been divulged by servants,
She died of vexation, July 20, 1768,
Aged 48 years.
Her worn-out husband survived her four months
and two days, and departed this life November 28, 1768,
in the 54th year of his age.
William Bond, brother to the deceased, erected
this stone,
a *weekly monitor* to the surviving wives of this
parish, that they may avoid the infamy
of having their memories handed down to posterity
with a *patch-work* character.

CHAPTER XXVII.

" To where the broken landscape, by degrees
   Ascending, roughens into rigid hills ;
   O'er which the Cambrian mountains, like far clouds
   That skirt the blue horizon, dusky rise."
                          THOMSON.

I HAVE visited few places where I found warmer
friends, or felt myself more at home, than in Aberdeen.
The dwellings, being built mostly of granite, remind
one of Boston, especially in a walk down Union-street,
which is thought to be one of the finest promenades in
Europe. The town is situated on a neck of land between the rivers Dee and Don, and is the most important
commercial place in the north of Scotland.

During our stay in the city we visited, among other
places, the old bridge of Don, which is not only resorted
to owing to its antique celebrity and peculiar appearance, but also for the notoriety that it has gained by Lord
Byron's poem for the " Bridge of Don." His lordship
spent several years here during his minority, and this
old bridge was a favorite resort of his. In one of his
notes he alludes to how he used to hang over its one
arch, and the deep black salmon stream below, with a

mixture of childish terror and delight. While we stood upon the melancholy bridge, and although the scene around was severely grand and terrific,— the river swollen, the wind howling amongst the leafless trees, the sea in the distance,— and although the walk where Hall and Mackintosh were wont to melt down hours to moments in high converse was in sight, it was, somehow or other, the figure of the mild lame boy leaning over the parapet that filled our fancy; and the chief fascination of the spot seemed to breathe from the genius of the author of " Childe Harold."

To Anthony Cruikshank, Esq., whose hospitality we shared in Aberdeen, we are indebted for showing us the different places of interest in the town and vicinity. An engagement, however, to be in Edinburgh, cut short our stay in the north. The very mild state of the weather, and a wish to see something of the coast between Aberdeen and Edinburgh, induced us to make the journey by water. Consequently, after delivering a lecture before the Mechanics' Institute, with His Honor the Provost in the chair, on the evening of February 15th, we went on board the steamer bound for Edinburgh. On reaching the vessel we found the drawing-saloon almost entirely at our service, and, prejudice against color being unknown, we had no difficulty in obtaining the best accommodation that the steamer afforded. This was so unlike the pro-slavery, negro-hating spirit of America, that my colored friends who were with me were almost bewildered by the transition. The night was a glorious one. The sky was cloudless, and the clear, bracing air had a buoyancy I have seldom seen. The moon was in its zenith; the steamer and surrounding objects were beautiful in the extreme. The boat left her moorings at half-past twelve, and we were soon out at sea. The " Queen " is a splendid craft, and, without the aid of sails, was able to make fifteen miles within the hour. I was up the next morning extremely early,— indeed, before any of my fellow-passengers,— and found the sea, as on the previous night, as calm and as smooth as a mirror.

> " There was no sound upon the deep,
>   The breeze lay cradled there ;
> The motionless waters sank to sleep
>   Beneath the sultry air ;
> Out of the cooling brine to leap
>   The dolphin scarce would dare."

It was a delightful morning, more like April than February; and the sun, as it rose, seemed to fire every peak of the surrounding hills. On our left lay the Island of May, while to the right was to be seen the small fishing-town of Anstruther, twenty miles distant from Edinburgh. Beyond these, on either side, was a range of undulating blue mountains, swelling, as they retired, into a bolder outline and a loftier altitude, until they terminated some twenty-five or thirty miles in the dim distance. A friend at my side pointed out a place on the right, where the remains of an old castle or look-out house, used in the time of the border wars, once stood, and which reminded us of the barbarism of the past.

But these signs are fast disappearing. The plough and roller have passed over many of these foundations, and the time will soon come when the antiquarian will look in vain for those places that history has pointed out to him as connected with the political and religious struggles of the past. The steward of the vessel came round to see who of the passengers wished for breakfast; and as the keen air of the morning had given me an appetite, and there being no prejudice on the score of color, I took my seat at the table, and gave ample evidence that I was not an invalid. On our return to the deck again, I found that we had entered the Frith of Forth, and that "Modern Athens" was in sight; and far above every other object, with its turrets almost lost in the clouds, could be seen Edinburgh Castle.

After landing, and a pleasant ride over one of the finest roads in Scotland, with a sprinkling of beautiful villas on either side, we were once more at Cannon's Hotel. While in the city, on this occasion, we went on the Calton Hill, from which we had a delightful view of the place and surrounding country.

I had an opportunity, during my stay in Edinburgh, of visiting the Infirmary; and was pleased to see among the two or three hundred students three colored young men, seated upon the same benches with those of a fairer complexion, and yet there appeared no feeling on the part of the whites towards their colored associates, except of companionship and respect. One of the cardinal truths, both of religion and freedom, is the equality and brotherhood of man. In the sight of God and all just institutions, the whites can claim no precedence or privilege on account of their being white; and if colored men are not treated as they should be in the educational institutions in America, it is a pleasure to know that all distinction ceases by crossing the broad Atlantic. I had scarcely left the lecture-room of the Institute and reached the street, when I met a large number of the students on their way to the college, and here again were seen colored men arm in arm with whites. The proud American who finds himself in the splendid streets of Edinburgh, and witnesses such scenes as these, can but behold in them the degradation of his own country, whose laws would make slaves of these same young men, should they appear in the streets of Charleston or New Orleans.

During my stay in Edinburgh I accepted an invitation to breakfast with George Combe, Esq., the distinguished philosophical phrenologist, and author of "The Constitution of Man." Although not far from seventy years of age, I found him apparently as active and as energetic as many men of half that number of years. Mr. Combe feels a deep interest in the cause of the American slave. I have since become more intimately acquainted with him, and am proud to reckon him amongst the warmest of my friends. In all of Mr. Combe's philanthropic exertions he is ably seconded by his wife, a lady of rare endowments, of an attractive person and engaging manners, and whose greatest delight is in doing good. She took much interest in Ellen Craft, who formed one of the breakfast party; and was often moved to tears on the recital of the thrilling narrative of her escape from slavery.

CHAPTER XXVIII.

" Look here, upon this picture, and on this."

HAMLET.

No one accustomed to pass through Cheapside could fail to have noticed a good-looking man, neither black nor white, engaged in distributing bills to the thousands who throng that part of the city of London. While strolling through Cheapside, one morning, I saw, for the fiftieth time, Joseph Jenkins, the subject of this chapter, handing out his bills to all who would take them as he thrust them into their hands. I confess that I was not a little amused, and stood for some moments watching and admiring his energy in distributing his papers. A few days after, I saw the same individual in Chelsea, sweeping a crossing; here, too, he was equally as energetic as when I met him in the city. Some days later, while going through Kensington, I heard rather a sweet, musical voice singing a familiar psalm, and on looking round was not a little surprised to find that it was the Cheapside bill-distributor and Chelsea crossing-sweeper. He was now singing hymns, and selling religious tracts. I am fond of patronizing genius, and therefore took one of his tracts and paid him for a dozen.

During the following week, I saw, while going up the city road, that Shakspeare's tragedy of Othello was to be performed at the Eagle Saloon that night, and that the character of the Moor was to be taken by "*Selim, an African prince.*" Having no engagement that evening, I resolved at once to attend, to witness the performance of the "African Roscius," as he was termed on the bills. It was the same interest that had induced me to go to the Italian opera to see Madames Sontag and Grisi in Norma, and to visit Drury Lane to see Macready take leave of the stage. My expectations were screwed up to the highest point. The excitement caused by the publication of "Uncle Tom's Cabin" had prepared the public for anything in the African line, and I felt that the *prince* would be sure of a good audience; and in this I was not disappointed, for, as I took my seat in one of the boxes near the stage, I saw that the house was crammed with an orderly company. The curtain was already up when I entered, and Iago and Roderigo were on the stage. After a while Othello came in, and was greeted with thunders of applause, which he very gracefully acknowledged. Just black enough to take his part without coloring his face, and being tall, with a good figure and an easy carriage, a fine, full and musical voice, he was well adapted to the character of Othello. I immediately recognized in the countenance of the Moor a face that I had seen before, but could not at the moment tell where. Who could this "prince" be, thought I. He was too black for Douglass, not black enough for Ward, not tall enough for Garnet, too calm for Delany, figure, though fine, not genteel enough for Remond. However, I was soon satisfied as to who the *star* was. Reader, would you think it? it was no less a person than Mr. Jenkins, the bill-distributor from Cheapside, and crossing-sweeper from Chelsea! For my own part, I was over-whelmed with amazement, and it was some time before I could realize the fact. He soon showed that he possessed great dramatic power and skill; and his description to the senate of how he won the affections of the gentle Desdemona stamped him at once as an actor of merit. "What a pity," said a lady near me to a gentleman that was by her side, "that a prince of the royal blood of Africa should have to go upon the stage for a living! It it is indeed a shame!" When he came to the scene,

> "O, cursed, cursed slave!—whip me, ye devils,
> From the possession of this heavenly sight!
> Blow me about in winds, roast me in sulphur!
> Wash me in steep-down gulfs of liquid fire!
> O, Desdemona! Desdemona! dead?
> Dead? O! O! O!"

the effect was indeed grand. When the curtain fell, the prince was called upon the stage, where he was received with deafening shouts of approbation, and a number of *bouquets* thrown at his feet, which he picked up, bowed, and retired. I went into Cheapside the next morning, at an early hour, to see if the prince had given up his old trade for what I supposed to be a more lucrative one; but I found the hero of the previous night at his post, and giving out his bills as energetically as when I had last seen him. Having to go to the provinces for some months, I lost sight of Mr. Jenkins, and on my return to town did not trouble myself to look him up. More than a year after I had witnessed the representation of Othello at the Eagle, I was walking, one pleasant Sabbath evening, through one of the small streets in the borough, when I found myself in front of a little chapel, where a number of persons were going in. As I was passing on slowly, an elderly man said to me, "I suppose you have come to hear your colored brother preach." "No," I answered; "I was not aware that one was to be here." "Yes," said he; "and a clever man he is, too." As the old man offered to find me a seat, I concluded to go in and hear this son of Africa. The room, which was not large, was already full. I had to wait but a short time before the reverend gentleman made his appearance. He was nearly black, and dressed in a black suit, with high shirt-collar, and an intellectual-looking cravat, that nearly hid his chin. A pair of spectacles covered his eyes. The preacher commenced by reading a portion of Scripture; and then announced that they would sing the twenty-eighth hymn in "the arrangement." O, that voice! I felt sure that I had heard that musical voice before; but where, I could not tell. I was not aware that any of my countrymen were in London; but felt that, whoever he was, he was no discredit to the race; for he was a most eloquent and accomplishéd orator. His sermon was against the sale and use of intoxicating drinks, and the bad habits of the working classes, of whom his audience was composed.

Although the subject was intensely interesting, I was impatient for it to come to a close, for I wanted to speak to the preacher. But, the evening being warm, and the room heated, the reverend gentleman, on wiping the perspiration from his face (which, by the way, ran very freely), took off his spectacles on one occasion, so that I immediately recognized him, and saved me from going up to the pulpit at the end of the service. Yes; it was the bill-distributor of Cheapside, the crossing-sweeper of Chelsea, the tract-seller and psalm-singer of Kensington, and the Othello of the Eagle Saloon. I could scarcely keep from laughing right out when I discovered this to be the man that I had seen in so many characters. As I was about leaving my seat at the close of the services, the old man who showed me into the chapel asked me if I would not like to be introduced to the minister, and I immediately replied that I would. We proceeded up the aisle, and met the clergyman as he was descending. On seeing me, he did not wait for a formal introduction, but put out his hand and said, "I have seen you so often, sir, that I seem to know you." "Yes," I replied; "we have met several times, and under different circumstances." Without saying more, he invited me to walk with him towards his home, which was in the direction of my own residence. We proceeded; and, during the walk, Mr. Jenkins gave me some little account of his early history. "You think me rather an odd fish, I presume," said he. "Yes," I replied. "You are not the only one who thinks so," continued he. "Although I am not as black as some of my countrymen, I am a native of Africa. Surrounded by some beautiful mountain scenery, and situated between Darfour and Abyssinia, two thousand miles in the interior of Africa, is a small valley going by the name of Tegla. To that valley I stretch forth my affections, giving it the endearing appellation of my native home and fatherland. It was there that I was born, it was there that I received the fond looks of a loving mother, and it was there that I set my feet, for the first time, upon a world full of cares, trials, difficulties and dangers. My father being a farmer, I used to be sent out to take care of his goats. This service I did when I was between seven and eight years of age. As I was the eldest of the boys, my pride was raised in no small degree when I beheld my father preparing a farm for me. This event filled my mind with the grand anticipation of leaving the care of the goats to my brother, who was then beginning to work a little. While my father was making these preparations, I had the constant charge of the goats; and, being accompanied by two other boys, who resided near my father's house, we wandered many miles from home, by which means we acquired a knowledge of the different districts of our country.

"It was while in these rambles with my companions

that I became the victim of the slave-trader. We were tied with cords, and taken to Tegla, and thence to Kordofan, which is under the jurisdiction of the Pacha of Egypt. From Kordofan I was brought down to Dongola and Korti, in Nubia, and from thence down the Nile to Cairo; and, after being sold nine times, I became the property of an English gentleman, who brought me to this country and put me into school. But he died before I finished my education, and his family feeling no interest in me, I had to seek a living as best I could. I have been employed for some years in distributing hand-bills for a barber in Cheapside in the morning, go to Chelsea and sweep a crossing in the afternoon, and sing psalms and sell religious tracts in the evening. Sometimes I have an engagement to perform at some of the small theatres, as I had when you saw me at the Eagle. I preach for this little congregation over here, and charge them nothing; for I want that the poor should have the Gospel without money and without price. I have now given up distributing bills; I have settled my son in that office. My eldest daughter was married about three months ago; and I have presented her husband with the Chelsea crossing, as my daughter's wedding portion."
" Can he make a living at it?" I eagerly inquired. " O, yes! that crossing at Chelsea is worth thirty shillings a week, if it is well swept," said he. " But what do you do for a living for yourself?" I asked. " I am the leader of a band," he continued; "and we play for

balls and parties, and three times a week at the Holborn Casino.''

By this time we had reached a point where we had to part; and I left Joseph Jenkins, impressed with the idea that he was the greatest genius that I had met in Europe.

CHAPTER XXIX.

"Farewell ! we did not know thy worth ;
    But thou art gone; and now 't is prized.
So angels walked unknown on earth,
    But when they flew were recognized."

THOMAS HOOD.

IT was on Tuesday, July 18, 1854, that I set out for
Kensall Green Cemetery, to attend the inauguration of
the monument erected to the memory of Thomas Hood,
the poet.   It was the first pleasant day we had had for
some time, and the weather was exceedingly fine.   The
company was large, and many literary characters were
present.   Near the monument sat Eliza Cook, author
of the "Old Arm Chair," with her hair cut short and
parted on one side like a man's.   She is short in stature,
and thick-set, with fair complexion, and bright eyes.
Not far from Miss Cook was Mrs. Balfour, author of
the "Working Women of the Last Half-century,"
"Morning Dew Drops," etc. etc.   Mrs. Balfour is both
taller and stouter than Miss Cook; and both are about the
same age,— not far from forty.   Murdo Young, Esq.,
of *The Sun*, and George Cruikshank, stood near the
monument.   Horace Mayhew, author of "London Labor

and London Poor," was by the side of Cruikshank. The
Hon. Mrs. Milnes sat near Eliza Cook. As the ceremony was about to commence, a short, stout man, with
dark complexion, and black hair, took his stand on a
tomb near by; this was R. Monckton Milnes, Esq.,
author of "Poetry for the People," and M.P. for
Pontefract. He was the orator of the occasion.

The monument, which has been ably executed by Mr.
Matthew Noble, consists of a bronze bust of the poet
elevated on a pedestal of highly-polished red granite, the
whole being twelve feet high. In front of the bust are
placed wreaths in bronze, formed of the laurel, the
myrtle, and the *immortelle;* and on a slab beneath the
bust appears that well-known line of the poet, which he
desired should be used as his epitaph:

> "He sang the Song of the Shirt."

Upon the front of the pedestal is carved this inscription:

> "In memory of Thomas Hood, born 23d May, 1798; died 3d May,
> 1845. Erected by public subscription, A. D. 1854."

At the base of the pedestal a lyre and comic mask in
bronze are thrown together, suggesting the mingled
character of Hood's writings; whilst on the sides of the
pedestal are bronze medallions illustrating the poems of
"The Bridge of Sighs" and "The Dream of Eugene
Aram." The whole design is worthy of the poet and
the sculptor, and it is much to the honor of the latter

that his sympathy with the object has entirely destroyed all hope of profit from the work.

Mr. Milnes was an intimate friend of the poet, and his selection as orator was in good taste. He spoke with great delicacy and kindness of Hood's personal characteristics, and with much taste upon the artistic value of the dead humorist's works. He touched with great felicity and subtlety upon the value of humor. He defined its province, and showed how closely it was connected with the highest forms in which genius manifests itself. Mr. Milnes spoke, however, more as a friend than as a critic, and his genial utterances excited emotions in the hearts of his hearers which told how deep was their sympathy both with the orator and the subject of his eulogium. There were not many dry eyes amongst his hearers when he quoted one or two exquisite portions of Hood's poems. It was evident that the greater part of the audience were well acquainted with the works of the poet, and were delighted to hear the quotations from poems which had afforded them exquisite gratification in the perusal.

Hood was not a merely ephemeral writer. He did not address himself to the feelings which mere passing events generated in the minds of his readers. He smote deep down into the hearts of his admirers. Had he been nothing more than a literary man, the ceremony on this occasion would have been an impertinence. The nation cannot afford to have its time taken up by eulogiums on every citizen who does his work well in his own particular line. Nevertheless, when a man not only does his own work well, but acts powerfully on the national mind, then his fame is a national possession, and may be with all propriety made the subject of public commemoration. A great author is distinguished from the merely professional scribe by the fact of adding something to the stock of national ideas. Who can tell how much of the national character is due to the operation of the works of Shakspeare? The flood of ideas with which the great dramatist inundated the national mind has enriched it and fertilized it. We are most of us wiser and better by the fact of Shakspeare having lived and written. It would not be difficult to find in most modern works traces of the influence which Shakspeare has exercised over the writers. A great author, such as Shakspeare, is, then, a great public educator. The national mind is enlarged and enriched by the treasures which he pours into it. There is, therefore, a great propriety in making such a writer the subject of public eulogium.

Hood was one of those who not only enriched the national literature, but instructed the national mind. His conceptions, it is true, were not vast. His labors were not, like those of Shakspeare, colossal. But he has produced as permanent an effect on the nation as many of its legislators.

Englishmen are wiser and better because Hood has lived. In one of his own poems, "The Death-Bed," how sweetly he sang:

" We watched her breathing through the night,
　　Her breathing soft and low,
　As in her breast the wave of life
　　Kept heaving to and fro.

" So silently we seemed to speak,
　　So slowly moved about,
　As we had lent her half our powers
　　To eke her living out.

" Our very hopes belied our fears,
　　Our fears our hopes belied ;
　We thought her dying when she slept,
　　And sleeping when she died.

" For when the morn came dim and sad,
　　And chill with early showers,
　Her quiet eyelids closed — she had
　　Another morn than ours."

Thomas Hood has another morn ; may that morn have
brightened into perfect day ! It is well known that the
poet died almost on the verge of starvation. Being
seized, long before his death, with a malady that kept
him confined to his bed the greater part of the time, he
became much embarrassed. Still, in defiance of anguish
and weakness, he toiled on, until nature could endure no
more. Many of Hood's humorous pieces were written
upon a sick bed, and taken out and sold to the publishers,
that his family might have bread. Little did those who
laughed over these comical sayings think of the pain
that it cost the poet to write them. And, now that he is
gone, we often hear some one say, " *Poor Hood !*" But

peace to his ashes! He now lies in the finest cemetery in the world, and in one of its greenest spots. At the close of the inauguration, a rush was made to get a view of Eliza Cook, as being the next great novelty after the monument, if not its equal.

CHAPTER XXX.

" Dull rogues affect the politician's part,
    And learn to nod, and smile, and shrug, with art ;
    Who nothing has to lose, the war bewails ;
    And he who nothing pays, at taxes rails."

                                              CONGREVE.

THE Abbey clock was striking nine, as we entered
the House of Commons, and, giving up our ticket, were
conducted to the strangers' gallery. We immediately
recognized many of the members, whom we had met in
private circles or public meetings. Just imagine,
reader, that we are now seated in the strangers' gallery,
looking down upon the representatives of the people of
the British empire.

There, in the centre of the room, shines the fine, open,
glossy brow and speaking face of Alexander Hastie, a
Glasgow merchant, a mild and amiable man, of modest
deportment, liberal principles, and religious profession. He
has been twice elected for the city of Glasgow, in which he
resides. He once presided at a meeting for us in his own
city.

On the right of the hall, from where we sit, you see
that small man, with fair complexion, brown hair, gray
eyes, and a most intellectual countenance. It is Layard,

with whom we spent a pleasant day at Hartwell Park, the princely residence of John Lee, Esq., LL.D. He was employed as consul at Bagdad, in Turkey. While there he explored the ruins of ancient Nineveh, and sent to England the Assyrian relics now in the British Museum. He is member for Aylesbury. He takes a deep interest in the Eastern question, and censures the government for their want of energy in the present war.

Not far from Layard you see the large frame and dusky visage of Joseph Hume. He was the son of a poor woman who sold apples in the streets of London. Mr. Hume spent his younger days in India, where he made a fortune; and then returned to England, and was elected a member of the House of Commons, where he has been ever since, with the exception of five or six years. He began political life as a tory, but soon went over to radicalism. He is a great financial reformer, and has originated many of the best measures of a practical character that have been passed in Parliament during the last thirty years. He is seventy-five years old, but still full of life and activity — capable of great endurance and incessant labor. No man enjoys to an equal extent the respect and confidence of the legislature. Though his opinions are called extreme, he contents himself with realizing, for the present, the good that is attainable. He is emphatically a progressive reformer; and the father of the House of Commons.

To the left of Mr. Hume you see a slim, thin-faced man, with spectacles, an anxious countenance, his hat on

another seat before him, and in it a large paper rolled
up. That is Edward Miall. He was educated for the
Baptist ministry, and was called when very young to be
a pastor. He relinquished his charge to become the con-
ductor of a paper devoted to the abolition of the state
church, and the complete political enfranchisement of the
people. He made several unsuccessful attempts to go into
Parliament, and at last succeeded Thomas Crawford in the
representation of Rochdale, where in 1852 he was elected
free of expense. He is one of the most democratic members of the legislature. Miall is an able writer and
speaker —a very close and correct reasoner. He stands
at the very head of the Nonconformist party in Great
Britain ; and *The Nonconformist*, of which he is editor,
is the most radical journal in the United Kingdom.

Look at that short, thick-set man, with his hair parted
on the crown of his head, a high and expansive forehead,
and an uncommon bright eye. That is William Johnson
Fox. He was a working weaver at Norwich; then went
to Holton College, London, to be educated for the Orthodox Congregational ministry ; afterwards embraced Unitarian views. He was invited to Finsbury Chapel, where
for many years he lectured weekly upon a wide range of
subjects, embracing literature, political science, theology,
government and social economy. He is the writer of
the articles signed "Publicola" in the *Weekly Dispatch*, a democratic newspaper. He has retired from
his pulpit occupations, and supports himself exclusively
by his pen, in connection with the liberal journals of the

metropolis. Mr. Fox is a witty and vigorous writer, an animated and brilliant orator.

Yonder, on the right of us, sits Richard Cobden. Look at his thin, pale face, and spare-made frame. He started as a commercial traveller; was afterwards a calico-printer and merchant in Manchester. He was the expounder, in the Manchester Chamber of Commerce and in the town council, of the principles of free trade. In the council of the Anti-Corn-Law League, he was the leader, and principal agitator of the question in public meetings throughout the kingdom. He was first elected for Stockport. When Sir Robert Peel's administration abolished the corn-laws, the prime minister avowed in the House of Commons that the great measure was in most part achieved by the unadorned eloquence of Richard Cobden. He is the representative of the non-intervention or political peace party; holding the right and duty of national defence, but opposing all alliances which are calculated to embroil the country in the affairs of other nations. His age is about fifty. He represents the largest constituency in the kingdom — the western division of Yorkshire, which contains thirty-seven thousand voters. Mr. Cobden has a reflective cast of mind; and is severely logical in his style, and very lucid in the treatment of his subjects. He may be termed the leader of the radical party in the House.

Three seats from Cobden you see that short, stout person, with his high head, large, round face, good-sized eyes. It is Macaulay, the poet, critic, historian and statesman.

If you have not read his Essay on Milton, you should do so immediately ; it is the finest thing of the kind in the language. Then there is his criticism on the Rev. R. Montgomery. Macaulay will never be forgiven by the divine for that onslaught upon his poetical reputation. That review did more to keep the reverend poet's works on the publisher's shelves than all other criticisms combined. Macaulay represents the city of Edinburgh.

Look at that tall man, apparently near seventy, with front teeth gone. That is Joseph Brotherton, the member for Salford. He has represented that constituency ever since 1832. He has always been a consistent liberal, and is a man of business. He is no orator, and seldom speaks, unless in favor of the adjournment of the House when the hour of midnight has arrived. At the commencement of every new session of Parliament he prepares a resolution that no business shall be entered upon after the hour of twelve at night, but has never been able to carry it. He is a teetotaller and a vegetarian, a member of the Peace Society, and a preacher in the small religious society to which he belongs.

In a seat behind Brotherton you see a young-looking man, with neat figure, white vest, frilled shirt, with gold studs, gold breast-pin, a gold chain round the neck, white kid glove on the right hand, the left bare with the exception of two gold rings. It is Samuel Morton Peto. He is of humble origin — has made a vast fortune as a builder and contractor for docks and railways. He is a Baptist, and contributes very largely to his own and other dissenting denominations. He has built several Baptist chapels in London and elsewhere. His appearance is that of a gentleman; and his style of speaking, though not elegant, yet pleasing.

Over on the same side with the liberals sits John Bright, the Quaker statesman, and leader of the Manchester school. He is the son of a Rochdale manufacturer, and first distinguished himself as an agitator in favor of the repeal of the corn-laws. He represents the city of Manchester, and has risen very rapidly. Mr. Cobden and he invariably act together, and will, doubtless, sooner or later, come into power together. Look at his robust and powerful frame, round and pleasing face. He is but little more than forty; an earnest and eloquent speaker, and commands the fixed attention of his audience.

See that exceedingly good-looking man just taking his seat. It is William Ewart Gladstone. He is the son of a Liverpool merchant, and represents the University of Oxford. He came into Parliament in 1832, under the auspices of the tory Duke of Newcastle. He was a disciple of the first Sir R. Peel, and was by that statesman introduced into official life. He has been Vice-president and President of the Board of Trade, and is now Chancellor of the Exchequer. Mr. Gladstone is only forty-four. When not engaged in speaking he is of rather unprepossessing appearance. His forehead appears low, but his eye is bright and penetrating. He is one of the ablest debaters in the House, and is master

of a style of eloquence in which he is quite unapproached.
As a reasoner he is subtle, and occasionally jesuitical;
but, with a good cause and a conviction of the right, he
rises to a lofty pitch of oratory, and may be termed the
Wendell Phillips of the House of Commons.

There sits Disraeli, amongst the tories.   Look at that
Jewish face, those dark ringlets hanging round that marble brow.   When on his feet he has a cat-like, stealthy
step; always looks on the ground when walking.   He is
the son of the well-known author of the " Curiosities of
Literature."   His ancestors were Venetian Jews.   He
was himself born a Jew, and was initiated into the Hebrew faith.   Subsequently he embraced Christianity.
His literary works are numerous, consisting entirely of
novels, with the exception of a biography of the late
Lord George Bentinck, the leader of the protectionist
party, to whose post Mr. Disraeli succeeded on the death
of his friend and political chief.   Mr. Disraeli has been
all round the compass in politics.   He is now professedly
a conservative, but is believed to be willing to support
any measures, however sweeping and democratical, if by
so doing he could gratify his ambition — which is for
office and power.   He was the great thorn in the side of
the late Sir R. Peel, and was never so much at home as
when he could find a flaw in that distinguished statesman's political acts.   He is an able debater and a finished orator, and in his speeches wrings applause even
from his political opponents.

Cast your eyes to the opposite side of the House, and

take a good view of that venerable man, full of years, just rising from his seat. See how erect he stands; he is above seventy years of age, and yet he does not seem to be forty. That is Lord Palmerston. Next to Joseph Hume, he is the oldest member in the House. He has been longer in office than any other living man. All parties have, by turns, claimed him, and he has belonged to all kinds of administrations; tory, conservative, whig, and coalition. He is a ready debater, and is a general favorite, as a speaker, for his wit and adroitness, but little trusted by any party as a statesman. His talents have secured him office, as he is useful as a minister, and dangerous as an opponent.

That is Lord Dudley Cutts Stuart speaking to Mr. Ewart. His lordship represents the populous and wealthy division of the district of Marylebone. He is a radical, the warm friend of the cause of Poland, Hungary and Turkey. He speaks often, but always with a degree of hesitation which makes it painful to listen to him. His solid frame, strongly-marked features, and unmercifully long eye-brows are in strange contrast to the delicate face of Mr. Ewart.

The latter is the representative for Dumfries, a Scotch borough. He belongs to a wealthy family, that has made its fortune by commerce. Mr. Ewart is a radical, a stanch advocate of the abolition of capital punishment, and a strenuous supporter of all measures for the intellectual improvement of the people.

Ah! we shall now have a speech. See that little man

rising from his seat; look at his thin black hair, how it seems to stand up; hear that weak, but distinct voice. O, how he repeats the ends of his sentences! It is Lord John Russell, the leader of the present administration. He is now asking for three million pounds sterling to carry on the war. He is a terse and perspicuous speaker, but avoids prolixity. He is much respected on both sides of the House. Though favorable to reform measures generally, he is nevertheless an upholder of aristocracy, and stands at the head and firmly by his order. He is brother to the present Duke of Bedford, and has twice been Premier; and, though on the sunny side of sixty, he has been in office, at different times, more than thirty years. He is a constitutional whig and conservative reformer. See how earnestly he speaks, and keeps his eyes on Disraeli! He is afraid of the Jew. Now he scratches the bald place on his head, and then opens that huge roll of paper, and looks over towards Lord Palmerston.

That full-faced, well-built man, with handsome countenance, just behind him, is Sir Joshua Walmesley. He is about the same age of Lord John; and is the representative for Leicester. He is a native of Liverpool, where for some years he was a poor teacher, but afterwards became wealthy in the corn trade. When mayor of his native town, he was knighted. He is a radical reformer, and always votes on the right side.

Lord John Russell has finished and taken his seat. Joseph Hume is up. He goes into figures; he is the arithmetician of the House of Commons. Mr. Hume is in the Commons what James N. Buffum is in our Anti-Slavery meetings, the *man of facts*. Watch the old man's eye as he looks over his papers. He is of no religious faith, and said, a short time since, that the world would be better off if all creeds were swept into the Thames. His motto is that of Pope :

> " For modes of faith let graceless zealots fight :
> His can't be wrong whose life is in the right."

Mr. Hume has not been tedious; he is done. Now for Disraeli. He is going to pick Lord John's speech to pieces, and he can do it better than any other man in the House. See how his ringlets shake as he gesticulates ! and that sarcastic smile ! He thinks the government has not been vigorous enough in its prosecution of the war. He finds fault with the inactivity of the Baltic fleet ; the allied army has made no movement to suit him. The Jew looks over towards Lord John, and then makes a good hit. Lord John shakes his head ; Disraeli has touched a tender point, and he smiles as the minister turns on his seat. The Jew is delighted beyond measure. " The Noble Lord shakes his head ; am I to understand that he did not say what I have just repeated ?" Lord John : "The Right Hon. Gentleman is mistaken; I did not say what he has attributed to me." Disraeli : "I am glad that the Noble Lord has denied what I thought he had said." An attack is made on another part of the minister's speech. Lord John shakes his head again. " Does the Noble Lord deny that, too ? " Lord John : " No, I don't, but your criticism is unjust."

Disraeli smiles again : he has the minister in his hands, and he shakes him well before he lets him go. What cares he for justice ? Criticism is his forte ; it was that that made him what he is in the House. The Jew concludes his speech amid considerable applause.

All eyes are turned towards the seat of the Chancellor of the Exchequer : a pause of a moment's duration, and the orator of the House rises to his feet. Those who have been reading *The Times* lay it down ; all whispering stops, and the attention of the members is directed to Gladstone, as he begins. Disraeli rests his chin upon his hat, which lies upon his knee : he too is chained to his seat by the fascinating eloquence of the man of letters. Thunders of applause follow, in which all join but the Jew. Disraeli changes his position on his seat, first one leg crossed, and then the other, but he never smiles while his opponent is speaking. He sits like one of those marble figures in the British Museum. Disraeli has furnished more fun for *Punch* than any other man in the empire. When it was resolved to have a portrait of the late Sir R. Peel painted for the government, Mr. Gladstone ordered it to be taken from one that appeared in *Punch* during the lifetime of that great statesman. This was indeed a compliment to the sheet of fun. But now look at the Chancellor of the Exchequer. He is in the midst of his masterly speech, and silence reigns throughout the House.

> " His words of learned length and thundering sound
> Amazed the gazing rustics ranged around ;

And still they gazed, and still the wonder grew
That one small head could carry all he knew."

Let us turn for a moment to the gallery in which we are seated. It is now near the hour of twelve at night. The question before the House is an interesting one, and has called together many distinguished persons as visitors. There sits the Hon. and Rev. Baptist W. Noel. He is one of the first of the Nonconformist ministers in the kingdom. He is about fifty years of age; very tall, and stands erect; has a fine figure, complexion fair, face long and rather pale, eyes blue and deeply set. He looks every inch the gentleman. Near by Mr. Noel you see the Rev. John Cumming, D.D. We stood more than an hour last Sunday in his chapel in Crown-court to hear him preach; and such a sermon we have seldom ever heard. Dr. Cumming does not look old. He has rather a bronzed complexion, with dark hair, eyes covered with spectacles. He is an eloquent man, and seems to be on good terms with himself. He is the most ultra Protestant we have ever heard, and hates Rome with a perfect vengeance. Few men are more popular in an Exeter Hall meeting than Dr. Cumming. He is a most prolific writer; scarce a month passes by without something from his pen. But they are mostly works of a sectarian character, and cannot be of long or of lasting reputation.

Further along sits a man still more eloquent than Dr. Cumming. He is of dark complexion, black hair, light blue eyes, an intellectual countenance, and when standing looks tall. It is the Rev. Henry Melville. He is considered the finest preacher in the Church of England. There, too, is Washington Wilks, Esq., author of " The Half-century." His face is so covered with beard that I will not attempt a description; it may, however, be said that he has literally entered into the *Beard Movement*.

Come, it is time for us to leave the House of Commons. Stop a moment! Ah! there is one that I have not pointed out to you. Yonder he sits amongst the tories. It is Sir Edward Bulwer Lytton, the renowned novelist. Look at his trim, neat figure; his hair done up in the most approved manner; his clothes cut in the latest fashion. He has been in Parliament twenty-five years. Until the abolition of the corn-laws, he was a liberal; but as a land-owner he was opposed to free trade, and joined the protectionists. He has two country-seats, and lives in a style of oriental magnificence that is not equalled by any other man in the kingdom; and often gathers around him the brightest spirits of the age, and presses them into the service of his private theatre, of which he is very fond. In the House of Commons he is seldom heard, but is always listened to with profound attention when he rises to speak. He labors under the disadvantage of partial deafness. He is undoubtedly a man of refined taste, and pays a greater attention to the art of dress than any other public character I have ever seen. He has a splendid fortune, and his income from the labors of his pen is very great. His title was given to him by the queen, and his rank as a baronet he owes to his high literary attainments. Now take a farewell view of this assembly of senators. You may go to other climes, and look upon the representatives of other nations. but you will never see the like again.

CHAPTER XXXI.

" Take the spade of Perseverance,
    Dig the field of Progress wide ;
Every bar to true instruction
    Carry out and cast aside.''

THE anniversary of West India emancipation was
celebrated here on Monday last. But little notice of the
intended meeting had been given, yet the capacious lecture-room of St. Martin's Hall was filled at an early
hour with a most respectable audience, who appeared to
have assembled for the sake of the cause.

Our old and well-tried friend, Geo. Thompson, Esq.,
was unanimously called to preside, and he opened the
proceedings with one of his characteristic speeches. The
meeting was then addressed by the Rev. Wm. Douglass,
a colored clergyman of Philadelphia, in a most eloquent
and feeling manner. Mr. Douglass is a man of fine
native talent.

Francis W. Kellogg, of the United States, was the
next speaker. Mr. Kellogg is an advocate of temperance, of some note, I believe, in his own country, and
has been lecturing with considerable success in Great

Britain. He is one of the most peculiar speakers I have ever heard. Born in Massachusetts, and brought up in the West, he has the intelligence of the one and the roughness of the other. He has the retentive memory of Wendell Phillips, the overpowering voice of Frederick Douglass, and the too rapid gestures of Dr. Delany. He speaks faster than any man I ever heard, except C. C. Burleigh. His speech, which lasted more than an hour, was one stream of fervid eloquence. He gave the audience a better idea of a real American stump orator than they ever had before. Altogether, he is the best specimen of the rough material out of which great public speakers are manufactured that I have yet seen. Mr. Kellogg's denunciations of Clay and Webster (the dead lion and the living dog) reminded us of Wendell Phillips; his pictures of slavery called to memory Frederick Douglass in his palmiest days; and his rebuke of his own countrymen for their unchristian prejudice against color brought before us the favorite topic and best speeches of C. L. Remond. It was his maiden speech on the subject of slavery, yet it was the speech of the evening.

Hatred to oppression is so instilled into the minds of the people in Great Britain, that it needs but little to arouse their enthusiasm to its highest point; yet they can scarcely comprehend the real condition of the slaves of the United States. They have heard of the buying and selling of men, women and children, without any regard to the tenderest ties of nature; of the passage and execution of the infamous Fugitive Slave Law; and, as we walk through the streets of London, they occasionally meet an American slave, who reminds them of the fact that while their countrymen are boasting of their liberty, and offering an asylum to the exiled of other countries, they refuse it to their own citizens.

Much regret has been expressed on this side of the Atlantic that Kossuth should have kept so silent on the slavery question while in America; and this act alone has, to a great extent, neutralized his further operations in this country. He certainly is not the man now that he was before his visit to the New World.

I seldom pass through the Strand, or other great thoroughfares of the metropolis, without meeting countrymen of mine. I encountered one, a short time since, under peculiar circumstances. It was one of those days commonly experienced in London, of half cloud and half sunshine, with just fog enough to give everything a gray appearance, that I was loitering through Drury Lane, and came upon a crowd of poor people and street beggars, who were being edified by an exhibition of Punch and Judy, on the one hand, and an organ-grinder, with a well-dressed and intelligent-looking monkey, on the other. Punch looked happy, and was performing with great alacrity, while the organ-grinder, with his loud-toned instrument, was furnishing music for the million. Pushing my way through the crowd, and taking the middle of the street for convenience' sake, I was leaving the infected district in greater haste than I entered it. I had scarcely taken my eyes off the motley group, when I observed a figure approaching me from the opposite direction, and walking with a somewhat hasty step. I have seen so much oddity in dress, and the general appearance of members of the human family, that my attention is seldom ever attracted by the uncivilized look of any one. But this being whom I was meeting, and whose appearance was such as I had not seen before, threw the monkey and his companions entirely in the shade. In fact, all that I had beheld in the Great Exhibition, of a ludicrous nature, dwindled away into utter insignificance when compared to this Robinson Crusoe looking man; for, after all, it turned out to be a man. He was of small stature, and, although not a cold day, his person was enveloped in a heavy over-coat, which looked as if it had seen some service, and had passed through the hands of some of the second-hand gentlemen of Brattle-street, Boston. The trousers I did not see, as they were benevolently covered by the long skirts of the above garment. A pair of patent-leather boots covered a small foot. The face was entirely hidden by a huge beard, apparently from ten to fifteen inches in length, and of a reddish color. Long, dark hair joined the beard, and upon the head was thrown, in a careless manner, one of those hats known in America as the wide-awake, but here as the billy-cock. A pair of bright eyes were entirely hid by the hair around the face. I was not more attracted by his appearance than astonished at the man's stopping before me, as if he knew me. I now observed something like smoke emanating from the long beard round the mouth. I was immediately seized by the individual by his right hand, while the left hand took from his mouth a pipe about three inches in length, stem included, and, in a sharp, shrill voice, sounding as if it came from the interior of a hogshead or from a sepulchre, he called me by my name. I stood for a moment and eyed the figure from head to foot, "from top to toe," to see if I could discover the resemblance of any one I had ever seen before. After satisfying myself that the object was new, I said, "Sir, you have the advantage of me." "Don't you know me?" he exclaimed, in a still louder voice. I looked again, and shook my head. "Why," said he, "it is C——." I stepped back a few feet, and viewed him once more from top to bottom, and replied, "You don't mean to say that this is H. C——?" "Yes, it is he, and nobody else." After taking another look, I said, "An't you mistaken, sir, about this being H. C——?" "No," said he, "I am sure I know myself." So I very reluctantly had to admit that I was standing in presence of the ex-editor of the "L. P. and H. of F." Indeed, one meets with strange faces in a walk through the streets of London. But I must turn again to the question of slavery.

Some months since a lady, apparently not more than fifty years of age, entered a small dwelling on the estate of the Earl of Lovelace, situated in the county of Surrey. After ascending a flight of stairs, and passing through a narrow passage, she found herself in a small but neat room, with plain furniture. On the table lay copies of

the *Liberator* and *Frederick Douglass' Paper*. Near
the window sat a young woman, busily engaged in sew-
ing, with a spelling-book laying open on her lap. The
light step of the stranger had not broken the silence
enough to announce the approach of any one, and the
young woman still sat at her task, unconscious that any
one was near. A moment or two, and the lady was observed, when the diligent student hastily rose, and apolo-
gized for her apparent inattention. The stranger was
soon seated, and in conversation with the young woman.
The lady had often heard the word "slave," and knew
something of its application, but had never before seen
one of her own sex who had actually been born and
brought up in a state of chattel slavery; and the one
in whose company she now was was so white, and had so
much the appearance of an educated and well-bred lady,
that she could scarcely realize that she was in the presence of an American slave. For more than an hour the
illustrious lady and the poor exile sat and carried on a
most familiar conversation. The thrilling story of the
fugitive often brought tears to the eyes of the stranger.
O, how I would that every half-bred, aristocratic,
slave-holding, woman-whipping, negro-hating woman of
America could have been present and heard what passed
between these two distinguished persons ! They would,
for once, have seen one who, though moving in the most
elevated and aristocratic society in Europe, felt it an
honor to enter the small cottage and take a seat by the
side of a poor, hunted and exiled American fugitive slave.

Let it be rung in the ears of the thin-skinned aristocracy of the United States, who would rather receive a flogging from the cat-o'-nine-tails than to sit at the table of a negro, that Lady Noel Byron, widow of the great poet, felt it a peculiar pleasure to sit at the table and take tea with Ellen Craft. It must, indeed, be an interesting fact to the reader, and especially to those who are acquainted with the facts connected with the life and escape of William and Ellen Craft, to know that they are industrious students in a school, and attracting the attention of persons occupying the most influential positions in society. The wonderful escape of William and Ellen Craft is still fresh in the minds of all who take an interest in the cause of humanity; and their eluding the pursuit of the slave-hunters at Boston, and final escape from the Athens of the New World, will not be soon forgotten.

Every American should feel a degree of humiliation when the thought occurs to him that there is not a foot of soil over which the *Stars and Stripes* wave upon which Ellen Craft can stand and be protected by the constitution or laws of the country. Yet Ellen Craft is as white as most white women. Had she escaped from Austrian tyranny, and landed on the shores of America, her reception would have been scarcely less enthusiastic than that which greeted the arrival of Jenny Lind. But Ellen Craft had the misfortune to be born in one of the Slave States of the American Union, and that was enough to cause her to be driven into *exile* for daring to escape from American despotism.

CHAPTER XXXII.

"——when I left the shore,
   The distant shore, which gave me birth,
I hardly thought to grieve once more,
   To quit another spot on earth."

                                    BYRON.

WHAT a change five years make in one's history!
The summer of 1849 found me a stranger in a foreign
land, unknown to its inhabitants; its laws, customs and
history, were a blank to me. But how different the summer of 1854! During my sojourn I had travelled over
nearly every railroad in England and Scotland, and had
visited Ireland and Wales, besides spending some weeks
on the continent. I had become so well acquainted with
the British people and their history, that I had begun to
fancy myself an Englishman by habit, if not by birth.
The treatment which I had experienced at their hands
had endeared them to me, and caused me to feel myself
at home wherever I went. Under such circumstances, it
was not strange that I commenced with palpitating heart
the preparation to return to my *native land*. Native
land! How harshly that word sounds to my ears!
True, America was the land of my birth; my grand-

father had taken part in her Revolution, had enriched the
soil with his blood, yet upon this soil I had been worked
as a slave.   I seem still to hear the sound of the auc-
tioneer's rough voice, as I stood on the block in the
slave-market at St. Louis.   I shall never forget the savage grin with which he welcomed a higher bid, when he
thought that he had received the last offer.   I had seen
a mother sold and taken to the cotton-fields of the far
South; three brothers had been bartered to the soul-
driver in my presence; a dear sister had been sold to the
negro-dealer, and driven away by him; I had seen the
rusty chains fastened upon her delicate wrists; the whip
had been applied to my own person, and the marks of
the brutal driver's lash were still on my body.   Yet this
was my native land, and to this land was I about to
embark.

In Edinburgh, I had become acquainted with the
Wighams; in Glasgow, the Patons and Smeals; in Manchester, the Langdons; in Newcastle, the Mawsons and
Richardsons.   To Miss Ellen Richardson, of this place, I
was mainly indebted for the redemption of my body from
slavery, and the privilege of again returning to my native country.   I had also met, and become acquainted
with, John Bishop Estlin, Esq., of Bristol, and his kind-
hearted and accomplished daughter.   Of the hundreds
of British Abolitionists with whom I had the pleasure of
shaking hands while abroad, I know of none whose hearts
beat more fervently for the emancipation of the American
slave than Mr. Estlin's.   He is indeed a model Chris-

tian. His house, his heart and his purse, were always open to the needy, without any regard to sect, color or country. When those distinguished fugitive slaves, William and Ellen Craft, arrived in England, unknown and without friends, Mr. Estlin wrote to me and said, "If the Crafts are in want, send to me. If you cannot find a home for them, let them come to Bristol, and I will keep them, at my expense, until something better turns up." And nobly did he keep his word. He put the two fugitives in school, and saw that they did not want for the means of support. I have known him to keep concealed what he had given to benevolent objects. To Mr. Estlin I am indebted for many acts of kindness; and now that the broad Atlantic lies between us, and in all probability we shall never again meet on earth, it is with heartfelt gratitude and pleasure that I make this mention of him.

And last, though not the least, I had become intimate with that most generous-hearted philanthropist, George Thompson, who never feels so well as when giving a welcome to an American fugitive slave. I had spent hours at the hospitable firesides of Harriet Martineau, R. D. Webb, and other distinguished authors. You will not, reader, think it strange that my heart became sad at the thought of leaving all these dear friends, to return to a country in which I had spent some of the best days of my life as a slave, and where I knew that prejudice would greet me on my arrival.

Most of the time I had resided in London. Its streets,

parks, public buildings and its fog, had become "as familiar as household words." I had heard the deep, bass voice of the Bishop of London, in St. Paul's Cathedral. I had sat in Westminster Abbey, until I had lost all interest in the services, and then wandered about amongst the monuments, reading the epitaphs placed over the dead. Like others, I had been locked in the Temple Church, and compelled to wait till service was over, whether I liked it or not. I had spent days in the British Museum and National Gallery, and in all these I had been treated as a man. The "negro pew," which I had seen in the churches of America, was not to be found in the churches of London. There, too, were my daughters. They who had been denied education upon equal terms with children of a fairer complexion, in the United States, had been received in the London schools upon terms of perfect equality. They had accompanied me to most of the noted places in the metropolis. We had strolled through Regent-street, the Strand, Piccadilly and Oxford-street, so often, that sorrow came over me as the thought occurred to me that I should never behold them again.

Then the English manner of calling on friends before one's departure. I can meet an enemy with pleasure, but it is with regret that I part with a friend. As the time for me to leave drew near, I felt more clearly my identity with the English people. By and by the last hour arrived that I was to spend in London. The cab stood at the door, with my trunks on its top; and, bidding the household "good-by," I entered the vehicle, the driver raised his whip, and I looked for the last time on my old home in Cecil-street. As we turned into the Strand, Nelson's monument, in Trafalgar-square, greeted me on the left, and Somerset House on the right. I took a farewell look at Covent Garden Market, through whose walks I had often passed, and where I had spent many pleasant hours. My youngest daughter was in France, but the eldest met me at the depôt, and after a few moments the bell rang, and away we went.

As the train was leaving the great metropolis of the world behind, I caught a last view of the dome of St. Paul's, and the old pile of Westminster Abbey.

In every town through which we passed on our way to Liverpool I could call to mind the name of some one whose acquaintance I had made, and whose hospitality I had shared. The steamer City of Manchester had her fires kindled when we arrived, and we went immediately on board. We found one hundred and seventy-five passengers in the cabin, and above five hundred in the steerage. After some delay, the ship weighed anchor, the machinery was put in motion, and, bidding Liverpool a long farewell, the vessel moved down the Mersey, and was in a short time out at sea. The steam tender accompanied the ship about thirty miles, during which time search was made throughout the Manchester to see that no "stow-aways" were on board. No vessel ever leaves an English port without some one trying to get his passage out without pay. When the crew are at work, or

not on the watch, these persons come on board, hide
themselves under the berths in the steerage cabin, or
amongst the freight, until the vessel is out to sea, and
then they come out. As they are always poor persons,
without either baggage or money, they succeed in getting their passage without giving anything in return. As
the tender was about quitting us to return to Liverpool,
it came along-side to take on board those who had come
with the vessel to see their friends off. Any number of
white napkins were called into requisition, as friends
were shaking hands with each other, and renewing their
promises to write by the first post. One young man
had come out to spend a few more hours with a handsome Scotch lass, with whom he, no doubt, had a matrimonial engagement. Another, an English lady, seemed
much affected when the last bell of the tender rung, and
the captain cried "All on board." Having no one to
look after, I found time to survey others. The tender let
go her cables amid three hearty cheers, and a deafening
salute from the two-pounder on board the City of Manchester. A moment more, and the two steamers were
leaving each other with rapid speed. The two young
ladies of whom I have already made mention, together
with many others, had their faces buried in their hand-
kerchiefs, and appeared to be dying with grief. However, all of them seemed to get over it very soon. On
the second day out at sea I saw the young English lady
walking the quarter-deck with a fine-looking gentleman,
and holding as tightly to his arm as if she had left no

one behind ; and as for the Scotch lass, she was seated on a settee with a countryman of hers, who had made her acquaintance on board, and, from all appearance, had entirely forgotten her first love. Such is the waywardness of man and woman, and the unfaithfulness of the human heart.

In the latter part of the second day a storm overtook us, and for the ten succeeding days we scarcely knew whether we were on our heads or our heels. The severest part of the gale was on the eighth and ninth nights out. On one of those evenings a fellow-roommate came in and said, "If you wish to see a little fun, go into the forward steerage." It was about eight o'clock, and most of the passengers were either in bed, or preparing for the night's rest, such as is to be had on board a ship in a gale of wind. This cabin contained about two hundred and fifty persons; some Germans, some Irish, and twenty-five or thirty Gypsies. Forty or fifty of these were on their knees in their berths, engaged in prayer. No camp-meeting ever presented a more noisy spectacle than did this cabin. The ship was rolling, and the sea running mountains high, and many of these passengers had given up all hope of ever seeing land again. The Gypsies were foremost amongst those who were praying; indeed, they seemed to fancy themselves in a camp-meeting, for many of them shouted at the top of their voices. One of them, known as the "Queen of the Gypsies," came to me and said, " O, Master ! do get down and help us to ask God to stop the wind ! You are a black man ; may be he 'll pay more

attention to what you say. Now do, master, do! and
when the storm is over I will tell your fortune for
nothing.'' At this juncture one of the chests which had
been fastened to the floor broke away from its moorings,
and came sliding across the cabin at the rate of about
twenty miles per hour; soon another got loose, and these
two locomotives broke up the prayer-meeting. Trunk
after trunk became unfastened, until some eight or ten
were crossing the cabin every time the vessel went over.
At last the loose boxes upset the tables, on which were
some of the passengers' eatables, and in a short time the
whole cabin was in splendid confusion. The lamps, one
after another, were knocked down and extinguished, so
that the cabin was in total darkness. As I turned to
retrace my steps, I heard the company joining in the
prayer, and I was informed the next day that it was
kept up during most of the night.

With all the watchfulness on the day of sailing, several persons succeeded in stowing themselves away. First
one came out, and then another, until not less than five
made their appearance on deck. As fast as these men
were discovered they were put to work; so that labor, if
not money, might be obtained for their passage. On the
sixth day out I missed a small leather trunk, and search
was immediately made in every direction, but no tidings
of it could be found. However, after its being lost two
days, I offered a reward for its recovery, and it was soon
found, hid away in the forecastle. It had been broken
open, and a few things, together with a little money, had

been taken.   The ships Chieftain and Harmony were the only vessels we met during the first ten days.   An iceberg made its appearance while we were on the banks, but it was some distance to the larboard.

After a long passage of twenty days we arrived at the mouth of the Delaware, and took a pilot on board.   The passengers were now all life; the Irish were basking in the sun, the Germans were singing, and the Gypsies were dancing.   Some fifteen miles below Philadelphia, the officers came on board, to see that no sickness was on the vessel; and, after being passed by the doctors, each person began to get his luggage on deck, and prepare to go on shore.   About four o'clock, on the twenty-sixth day of September, 1854, the City of Manchester hauled alongside the Philadelphia wharf, and the passengers all on the move; the Scotch lass clinging to the arm of her new Highland laddie, and the young English lady in company with her " fresh " lover.   It is a dangerous thing to allow the Atlantic Ocean to separate one from his or her " affectionate friend."   The City of Manchester, though not a fast steamer, is, nevertheless, a safe one.   Her officers are men of experience and activity. Captain Wyly was always at his post; the first officer was an able seaman, and Mr. John Mirehouse, the second officer, was a most gentlemanly and obliging, as well as experienced officer.   To this gentleman I am much indebted for kind attention shown me on the voyage.   I had met him on a former occasion at Whitehaven.   He is a stanch friend of humanity.

At Philadelphia I met with a most cordial reception at the hands of the Motts, J. M. M'Kim, the Stills, the Fortens, and that distinguished gentleman and friend of the slave, Robert Purvis, Esq. There is no colored man in this country to whom the Anti-slavery cause is more indebted than to Mr. Purvis. Endowed with a capacious and reflective mind, he is ever in search after truth; and, consequently, all reforms find in him an able and devoted advocate. Inheriting a large fortune, he has had the means, as well as the will, to do good. Few men in this country, either colored or white, possess the rare accomplishments of Robert Purvis. In no city in the Free States does the Anti-slavery movement have more bitter opponents than in Philadelphia. Close to two of our Southern States, and connected as it is in a commercial point of view, it could scarcely be otherwise. Colorphobia is more rampant there than in the pro-slavery, negro-hating city of New York. I was not destined to escape this unnatural and anti-christian prejudice. While walking through Chestnut-street, in company with two of my fellow-passengers, we hailed an omnibus going in the direction which we wished to go. It immediately stopped, and the white men were furnished with seats, but I was told that "We don't allow niggers to ride in here." It so happened that these two persons had rode in the same car with me from London to Liverpool. We had put up at the same hotel at the latter place, and had crossed the Atlantic in the same steamer. But as soon as we touch the soil of America we can no longer ride in the same conveyance, no longer eat at the same table, or be regarded with equal justice, by our thin-skinned democracy. During five years' residence in monarchical Europe I had enjoyed the rights allowed to all foreigners in the countries through which I passed; but on returning to my NATIVE LAND the influence of slavery meets me the first day that I am in the country. Had I been an escaped felon, like John Mitchell, no one would have questioned my right to a seat in a Philadelphia omnibus. Neither of the foreigners who were allowed to ride in this carriage had ever visited our country before. The constitution of these United States was as a blank to them; the Declaration of Independence, in all probability, they had never seen,— much less, read. But what mattered it? They were white, and that was enough. The fact of my being an American by birth could not be denied; that I had read and understood the constitution and laws, the most pro-slavery, negro-hating professor of Christianity would admit; but I was colored, and that was enough. I had partaken of the hospitality of noblemen in England, had sat at the table of the French Minister of Foreign Affairs; I had looked from the strangers' gallery down upon the great legislators of England, as they sat in the House of Commons; I had stood in the House of Lords, when Her Britannic Majesty prorogued her Parliament; I had eaten at the same table with Sir Edward Bulwer Lytton, Charles Dickens, Eliza Cook, Alfred Tennyson, and the son-in-law of Sir Walter Scott: the omnibuses of

Paris, Edinburgh, Glasgow and Liverpool, had stopped to take me up; I had often entered the "Caledonia," "Bayswater," "Hammersmith," "Chelsea," "Blue-bell," and other omnibuses that rattle over the pavements of Regent-street, Cheapside, and the west end of London,— but what mattered that? My face was not white, my hair was not straight; and, therefore, I must be excluded from a seat in a third-rate American omnibus. Slavery demanded that it should be so. I charge this prejudice to the pro-slavery pulpits of our land, which first set the example of proscription by erecting in their churches the "negro pew." I charge it to that hypocritical profession of democracy which will welcome fugitives from other countries, and drive its own into exile. I charge it to the recreant sons of the men who carried on the American revolutionary war, and who come together every fourth of July to boast of what their fathers did, while they, their sons, have become associated with bloodhounds, to be put at any moment on the track of the fugitive slave.

But I had returned to the country for the express purpose of joining in the glorious battle against slavery, of which this Negrophobia is a legitimate offspring. And why not meet it in its stronghold? I might have remained in a country where my manhood was never denied; I might have remained in ease in other climes; but what was ease and comfort abroad, while more than three millions of my countrymen were groaning in the prison-house of slavery in the Southern States? Yes, I came back to the land of my nativity, not to be a spectator, but a soldier — a soldier in this moral warfare against the most cruel system of oppression that ever blackened the character or hardened the heart of man. And the smiles of my old associates, and the approval of my course while abroad by my colored fellow-citizens, has amply compensated me for the twenty days' rough passage on my return.

OPINIONS OF THE BRITISH PRESS.

"While all the world is reading ' Uncle Tom's Cabin,' it is quite possible that what a real fugitive slave has to say for himself may meet with less attention than it deserves. Mr. Brown's book is pleasingly written."— *The Critic*, Dec. 16, 1852.

" When he writes on the wrongs of his race, or the events of his own career, he is always interesting or amusing."— *The Athenæum*, Nov. 15, 1852.

" The appearance of this book is too remarkable a literary event to pass without a notice. At the moment when attention in this country is directed to the state of the colored people in America, the book appears with additional advantage ; if nothing else were attained by its publication, it is well to have another proof of the capability of the negro intellect. Altogether, Mr. Brown has written a pleasing and amusing volume. Contrasted with the caricature and bombast of his white countryman Mr. Willis' description of ' People he has Met,' a comparison suggested by the similarity of the title, it is both in intellect and in style a superior performance, and we are glad to bear this testimony to the literary merit of a work by a negro author."— *The Literary Gazette*, Oct. 2, 1852.

" That a man who was a slave for the first twenty years of his life, and who has never had a day's schooling, should produce such a book as this, cannot but astonish those who speak disparagingly of the African race."— *The Weekly News and Chronicle*, Sept. 6, 1852.

" It is something new for a self-educated slave to publish such a work,

It is really wonderful how one who has had to surmount so many difficulties in his literary career should have been able to produce a volume
of so sparkling a character. The author is personally known to many
of our readers, and, therefore, we need not enlarge respecting his abilities or his merits. We recommend them to procure his book, and are
induced to do so by the consideration that his main object in bringing
out the work is to enable him to educate his family ; an object at all
times honorable and praiseworthy, but in one occupying the position
of William Wells Brown eminently commendable, and in which every
friend of humanity must wish him success."— *British Friend*, Aug. 1852.

" This remarkable book of a remarkable man cannot fail to add to the
practical protests already entered in Britain against the absolute bondage of three millions of our fellow-creatures. The impressions of a self-
educated son of slavery, here set forth, must hasten the period when the
senseless and impious denial of common claims to a common humanity,
on the score of color, shall be scouted with scorn in every civilized and
Christian country. And when this shall be attained, among the means
of destruction of the hideous abomination his compatriots will remember with respect and gratitude the doings and sayings of William Wells
Brown. The volume consists of a sufficient variety of scenes, persons,
arguments, inferences, speculations and opinions, to satisfy and amuse
the most *exigeant* of those who read *pour se desennuyer;* while those who
look deeper into things, and view with anxious hope the progress of
nations and of mankind, will feel that the good cause of humanity and
freedom, of Christianity, enlightenment and brotherhood, cannot fail to
be served by such a book as this." — *Morning Advertiser*, Sept. 10, 1852.

" He writes with ease and ability, and his intelligent observations
upon the great question to which he has devoted and is devoting his
life will be read with interest, and will command influence and respect."
— *Daily News*, Sept. 24, 1852.

" The extraordinary excitement produced by ' Uncle Tom's Cabin '
will, we hope, prepare the public of Great Britain and America for this
lively book of travels by a real fugitive slave. Though he never had a
day's schooling in his life, he has produced a literary work not unwor-
thy of a highly-educated gentleman. Our readers will find in these letters much instruction, not a little entertainment, and the beatings of a

manly heart, on behalf of a down-trodden race, with which they will not fail to sympathize."—*The Eclectic Review*, Nov. 1852.

" We have read this book with an unusual measure of interest. Seldom, indeed, have we met with anything more captivating. It somehow happens that all these fugitive slaves are persons of superior talents. The pith of the volume consists in narratives of voyages and journeys made by the author in England, Scotland, Ireland and France ; and we can assure our readers that Mr. Brown has travelled to some purpose. The number of white men is not great who could have made more of the many things that came before them. There is in the work a vast amount of quotable matter, which, but for want of space, we should be glad to extract. As the volume, however, is published with a view to promote the benefit of the interesting fugitive, we deem it better to give a general opinion, by which curiosity may be whetted, than to gratify it by large citation. A book more worth the money has not, for a considerable time, come into our hands."—*British Banner*, Dec. 15, 1852.

" THREE YEARS IN EUROPE. — The remarkable man who is the author of this work is not unknown to many of our readers. He was received with kindness in this city, and honored with various marks of respect by many eminent characters in the sister country. Since his arrival Mr. Brown has contributed much to the press ; and the work before us, though small and unpretending, is of a high character, and evinces a superior and cultivated mind."— *Dublin General Advertiser*, October 30, 1852.

" This is a thrilling book, independent of adventitious circumstances, which will enhance its popularity. The author of it is not a man in America, but a chattel, a thing to be bought, and sold, and whipped: but in Europe he is an author, and a successful one, too. He gives in this book an interesting and graphic description of a three years' residence in Europe. The book will no doubt obtain, as it well deserves, a rapid and wide popularity."— *Glasgow Examiner*.

" The above is the title of an intelligent and otherwise well-written book, in which the author details, in a pleasing and highly-interesting manner, an account of places he has seen and people he has met; and we take much pleasure in recommending it to our readers."— *Weekly Dispatch*.

" This is an interesting volume, ably written, bearing on every page
the impress of honest purpose and noble aspiration. One is amused by
the well-told anecdotes, and charmed with the painter-like descriptions
of towns, cities and natural scenery. Indeed, our author gives many
very recognizable sketches of the places he has seen and people he has
met. His three years in Europe have been well spent. The work will
be appreciated by all the friends of the negro."— *The Leader.*

" W. Wells Brown is no ordinary man, or he could not have so
remarkably surmounted the many difficulties and impediments of his
training as a slave. By dint of resolution, self-culture and force of character, he has rendered himself a popular lecturer to a British audience,
and vigorous expositor of the evils and atrocities of that system whose
chains he has shaken off so triumphantly and forever. We may safely
pronounce William Wells Brown a remarkable man, and a full refutation of the doctrine of the inferiority of the negro."— *Glasgow Citizen.*

" We can assure those who are inclined to take up this volume that
they will find it written with commendable care, as well as fluency, and
will derive much pleasure from a perusal of it."— *Bristol Mercury.*

" The profound Anti-slavery feeling produced by ' Uncle Tom's Cabin '
needed only such a book as this, which shows so forcibly the powers
and capacity of the negro intellect, to deepen the impression. The work
certainly exhibits a most favorable contrast to the more ambitious productions of many of his white countrymen, N. P. Willis among others."
—*Caledonian Mercury.*